THE DEVIL'S BACKBONE

The Story of the Natchez Trace

JONATHAN DANIELS

PELICAN PUBLISHING COMPANY
GRETNA 2018

Copyright © 1962, 1990
By Jonathan Daniels
All rights reserved

Reprinted by arrangement with McGraw-Hill Book
Company.

First Pelican edition, August 1985
Second printing, October 1987
Third printing, August 1989
Fourth printing, October 1992
Fifth printing, June 1998
Sixth printing, September 2011
Seventh printing, May 2017
Eighth printing, September 2018

Library of Congress Cataloging in Publication Data

Daniels, Jonathan, 1902-81
    The devil's backbone.

    Reprint. Originally published: New York: McGraw-Hill,
1962.
    1. Natchez Trace.   2. Southern States—History
I. Title.
F217.N37D36   1985   976.2   84-3222
ISBN 9780882894386

Printed in Canada
Published by Pelican Publishing Company, Inc.
1000 Burmaster Street, Gretna, Louisiana 70053
www.pelicanpub.com

Contents

the Devil's Backbone

I: THE GRASPING HAND

WITH the tattered Cavalcade the pigs came, rooting and hunting. While men died of arrow wounds and the fevers, the hogs multiplied and fattened on the acorns under the great oaks of the wilderness.

Their grunting and the neighing of the horses echoed in the autumn forest in the company of Don Hernando de Soto, Knight Commander of the Order of St. James of Compostela, Governor of the Island of Cuba, Adelantado of Florida, and marquis of lands yet to be subdued. In the unknown reaches of southeastern North America his force moved with an increasing sense of ill omen. Yet it did not seem probable that the greatest danger which awaited them would be baited by the grunting swine.

De Soto found no simple savages. Perhaps in his pride and his rough greed he was more gullible than any of the copper-colored people whom he found. An Indian princess, called the Lady of Cofitachequi, met the possibility of his hostility with hospitality. She sought to placate him with pearls and was only taken prisoner for her pains. In modesty she retired to a canebrake and escaped with one of the Spaniard's Negro slaves. Perhaps that was a call of nature, too. Other Indians whom De Soto encountered on the twisting, still-disputed track of his wanderings met him with awe, then guile, then fury. All the tribes, among them Creeks and Cherokees, fought with a courage which the mounted and armored Spaniards remembered ever after with ungrudging admiration.

3

From the tangled woods warriors shouted menace. Their ceremonial drums sounded in the hot darkness. And they fought the Christians—as the chroniclers of the Spaniards always referred to themselves—from the canebrakes, on the hills, in the marshes, from a lake where they hid their painted heads among the water lilies. The Indians were killed by the thousands, but they inflicted wounds upon the surprised Spaniards which the Christians could not dress and heal with the fat of the savages they killed. In the fighting, not only clothes and equipment, but also Eucharistic ornaments, the vestments of the priests, and the sacramental wine were destroyed. Thereafter only a makeshift Mass was possible.

Under the Cross, the devout were disturbed by the ominous portent. They urged the shorter journey to the Gulf, where brigantines were waiting. But De Soto was "an inflexible man and dry of word." He disregarded mutterings. In October, 1540, as the forests chilled and reddened, he turned northward by the maze of trails made by the buffaloes and the Indians, for God, for glory, and for gold.

So they came by the paths to an ancient trail, in what is now northwest Mississippi, which ran by the villages of the Chickasaws, a people "very warlike and much dreaded." Running roughly north and south, it was only one of the many narrow lanes beaten through the brush, by the buffaloes and Indians, between tribal villages, hunting grounds and salt licks, shellfish shores, rivers and streams. By the time De Soto came along this path the Chickasaws had already cultivated fields. Furthermore, they seemed ready to greet the Spaniards in friendship. Their chiefs came with gifts of corn and game. In return the Spaniards feasted the Chickasaws on the first roast pork they had ever known from hogs which were part of the elaborate commissariat on the hoof which De Soto had brought from Cuba. So he roused an appetite which became the basis of anger. On nights thereafter Indians crept in the darkness to the houses for the hogs, a crossbow shot from the Spanish camp, "to kill and carry away what they could of them."

The "Child of the Sun," as De Soto had set himself up to be, was not to be so trifled with. When he caught such pilfering Indians, three were tied to posts and killed with arrows. He dealt differently with another. This red captive's arms were roped to a log. His pulsing arteries stood out like cords. Then in two swift strokes, an ax of keen Spanish steel cut through the hemp, the flesh, the bones of his wrists, and into the wood. With both hands neatly chopped off, the Indian thief was sent back to his chief. Fortunately on the old trail this was not a precedent always followed in dealing with the grasping hand.

The Chickasaws apparently accepted such punishment without protest. An ominous peace prevailed. The Spaniards built a substantial timbered winter camp. The snows fell and melted. The wisteria purpled the trees. The tiny red roses ran close to the ground. Then De Soto asked for the naked fury he got. He demanded 200 women as *tamenes,* or carriers.

Always, said one of the chroniclers of the expedition, the Spaniards sought the "young and least ugly women." He added, almost in confession, that "some died, and others ran away or were tired out, and so it was necessary to replenish their numbers and to take more; and the women were desired both as servants and for their foul uses and lewdness." The Chickasaws delayed fulfillment of the request for the women. Then De Soto received stealthy incendiarism and murderous attack in the night. With his surviving company, he was sent limping westward from the trail toward the greatest American river and to his death, after illness, beside it.

These lean and weary Spaniards are remembered as the discoverers of the Mississippi River, the currents of which constituted a ready route southward. The trail which they had crossed and from which they fled provided an indispensable way, first for Indians and then for a wide variety of white men, to return north. De Soto's bones were silt in the great stream when an increasing multitude made that path a road necessary to the development of a continent.

The original deep-rutted pathway followed ridges, so that water from often torrential rains was quickly shed. It avoided the swamps and found the easiest fording places at the streams. Hoofs and moccasined feet trampled the path deep into the ground. But beside it brush and cane and vine grew rank and high. Hoot and howl in the thickets—even bird song—might be mimicking Indian signals carrying always the danger of ambuscade. Diamond-marked snakes seemed hardly more poisonous than the insect swarms.

This trail which De Soto crossed ran northward 600 miles from the loess bluffs above the Mississippi where the Natchez tribe of Indians performed bloody rites at White Apple Village. This was to be the site of the town of Natchez. Through the wilderness the path twisted across the lands of the Choctaws and of the Chickasaws. Its northern terminus was in the game-rich hunting grounds of many tribes in Tennessee. There settlements on the Cumberland River were to grow into the city of Nashville.

This trail, which in its origin was only a combination of shorter ones, became the Natchez Trace. It was an essential link with similar paths which ran from the Great Lakes to the Gulf and from the crowding and restless Atlantic seaboard to the far southwest. It joined many paths to the North and East: the Kentucky Trace, the Great Lakes Trail, the Wilderness Road, the Cisca or Augustine Trail. Toward the far southwest El Camino Real, the Spanish royal road, which often seemed more a vague direction than a path, ran by way of Los Adais and San Antonio to viceregal Mexico City. North and eastward other trails, like the Great War Path, ran through the mountain gaps between Virginia and the Carolinas and Tennessee and Kentucky. Such paths long antedated often were followed by men like Daniel Boone when he blazed the Wilderness Road.

Many trails such as the Mohawk, the Oregon, and the Santa Fe led east and west. Much of the importance of the Natchez Trace was that in general the Middle American rivers flowed southward. Below the St. Lawrence country all the streams between the Appalachians and the Rockies poured their waters into the Mississippi. Downstream on all of them was a long journey often made difficult by turbulent currents. But the only way of return was overland, a painful, dangerous, laborious way through the wilderness along the old trails of which the Natchez Trace became the most famous. Pioneer travelers had to be both sailors and woodsmen.

Down the streams the first Americans who had pushed past the Appalachians brought the products of Kentucky and Indiana, Tennessee and Pennsylvania, and of the forests and clearings along the Cumberland, the Ohio, the Wabash, and even such a little stream as the Sangamon. By barge and keelboat and raft, they freighted southward flour and millstones and tobacco, pelts and iron and Monongahela whiskey. Down the Mississippi River they sold their cumbersome boats as lumber. And on the overland return by the Natchez Trace they sometimes brought back more gold clinking in their saddlebags than De Soto's Spaniards vainly sought. And some came only homesick, footsore, and afraid. Others, who thought they fared well, brought with them blindness and idiocy for their children as the bitter fruits of their frolics with white and yellow whores in the good-time houses of Natchez-under-the-Hill.

Not strangely it became a robbers' road. And there were rogues along it never labeled as bandits and never in danger of hemp. It was the thoroughfare of the hunted and the hunting—of men going to get what they wanted and of others fleeing from what they only too well deserved. Flatboatmen headed homeward met other men headed south. Among them were traders, medicine peddlers, and missionaries. And sometimes pretended preachers were the worst plunderers. They praised the Lord while confederates in their congregations picked pockets.

All merged in the march of pioneers—long men and lean women with towheaded children at their heels. On the way with the pioneer mothers were always the frontier bawds. There were also gentlemen and ladies, from Connecticut as well as the Carolinas, with coffled slaves in their train. Land hunger was in the eyes of them all. Some of the land seekers loudly complained that they were robbed by the Indians as they came to grab the Indians' land.

Doomed men and men of destiny moved along it. The path of both was a gamble with weather and fever, stumps and swamps, and river crossings. Still the stream of travelers thickened into what Thomas Jefferson called an "immense swarm." Their movement was not merely geographical along a north-south trail. It was also chronological through a history which included Indian resistance, French specula- tion in settlement, Spanish domination, and finally American expansion. Just as men passed each other on the road, so their stories ran side by side. Like the paths of which the Natchez Trace was composed and the branches which extended from it, its story is a maze in history, too.

Time upon it was not neatly dated as in most history books. Indeed, when Jefferson, as such books say, purchased the vast area called Louisiana, he bought only what plodding or galloping travelers upon the Trace had already inevitably taken with oar and pole, musket and plow, and with the long knife and pistol as well. Mr. Jefferson had to send his young secretary Meriwether Lewis on the famous Lewis and Clark expedition to find out what he had bought. Though that expedition did not move along the Trace in the truest sense, it started there. And Lewis came back to find his own dark destiny on the Natchez Trace itself.

An expansive Mississippi politician once said that the Natchez Trace was the oldest road in the world, made by the animals and the Indians long before the Romans built the

Appian Way. Political oratory has not always required documentation in Mississippi. The Trace's age is still a matter of guesswork for historians as well as politicians. It is certain that as white men after De Soto knew it, it was a road which flourished greatly and swiftly and, like many men upon it, died young too.

The Natchez Trace wore that name only briefly. It was sometimes called the Chickasaw Trace and sometimes, at its southern end, the Path to the Choctaw Nation. Amazingly it was even labeled the Path of Peace. When officials in Washington decided on its necessity as an improved route for the mails and the military from frontier Nashville to Natchez, then the most distant American outpost, they pompously christened it the Columbian Highway.

That was a name too fancy for either its character or its travelers. By those who moved over it, it was often simply called the Natchez Road or the Nashville Road, depending upon which direction they were headed. Its lasting name was finally fixed in the history and the folklore of the West by those veterans of the Battle of New Orleans who, upon this path, also gave Andrew Jackson his nickname of Old Hickory. Long afterwards, when these once valiant fighters had become garrulous gaffers, the Natchez Trace ran through many of their tallest tales.

The death of the old road can be more definitely dated. It was in effect doomed in a year which for more reasons than one was called the *annus mirabilis* of the Mississippi Valley. That was the year in which Indians were called most eloquently to retake the lands of their fathers. Even more important, the first steamboat proved its power to meet the Mississippi's currents and end the necessity of overland travel homeward. And nature seemed to celebrate both events with a trembling earth and a flaming sky.

Nevertheless the Trace died stubbornly. Men on foot and on Opelousas horses still passed by the stands or inns kept by the Choctaws, the Chickasaws, and a variety of half-breeds. Only gradually the old Trace began to fall apart into local and rural roads between new and growing settlements. Cotton blossomed where cane had hidden killers and corpses. Indeed, the relatively short, rambunctious life of the thoroughfare can almost be bounded by the names and dates of two then obscure men among the flatboatmen who added so much color to the Trace's story.

In March, 1806, such a man was hired to take a load of merchandise from Kentucky down the Ohio and Mississippi rivers. Already "Kaintuck" described a kind of man and not merely a place of habitation. General Jackson at the Battle of New Orleans described only their mildest marks of identification.

"I never met a Kentuckian," he said, "who did not have a rifle, a pack of cards and a bottle of whiskey."

Perhaps the man who set out in 1806 was such a man, perhaps not. Certainly then the only way he could get back home was to make his way by land through the wilderness—over the Trace. And this man was in a hurry to return to Kentucky where not long after he was to marry a lively, illiterate frontier girl named Nancy Hanks. His name was Thomas Lincoln.

Just 22 years later this Tom's tall boy, Abraham, then 19 years old, made a similar 1,000-mile trip down the rivers. He returned with a scar he wore all his life as the result of a rough and tumble fight with seven Negroes who tried to steal his flatboat's cargo. Also much legend has been made to the effect that his emancipation of the slaves long afterwards had its emotional origin when he saw brawny blacks and gold-tinted octoroons auctioned on the block. The important fact in the demise of the Trace is that as a flatboatman Abraham Lincoln did not walk home by any wilderness road. His employer paid his fare on one of the ornate, white-plumed, whistle-blowing steamboats which already crowded the stream—and on which even home-headed flatboatmen could ride for a small price if they slept on the deck and provided their own food.

The Trace was history then. Its legends of violence were

fully grown even if the code duello outlasted the desperadoes, and aristocrats were often rowdy after the flatboatmen had all but disappeared. The robbers had been hung. Cotton was king, and mansion-building Cotton Snobs were the lords of a country of broadcloth and crinoline, not of buckskin breeches and coon-tailed hats. Already angers were turning from Indians to abolitionists. Audubon did portraits for a living while he painted his birds. And the portraits hung in ornate halls. But the pioneer was still a pressing personage in the land.

Abraham Lincoln went down the river in 1828. And that same year the first pioneer West put one of its own into the White House as President of the United States. It put its spirit into American political power, too. The last of the Indians whom De Soto had found were about to follow the buffaloes across the Mississippi. Like the Cherokees, the Choctaws and the Chickasaws, too, followed a Trail of Tears. The West had been won, though it already seemed East to a new, farther West in which so many of its patterns would be endlessly repeated.

As great gamblers the old Westerners (soon to be called Southerners) had won, too. They had taken what they wanted. And perhaps in history, from De Soto and his pigs to an old, tough, quick-triggered border captain in the Presidency, the ancient trail was best symbolized as the highway of the grasping hand. The glove of grace was, even in the mansioned years, a gauntlet, too. Death and American destiny, high stakes and hair trigger, prancing nigger and punctilious pride, the duel and the development of a nation were never very far apart along the Natchez Trace.

If De Soto came to it as a doomed stranger, he was never alien to the proud, the predatory, the courageous, and the diverse company which on the trail sought treasure and spilt blood. The road to the American dream has always been rough. And the Natchez Trace was not only its pathway but its parable as well.

II. HARVEST OF HATRED

THE FRENCH came to Natchez at the southern end of the Trace as the first white settlers there.

In 1716 Jean Baptiste Le Moyne, Sieur de Bienville, built his Fort Rosalie (named after the beautiful Duchess of Pontchartrain, whose husband was the French minister of marine). As outpost of empire, he placed it on the high bluffs, beside the villages of the Natchez Indians, 300 miles up the Mississippi from the marshes where New Orleans was to be.

This great sun-bronzed Bienville was one of the nine Le Moyne brothers, whose father in Canada had been ennobled for his services to France. Bienville himself had fought for the king, from freezing Hudson Bay to the fever islands of the Caribbean, when France meant to make the heart of the continent its own. At eighteen he had come to the Mississippi country with his older brother, Pierre, Sieur d'Iberville. More than any other men, the Le Moynes made France in America—and this younger of the bold brothers lived to see most of it lost, too.

When Bienville's brother Pierre died of the yellow fever which the French had brought from fighting in the Spanish settlements, Jean Baptiste was only twenty-six. He was thirty-six when he built Fort Rosalie, and hardened. Not long before he came to Natchez something had happened to prevent his marriage to the daughter of the irritable, covetous, and grasping Governor Antoine de la Mothe Cadillac. It was in that embittered time that Cadillac, whose monument was to be an automobile not an empire, sent Bienville to reduce the Natchez Indians to obedience to the crown of France.

If Bienville left loss and quarrel behind him, he meant to have tranquility in the wilderness over which he presided. That was not only necessary to the safety of the mounting hopes of French settlement in America. It was also essential if the British on the Atlantic seaboard, whose traders were already slipping in to take furs and Indian slaves, were to be held back. Bienville went brusquely about his task.

He had an aptitude for learning the Indian languages and conciliating the tribesmen. Still, this time he knew that he had antagonism behind him, watching for any weakness. So when the Natchez Indians killed four Frenchmen and ransacked a depot of supplies, he retaliated with swift strategem and severity. He had only 49 men against the whole Natchez Nation. Still, undaunted and shrewd as he was brave, he captured by trick the Great Sun of the tribe. He forced the chief to deliver the leaders of the raid. They were promptly put to death. And as further retribution he required the tribe to supply him bark from 3,000 cypress trees and 2,500 pieces of acacia wood to be woven into wattles to strengthen his fort.

The fort was an outpost then in an unsubdued continent. In 1712, four years before Bienville built Rosalie, a count had shown that the entire European population, scattered from Mobile to the site of future New Orleans and up the big river to Natchez, numbered only 324 men. Far up the river the Long Hunters and the French fur traders had hardly begun to enter Kentucky and Tennessee. Daniel Boone had not even been born. Still Bienville had chosen his place well. The lands were fertile, made of an easily cut and cultivated soil composed of the dust of old glaciers blown by the river winds. When cut the roadbanks stood like a sliced cake. The sun blessed vine and tree. The fevers seemed farther away than at the river's muddy mouth.

The colony grew. Beside the fort settlers were brought to

the Concession de Sainte Catherine, which gave its name to St. Catherine's Creek north of the post. St. Catherine was the patron saint of wheelwrights and mechanics (some of whom were among the settlers) as well as the University of Paris. And the founding of the fort and colony came at about the time of the launching in Paris of the great hoax called "The Mississippi Bubble."

There the famous or infamous hard-drinking, dueling Scottish gambler John Law proposed to resuscitate the war-depleted finances of France. He built his speculations on the basis of the old delusion which De Soto followed to his death. Across Europe, in a program which can only be described in the modern terms of promotion and advertising, his government-sponsored Compagnie des Indes Occidentales spread its bait to the poor, the adventurous, and the hopeful. The lands were rich in precious metals. The Indians were eager to lead colonists to them and also to miraculous herbs providing remedies for "the most dangerous wounds, yes, also, so they say, infallible ones for the fruits of love."

L'amour, or its wilderness equivalents, was adding to Bienville's troubles. Close to his fort the Natchez, despite strange rites which their traditions said had come with them from an Aztec West, were an orderly, handsome people. Their women, by French accounts, were beautiful. And their appeal to lonely men disturbed not only the Jesuit and Capuchin priests but even the bachelor Bienville.

"Send me wives for my Canadians," he wrote, "they are running in the woods after Indian girls."

And sometimes when the kind of women who would come or could be sent from Paris arrived, some of the Frenchmen of the Old World and the New still preferred the Indian girls. The priests complained. Yet Mississippi historians long after preserved the romantic tradition of "the dusky maidens . . . their flashing eyes, and their voluptuous forms . . . their delicate hands and feet . . . their merry laugh, and their raven hair that brushed the dew drops as they walked." (Perhaps loneliness in the whole West built the picture of beautiful Indian women. Early travelers in Tennessee, at the northern end of the Trace, wrote of the Cherokee beauties who had "features formed with perfect symmetry and countenances cheerful and friendly." They were, one said, "tall, slender, erect, and of a delicate frame, moving with grace and dignity.") Undoubtedly the Natchez were handsome—and by Fort Rosalie they seemed as malleable as copper.

The whole Mississippi country seemed as appealing. In Paris the thrifty French invested in the shares of John Law's soaring scheme, commonly called the Mississippi Company, and watched them rise as others clamored to buy. Law promised to send 6,000 white colonists and 3,000 African slaves within 25 years. Many came: French, Swiss, numerous Germans. Not all died at sea, starved on the shores, or rotted in the wilderness. Neither did they find the Eden in which Indians poured gold into their hands. In 1720, 300 colonists were settled at Natchez. Frenchmen and sweating blacks cut back the canebrakes which on the richest land grew 30 feet high and two inches in diameter. The burning of the cut cane, John James Audubon said a century later, cracked and exploded with "sounds resembling discharges of musketry."

The first plantations were opened. Artisans and traders came. Ships moved to the Gulf Coast carrying tobacco, pelts, and bear grease. The colony was still growing beside the watching Natchez Indians in 1720, when, far off, John Law slipped secretly out of Paris as his Mississippi Bubble with its tumbling shares became an anger and a byword on the exchanges and in the cafés. In America, with little help, Bienville kept his courage, though now that he had become governor of the whole province jealous enemies multiplied around him. His task was still to help build France from Canada to the Caribbean.

Stupidity and stinginess might be in control down the river and across the sea, but he was confident at his Fort

Rosalie among the Natchez Indians and pleased about the situation to the north on the path which led to the wilderness and to the Choctaws, and the Chickasaws beyond them. These three tribes were all members of the Muskhogean linguistic group of Indians in the American Southeast. The Natchez and the Chickasaws were friends, and both were enemies of the Choctaws between them. Bienville depended upon the docility of the Natchez whom he thought he had subdued. In their villages about his fort they performed in intricate and brutal rites the most elaborate religious ceremonies that the Jesuits found among the North American Indians. French chroniclers described them best in terms of the funeral of Tattooed Serpent, brother of the Great Sun. Many of his friends and relatives were strangled to accompany him into eternity.

Northward through rich loess soil the trail of Bienville's concern ran to the Nation of the Choctaws, the best friends of the French. Their rites and rituals were less spectacular. Still, one of their customs seemed weird to the Europeans. The colonists called the Choctaws "Flatheads" because they put bags of sand on the heads of their infants to flatten their skulls. They were more given to farming and trade than to war, but they could be fierce in protecting their own—and also in fighting for the French.

Beyond them as the hills rose toward Tennessee were the handsome, more warlike Chickasaws, great hunters who troubled Bienville most and liked the British best. And across the wide, turbulent Tennessee River the Cherokees ranged over mountain and plain. To the great hunting ground there came also wandering bands of Creeks, from lands which were to be Georgia and Alabama, and other tribes from north of the Ohio. Bienville was most concerned with those on the path between the Mississippi and Tennessee rivers.

"The Choctaws, whom I have set in motion against the Chickasaws," Bienville wrote in 1723, "have destroyed entirely three villages of this ferocious Nation, which disturbed our commerce on the river. They have raised about 400 scalps and made 100 prisoners."

And he added with pride: "It has not cost one drop of French blood."

This was not the first time Bienville had used Indians against Indians. Perhaps syphilis and smallpox, and tafia, a rum made from the cane of the West Indies, were from the beginning the white man's chief weapons of destruction. But earlier Bienville had offered his friends the Choctaws ten "écus" for Indian scalps. He got them, but as other "hair buyers" later found, in the old Northwest as well as the South, canny seekers for scalp bounties learned fast. A full scalp taken just above the ears could be made into several smaller ones, equally negotiable. This time France was not impressed by the bargain Bienville made without a drop of French blood.

The Mississippi Company had no money and only recriminations to send him. New unrest among the Natchez had to be put down. Furthermore, all up and down the river and on the Gulf shore Bienville tried to deal, in what seems to us now a strange combination of Christianity and cruelty, with the thousands of Negroes who had survived the death-packed holds of the slave ships. In his Black Code miscegenation was a prohibition never to be enforced. Mulattoes and octoroons multiplied. Indeed, the French classified such mixed bloods in an elaborate scale extending all the way from sacatroes, with 87½ per cent Negro blood, through griffes, marabons, mulattoes, os rouges, tiercerons and quadroons to octoroons with only 12½ per cent Negro blood. Lack of genealogical records in breeding soon made such distinctions difficult. Still, special headdresses, or bright colored tignons, were required to be worn by all women of color. The Black Code's purpose was to guard white lives and protect black property. For acts from insubordination to insurrection the punishments provided in it ran the succession from the lash to the brand, to mutilation, on to the rack and the bone-cracking wheel.

Many of its provisions were long to persist. Still, before Natchez became part of the United States a governor in a proclamation observed "that the idleness of free negro, mulatto, and quarteroon women, resulting from their dependence for a livelihood on incontinence and libertinism, will not be tolerated." He complained: "The distinction which had been established in the headdress of females of color is disregarded, and urges that it is useful to enforce it; he forbids them to wear thereon any plumes or jewelry, and directs them to have their hair bound in a kerchief." And when the edict was not ignored the kerchiefs often became badges of their amiable availability.

Bienville did his best with the diverse Europeans Law had lured, and with the blacks and the Indians. Still as reward for his loyalty and his labors there was only ruin. He was recalled to France under charges in 1724. For the first time since its beginnings the lower Mississippi Valley was left without a Le Moyne. Others were in command when in its annual recurrence the time came for one of the most pleasing of the rites of the Natchez Indians in 1729.

Before the geese honked southward that autumn the corn dance was celebrated. It was the happiest of the customs which, according to their traditions, the Natchez had brought with them long before when they moved eastward from an Aztec West. On his litter the Great Sun of the tribe was borne swiftly by relays of bearers to the celebration of the harvest. Feasting and shouting, oratory and games filled the afternoon. Then, as the slow dark came, torches made of cane blazed as brightly as the last sun on the lowlands across the river.

A drummer began to beat a skin stretched across a pottery vessel. Around him circled the young women, then the warriors, each carrying a gourd filled with pebbles. The women moved from left to right and the men from right to left, all keeping time with their bodies and their gourds to the beat of the drum. As the dancers tired, men and women dropped out into the darkness beyond the torches. Others took their places. Celebrating the harvest, fulfillment, and fertility, the dance went on till dawn. But this year what the Natchez were about to celebrate was a harvest of hatred.

If this year there were misgivings among the colonists around Fort Rosalie, the French commander showed greed instead of fear. Word reached the Indians that this stupid and greedy gentleman, Sieur de Chopart, planned demands for more of the land of the Natchez, including even White Apple Village, where the ceremonial pyramidal mounds of the proud tribe stood. The resentment of the Natchez should have been no less secret than Chopart's purposes. There is a story that the French were warned of Natchez plans for French blood by an Indian woman who was in love with a soldier in the garrison at Fort Rosalie. If the tale is true, the warning was disregarded. The carefully planned massacre came on November 28, 1729.

Modern historians of the Natchez Trace report briefly that "more than 500 men, women and children were killed; a few women and slaves were taken prisoners." The news which sped down the river with the few half-crazed refugees must have been cried in terror. New Orleans reacted almost in panic. Perhaps the best contemporary report was one coldly written and formally dispatched by Diron d'Artaguiette, commandant at Mobile, to the frivolous young Comte de Maurepas, then in charge of the administration of the French navy. This D'Artaguiette knew the country and its people. He had traveled the river from New Orleans to the French settlements far north and had reported happier days when he had met pirogues of traders headed down the river with salt meat and bear oil. Now he wrote:

"My Lord:—My duty and the perfect attachment that I shall always retain for your Lordship induce me to relate to you what is happening to-day in this colony of Louisiana.

"The Natchez Indians, a nation established ninety leagues above New Orleans, having information toward the end of last November that the French wished to force them to abandon their villages and their lands in keeping with the order of Sieur de Chopart, who was in command at that fort, conspired to slaughter all the French who were established there."

The plot had been carefully planned. Early in the morning the Natchez came with word that the Choctaws were about to attack. The French must have been gullible to believe such a story about their best friends. Still they apparently listened to the announcement by the Natchez that they were ready in friendship to help the French resist the Choctaws. They even loaned guns to the Natchez. With them the Indians dispersed themselves into the houses of the colonists "in such a way that to those in which there were only one or two Frenchmen four Indians went." At the same time the Great Sun himself with several of his Honored People went to the residence of Sieur de Chopart. They had, they said, some fowl they wished to trade with him. The commander was not pleased. He wanted none of their birds. He stooped to pick up the game and throw it out. At that moment the Natchez chief gave his people the signal to fire. De Chopart was shot as he stooped. And in every other house the slaughter began.

"This lasted until four o'clock in the afternoon," wrote D'Artaguiette, "when the massacre ended. Then the Indians had all the heads of the French brought into the public square, with the booty that they had taken. The spoils they divided among themselves. As they had spared as many French women as they could during the massacre, they brought them all together and put them into two houses where they are being kept under surveillance. It is feared that the women may be slaughtered before they can be taken from that place. The Indians have likewise taken many negroes and negresses whom they also have with them."

Other reports differ as to details. D'Artaguiette was begging for troops and criticizing Etienne de Périer, who had succeeded Bienville as governor. In a report seven months after the massacre Father Philibert, a Capuchin priest and missionary, gave a gruesome list of the dead. He reported 144 men, 35 women, and 56 children killed. Some were mutilated before they were beheaded. "Burnt tortured" was his phrase. J.F.H. Claiborne, the Mississippi historian, from his study of old sources wrote that the Indians "spared but two white men; most of the women and half grown children, and the negroes were reserved for slaves, but they ripped open those that were pregnant, and killed all the infants." At the feet of the Great Sun, he added, "bodies after being mutilated were left to the dogs and the buzzards."

The revenge of Governor Périer could hardly be described as mild. Indeed, panic in New Orleans spurred a retaliation as hideous as the crime. The Choctaws, as friends of the French and old enemies of the Natchez, were quickly enlisted in the retaliation. The French-Choctaw force fell upon the Natchez while they were still celebrating their bloodletting. Four men and women of the Natchez Nation were brought to New Orleans to be burned at the stake in the Place d'Armes. There was no pity in the plaza. Still, some in the crowd of watching, outraged French noted that "even the women showed not the least trace of weakness as they were consumed by the flames."

The lust for vengeance was not sated. The Natchez Nation fled west across the river from whence they had come long before. There the French found them and, disregarding a flag of truce, destroyed the main body of the tribe. Some were sent to slow dying in West Indian slavery. Only a few warriors and their families were able to come back east across the river to the ancient trail which ran from Natchez north across Bayou Pierre, and by the Pearl River through the Nation of the Choctaws. So along the path which was to become the Natchez Trace, they reached the hospitality of the Chickasaws in northeastern Mississippi. Some, moving northward to oblivion, may have reached the rich hunting grounds where Nashville was to be.

Fear remained behind them. The year after the massacre, a Negro named Samba, who must also have found his way up the Trace, plotted slave insurrection with the Chickasaws. Red and black together could exterminate the French. Perhaps some Negro betrayed the plan. The whole plot may have been manufactured, as was often the case, out of the panic imagination of the whites. Still a Negro woman was hanged, and eight black men were killed by the slow breaking of their bones on the wheel.

It was not strange that the return of Bienville, in 1733, was hailed with "a joy and satisfaction without parallel." Still it was not the young Bienville who returned from humiliations. "Tranquility" was not easily re-created. He tried. Quickly he moved against the Chickasaws, whose alliance with the British and their westward-moving traders was all too clear. He directed his blows from the north as well as from the south. Southward with French troops came Pierre d'Artaguiette, commandant in Illinois and brother of the Diron d'Artaguiette who had reported to Paris the massacre at Natchez. Bienville himself with his Choctaw allies was to move from the Gulf. He was delayed in starting. Perhaps D'Artaguiette's Illinois *coureurs de bois* moved too fast on their downstream way. The two French forces never met.

Along Pontotoc Ridge, where De Soto had been almost destroyed two centuries before, the Chickasaws struck D'Artaguiette first, on March 24, 1736. There (near modern Tupelo) the French were completely defeated. D'Artaguiette, the priest of his forces, and twenty other Frenchmen were burned at the stake. Southern Indians knew how to torture as well as fight. They stuck their victims full of splinters of fat pine, until they were covered with quills like a porcupine. These they set on fire, sometimes with the red-hot barrels of guns English traders had furnished them in the contest with the French for furs. Men so executed lived long after the splinters had burned into their skins.

When Bienville finally arrived the Chickasaws were ready

for him, too. On May 26 he met this "ferocious nation" in the Battle of Ackia, not far from the scene where D'Artaguiette had been turned into a torch. Bienville was not destroyed, but his force was so badly mauled that he fell back to Mobile.

Some have said that this was one of the most decisive, though least remembered, battles in early American history. James Adair, the Irish trader, who lived with the Chickasaws before this time and after, always doing what he could to attach the Indians to the English and turn them against the French, believed so. Adair had some strange notions to the effect that the Indians were the descendants of the ancient Jews. Still, as a highly educated Irishman who lived long among the Chickasaws, there is much basis for his belief that this tribe's militant opposition to the French saved the land on the Cumberland and Tennessee rivers for the English. That was important to the outcome of the French and Indian War. It was important, too, to the settlers of Saxon stock who would soon begin to occupy the lands at the northern end of the Natchez Trace.

The dogged Bienville tried again after Ackia. He moved large forces north against the almost irresistible currents of the Mississippi to strike the Chickasaws from the west— from Chickasaw Bluffs, now Memphis. On shore, continual rains bogged his progress. Dissension among his Indian allies blunted his purposes. A truce was patched up. But Bienville and France were done when in 1743, sixty and weary, he left America never to return.

Still the Mississippi country remained in his stout old heart. As an old man in Paris in the year before his death in 1767, he joined in protests against the cession to Spain of the last remnant of that French empire in the American South which he had tried to build. He failed again. To bankrupt and self-indulgent Louis XV, it was good riddance to pass his Louisiana to his cousin, Charles III of Spain. That had the added merit of tricking the British, who had already taken Quebec, by giving the "Island of New Orleans" and all Louisiana lying west of the Mississippi to the Spanish. Left for England to take, in 1763, were only the French settlements east of the river, north of the 31st parallel, among them Natchez, which was no longer any settlement at all. It was as empty as this last sad, futile gesture Bienville made.

Perhaps after the massacre of 1729 some French troops remained at Natchez near their Choctaw friends. No colony, however, quickly grew again on the bloody site. Wilderness returned to the bluffs and to the shore below lapped by the muddy waters. The cane grew high again, sometimes as thick as a man's arm. The scene presented an aspect not dissimilar to that which greeted the ancestors of the Natchez when they came from the west to settle in this pleasant land.

It remained beautiful. And the bloody massacre on the edge of the lush wilderness remained, too, a source of lasting fascination. It seemed to have a special interest to those Frenchmen who never hacked their way through a canebrake or listened to Indian drums but who became fancifully concerned with the fashionable concept of Jean Jacques Rousseau: that primitive man was nobler and more sensitive than the highly civilized products of European society. Up from Natchez along the Trace that question was never to be adequately answered.

Yet, when François René, Vicomte de Chateaubriand, gave his romantic attention to the massacre sixty years after the bloody November day, he left a lasting romantic picture of the land. He was a little late as witness. Indeed, when he came to America in 1791, his observations of the Indians anywhere were limited. He never visited the lands where the Natchez killed and died. His *Atala, ou les amours de deux sauvages dans le désert* was not published until a decade later, in 1801. But similarly Daniel Boone was three years dead and his exploits far behind him when Lord Byron, in 1823, made the world image of him as the greatest American pioneer in the eighth canto of *Don Juan.*

The romantic portrait of the American West was always a part of its reality, too. Even the Long Hunters, before Boone and less talkative, brought back from Kentucky and Tennessee to the peopling and prosaic Eastern colonies reports of a beautiful land as well as one rich with pelts and of valleys ready for the plow. Chateaubriand was simply more sophisticated when he wrote three novels of this first French West as a wilderness never to be destroyed forever by bloodshed.

In his highly successful *Atala* he described the "trees of every form and color, and of every perfume . . . stretching up in the air to heights which weary the eye to follow." Wild vines, begonias, coloquintidas, he said, intertwined each other at the foot of these trees, escaladed their trunks, and crept along the extremities of their branches. They stretched from the maples to the tulip trees. In their wanderings from tree to tree, the creepers sometimes crossed the arm of a river, over which they threw a bridge of flowers. He mentioned early the scented tree which was to become the symbol of the land. "Out of the midst of these masses," he declared, "the magnolia, raising its motionless cone, surrounded by large white buds, commands all the forest."

If, as was true of the time about which he wrote, man primitive or man civilized killed each other off, and if it was difficult then or later to decide which killer was the most savage, Chateaubriand found life in nature beautiful, various, extravagant, and venomous, too. Others were to find it so.

"From the extremities of the avenues," he wrote with unrestrained exuberance, "may be seen bears; intoxicated with the grape, staggering upon the branches of the elm-trees; . . . black squirrels play among the thick foliage; mockingbirds, and Virginia pigeons not bigger than sparrows, fly down upon the turf reddened with strawberries; green parrots with yellow heads, purple woodpeckers, cardinals red as fire, clamber up to the very tops of the cypress trees; hummingbirds sparkle upon the jasmine . . . and bird catching serpents hiss while suspended to the domes of the woods, where they swing like vines."

His was not too imaginative a description of an Eden which spread where dogs and buzzards had eaten the ripped women, the headless men, and the mutilated children. There were plenty of horned creatures beside the lakes. Birds flashed and sang. Serpents tattooed by nature slithered among the flowers. It is not too much to believe that the turf was reddened by the strawberries. At the north end of the Trace to which the English, Scottish, and Irish settlers would soon be coming, early travelers described a land in which, during the late spring, the juice of wild strawberries reddened the legs of their horses up to the knees.

Certainly, after the massacre the vines spread where sweating, still jibbering Negroes fresh from African jungles had hacked the first plantations out of the oldest canebrakes. The land Chateaubriand described was the southern end of the path over which the Natchez had fled to hospitality and oblivion. Across bayous and rivers, over red hills, over the highland rim where the Cherokee followed the game to the salt licks, the Trace ran. Certainly, where the trail left the Mississippi to make the way north which currents prevented on the great river, it seemed a land too intoxicating for Puritans.

Yet, it was for the best people of the Pilgrim Fathers of New England that the luxuriating wilderness now waited. Its cane grew for the knives of Yankees more accustomed to rocky fields than to loess soils, more habituated to a hard religion than to the enervating ease of a land which knew more sun than snow. Still, where the French had failed and the Indians had died, the Puritans were coming.

And they, too, would find that the old Trace would be necessary as a way not merely for trade and travel, but, in turn, for flight when death seemed at their heels. And for all upon it, whichever way they moved, and from whatever motives, it marked the diversity of the human development of the West.

III: PILGRIM'S PROGRESS

JOHNNY Hutchins was born in 1774 in a house built on a mound where the old Natchez White Apple Village had been. Nearby ran the path to the Chocktaw Nation which, off beyond the Bayou Pierre and along the Pearl River, joined the trail to the Chickasaw towns and on to the great feeding grounds of Tennessee.

Johnny, as a child of an aristocracy which would grow very rich and perhaps too proud, marked by the years of his life the revival and growth of settlement in the Old Southwest. In effect, as a result of the Seven Years' War (which coincided with the French and Indian War in America), rule of the Mississippi Valley passed, in 1763, from Louis XV to George III. It was an uneasy rule, however, with Spain holding New Orleans, all the west bank of the Mississippi, and the east bank to a point north of Baton Rouge.

By proclamation George III's government made the Natchez District (including a great area which had been secured by treaty from the Choctaws) the only British area open to settlement west of the Appalachians. And Johnny's father, Col. Anthony Hutchins, a native of New Jersey who had served under Lord Jeffrey Amherst, got one of the first grants. As a reward for his services he received at least 1,434 acres from the king and was, under the British regime, one of the chief magistrates at Natchez.

The country had not greatly changed from the wilderness to which it had returned after massacre. When Colonel

Anthony came in 1772, and when his son was born two years later, the forest around the Hutchins' lands was almost impenetrable. Through it ran narrow creeks with high banks cut through the loess soil. The steep slopes to the streams were coated and protected by the matted roots of cane, which grew rank and thick beneath the big trees of the woods. Deep pools in the stream abounded with beaver and otter, trout and perch. Buffaloes still came to drink. And into this wild land, close to the town which had been wiped out by massacre, Johnny went often as a young boy with a black slave hunter.

It was not easy even for a small boy to move through the thickets of cane. Johnny learned early that the best way was to push himself backwards, wedging a way between the stems. But often the hunter had to hack little paths through the canebrake with his knife to find the game which was always most plentiful where on rich soil the cane grew thickest. During one winter when the brush often crackled with the sleet upon it, Johnny Hutchins and the black man killed 107 bears. By that time the boy had seen more excitement than bear hunting provided.

Johnny's father does not readily conform to the conventional image of the American pioneer. His house at Natchez could have been no cabin. It held furnishings which looting soldiery greedily carried off, and it was presided over by a lady whose grace was matched by her courage. Colonel Hutchins' position in America and in history is perhaps better marked by the fact that he was the brother of Thomas Hutchins, who was later made by Congress "geographer of the United States." Anthony was a Tory and a former soldier of the king. Thomas, caught in England when the Revolution began, preferred to go to prison rather than fight against the colonies.

The brothers later quarreled over lands. Important to both was the fact that Thomas, as one of the first scientific explorers of the American West, charted rivers and found good lands. He came down the Ohio and the Mississippi by

Natchez in 1766. He was exploring, in 1769, around the site where Nashville was to be. It was around that time, probably on the basis of his brother's exploration, that Colonel Anthony sought and got his lands.

Others sought the rich lands, too. Jedidiah Morse, who wrote the first geography to be published in the United States, spoke of the "opulent" families both in Natchez and the Cumberland settlements to which the Natchez Trace ran. Some of the families which had gone to Natchez between the French and Indian War and the American Revolution had as many as 200 slaves. Perhaps the most significant of these wealthy settlers were the Lymans and Dwights and other eminent descendants of the oldest American families in New England. First among them was Gen. Phineas Lyman. His interest had been aroused as an officer, as was Colonel Hutchins', to whom the British crown owed gratitude and its newly acquired lands offered reward.

General Lyman was regarded by the British as the ablest and most trustworthy Colonial general in the northern colonies in the French and Indian War. Still, he appeared most vividly in history when, in 1762, he attracted attention in "the finest coat ever seen in New York." And his prestige, if not his appearance, was enhanced by the fact that he was married to Eleanor, daughter of Col. Timothy Dwight of Northampton, Massachusetts, whose son and great-grandson were both to become presidents of Yale University.

In his "finest coat," or garments more suitable for hard fighting, Phineas Lyman went on from New York to command all the provincial troops in the British expedition against Havana. Soon after the fighting ended he was off to England seeking grants of land for colonization in the West. Much British red tape and vacillation of policy about colonization in the West met him there, but, in 1770, he obtained a grant of 20,000 acres near Natchez.

Phineas did not set out to take up his grant as quickly as

Colonel Hutchins did. He came back from England in ill health but full of talk about the Natchez lands. He must have talked much in the tavern of his old wartime comrade, Israel Putnam, later to become a popular hero of the patriots in the American Revolution. At any rate, Israel and his brother Rufus were stirred by the "false hopes" Phineas raised about the lands. They set out, representing other Yankees, on a voyage of inspection which carried them, in 1772–73, to the area Lyman had pictured as a promised land. The Putnams left a journal about their explorations but preferred to remain in New England. Lyman set out to establish his colony of Georgiana, named, of course, after George III, but soon after his arrival at Natchez died, in 1774, "leaving his wife and surviving children to continue his ill fortune."

They received it in full measure. Back in New England the clashes of loyalties were sharpening. The Putnams, whom Phineas had interested in his lands, were preoccupied for the moment with patriotic resistance to the king. However, Phineas' father-in-law, Colonel Dwight, and some others had little patience with hotheaded Liberty Boys. Those impertinent patriots would probably have hesitated in the case of Colonel Dwight, but the atmosphere, in which they were often ready with tar and feathers for Tories, could not have been pleasant for the colonel.

As a judge of probate he had sworn fealty to the crown. So to escape his scruples and perhaps his neighbors he bought part of the Mississippi grant of his deceased son-in-law Phineas. For a little while it was a happy retreat from the far-off war which had the effect of increasing immigration to the area. Plantations were multiplying, and planters established credits in London, Pensacola, and Jamaica. Not all who came, however, were the king's gentlemen. Some wished to be neutral. And some sympathized with the Revolution.

Many who began to fill the Southwest were not opulent by any means, then or later. Poor men came through the gaps in the mountains and down the rivers, some as hunters, rovers, or small traders. Others began to edge in as little farmers seeking a better chance than they had found in the piney hills of the East. No dreams of great domains pulled them. Debt and disadvantage, drought and thin soils pushed them. Most of them declined at the end of their trek ever to permit, between themselves and those who thought they were their betters, such distinctions as marked the Eastern differences between tidewater planters and the poor whites, or crackers. From the beginning they brought along, with their few possessions, the frontier democracy and insistent white equality which was to spread its power back even to the lands they left behind. Revolutionary notions made their way along the same paths and rivers as those over which Tories and Toryism came.

Even when Colonel Hutchins arrived, in 1772, irritations vere already growing in the Eastern colonies which would ;oon lead to the American Revolution. Not even Natchez was quarantined from new ideas about liberty. It was still British soil. So when the Revolution erupted, Tories fled from the Atlantic colonies. They found enough congenial company in the area where Britain, with Spain so close at hand, needed loyal men.

"The majority of those who came were men of intelligence and character," wrote the Mississippi historian John Francis Hamtramck Claiborne. As a grandson of Colonel Hutchins, Claiborne may have had some partiality for that gentleman and his social equals. He may also have been unduly critical of some who disagreed with the colonel.

"Bad men, outlaws and fugitives from justice came likewise," he said, "but they were outnumbered and restrained by the better class; and there was generally peace and order and security for property. . . the Natchez district was proverbial for its immunity from crimes and criminals."

As chief magistrate, Colonel Hutchins had much to do with the order in which, as in any community, happy boys like Johnny Hutchins were born and old men like Colonel Dwight died. And the safe distance of Natchez from the Revolutionary War, which was a civil war, too, was emphasized by the fact that it was a whole year after Colonel Dwight died on June 10, 1777, before the news of his death reached Massachusetts.

Obviously Johnny Hutchins was not big enough to be shooting bears then, though it did not take boys on the frontier long to learn to shoot. Before the Revolution was over, up at the other end of the Natchez Trace Jonathan Robertson, son of the founder of the Cumberland settlements, was at the age of twelve manning a porthole in an Indian attack. In that fight, survivors reported, he was as "good a soldier as ever pulled a trigger." No such chores at the time were required of Johnny Hutchins. Still, near Natchez he was closer to danger than his opulent parents expected.

The town was then only a village among the plantations. Its few buildings were all on the then-extensive river flats below the bluff which was later to become famous or infamous as Natchez-under-the-Hill. All of them were ordinary frame or log houses. There were only four merchants: Hanchett & Newman, Thomas Barber, and two others who were soon to become prominent in the troubles of the community.

One was Capt. John Blommart, a Swiss soldier of fortune who had served as a warrant officer in the British Royal Navy during the Seven Years' War. In 1765 he conducted a group of Swiss Protestants into the colony. Later he acquired Mount Locust, north of Natchez, and there built a house to meet one of the conditions of the grant: "one good Dwelling House to contain at least twenty feet in length, sixteen feet in breadth." By 1781 he was one of the wealthiest men in the Old Natchez District.

The fourth merchant was James Willing from Philadelphia. Johnny Hutchins must have known him, because, as was afterwards said with much indignation,

Willing was often a guest at the Hutchins' house. He did not do very well as a merchant. Arriving in Natchez in the same year in which Johnny was born, he was said to be "doing an indifferent business as a merchant and frittering away his fortune in dissolute living." His creditors in New Orleans were already doubtful about him in 1775.

However, James Willing had a brother, Thomas, in Philadelphia who was a partner of rich Robert Morris, the financier of the Revolution. As a patriot in 1775, this Willing was elected to the Second Continental Congress. And though in 1776 he voted against the resolution for independence and was not re-elected to the Congress, his firm was the most solid support Morris had in finding funds for the Colonial armies. Later, Thomas Willing's daughter Anne, famous for her wit and beauty, married William Bingham, one of the wealthiest men in America. She became the acknowledged leader of Federalist society in Philadelphia. In that staid continental capital, historians noted that "there was nothing of the democrat and nothing of the Puritan about Mrs. Bingham." Abigail Adams called her "the dazzling Mrs. Bingham." It was to her that George Washington gave his promise to sit for his portrait by Gilbert Stuart.

Obviously, therefore, Natchez merchant James Willing had influential friends in Philadelphia even if he was financially and morally bankrupt in Natchez. A respected Scottish aristocrat and planter, William Dunbar, said Willing often "indulged his natural propensity for getting drunk." Still maybe only patriotism moved him when the colonies declared their independence in 1776. In Natchez he tried to stir up interest in the cause of the colonies, but without success. He found more sympathetic company in Philadelphia in 1777.

There, with the backing of his influential family and friends, he was made a captain in the Navy to lead an expedition down the Mississippi. His instructions have been lost, but it seems clear that, among other things, he was "to make prize of all British Property on the Mississippi." And that he did with a vengeance never forgotten or forgiven. On an armed boat, *Rattletrap,* with a volunteer crew of about 30 men, he came down from Fort Pitt (now Pittsburgh), and on the sixteenth or seventeenth of February, 1778, he reached the plantation of Colonel Hutchins near Natchez.

Historian Claiborne, who passed on to posterity no kind words for Willing, says that the new naval officer had recruited "vagabonds and rascals" and that they not only plundered Colonel Hutchins' house of its plate, money, and other valuables, and "insulted the family," but dragged the colonel from "his sick bed, a close prisoner," though the colonel had sent his sons (probably not young Johnny) to state his readiness to take an oath of neutrality.

Virtually every account of Willing's expedition reported his readiness to loot. Though a chairman of the Tennessee Historical Commission described him as "bold and enterprising," other historians stated that he embarked on a "career of confiscation and cruelty." He ransacked houses and burned some of them. Many people even fled across the river to the Spanish to escape him. Willing's men killed hogs and cattle, gathered up slaves, and broke such bottles of wine as they did not drink. Then down the river he went, still attacking the residences of the British and effectively giving the impression that he was only the advance guard of a much bigger American force behind him. The only humorous detail recorded about his activities was that Henry Stuart, British Indian Commissioner for the Southern District, escaped only "in his shirt"—presumably without his pants.

Oliver Pollock, the able friend and financier of the colonies in New Orleans, reported that Willing had got 100 slaves in his seizures. In other respects his "pillaging was done on a grand scale." But before long even the patriotic Pollock was disgusted with Willing's methods and the dissipation he indulged in in New Orleans. In the face of the anger of the settlers whom he had looted on the way down, Willing could not safely go back up the river, and Pollock was much relieved when Willing finally left by sloop for Philadelphia and possible applause at that distance. George Rogers Clark, who before the advent of Willing had been receiving supplies up the valley from Pollock for his war against the British in the north, expressed his feelings about Willing strongly. He was undoubtedly speaking of that pillaging patriot when he wrote, "when plunder is the prevailing Passion of any Body of Troops whether Great or Small, their Country can expect but little service from them."

Perhaps, considering Willing's character and Colonel Hutchins' almost apoplectic indignation, it was not strange that the colonel broke his parole as prisoner in New Orleans. Soon after he was carried there, he learned that more men were to be sent up to Natchez to see that the oath of neutrality was observed. Hurrying home, he "excited the inhabitants of Natchez to take up arms, by declaring on OATH to the people, that this detachment was coming up with a determination of robbing the inhabitants without exception." Undoubtedly the colonel was overwrought, but when a party of Americans did arrive the Natchez settlers gave it a violent reception. Once more the British flag flew over Fort Panmure, as the British had rechristened Fort Rosalie. It was not to stay there long.

In June, 1779, Spain formally declared war on England. The Spanish governor then was the brilliant and vigorous Bernardo de Galvez. It was Galvez who later, as viceroy of Mexico, built the supposedly impregnable Castle of Chapultepec in Mexico City. It became the American target in 1846, but many Spaniards feared the westward push of Saxon settlers even in the eighteenth century. Now Galvez, who had long been co-operating secretly with Pollock, moved against the British posts up the river. Fort Panmure capitulated on October 5, 1779.

Unexpectedly lenient, Galvez gave the people of Natchez

guarantees of religious freedom, promised to purchase their tobacco crop, and gave them right to move to the United States whenever they desired. Fear of the Dons faded. When English agents among the Chickasaws first tried to form a company in the area to go to the aid of the British whom Galvez was hitting hard at Mobile and Pensacola in British-held West Florida, there was little response. However, in the Natchez area a lot of plotting was going on, much of which is still obscure.

Undoubtedly there was in Natchez much sympathy for Pensacola, which also had become a haven of Tories when the fleet of Galvez appeared before it. The British there had established the Scottish firm of Panton, Leslie and Company, which had close relations with the Indians, including the Scottish-born James Logan Colbert, who had settled among the Chickasaws in the late 1730s and had been adopted by them. He and his half-breed sons and grandsons became almost a dynasty along the Natchez Trace. Colbert was as violently anti-Spanish as any Tory in besieged Pensacola. And down the Indian path in Natchez, even after Willing, some settlers were eager to bring the territory from Spanish to American control.

Word came from the British general at Pensacola, perhaps by way of the Chickasaws on the Trace, that British success at Pensacola would be served by a diversion in the form of a revolt at Natchez. So suddenly Hutchins, the lean loyalist, and some revolutionary sympathizers, too, were all involved in revolt together. (Some historians give credit for the leadership of the revolt to Phineas Lyman. If so, he must have been a son of that name. The elder Phineas was already dead.)

None of the settlers around Natchez seem to have been disturbed at the time because the man who brought the commissions from the British was, as Colonel Hutchins said later, "a noted vagabond of bad character and abandoned principles." Maybe the colonel was at first not sufficiently informed. Perhaps he was brought late into the scheme and faced the cold alternative of joining the revolt or losing his life. However, his grandson, the historian, describes him as one of the "old soldiers" who undertook the small but disastrous rebellion. After it, according to the same grandson, he, together with the rich merchant John Blommart, who was given command, was effective in restraining the more bloodthirsty and avaricious of the rebels against Spain.

They took Fort Panmure by a trick on April 29, 1781. Unable to take the post by storm, they sent word by a supposed friend of the commander that the fort had been mined and would be blown up. That was possible. A ravine did lead to the foundations of the fort. The Spaniards capitulated, but the success was quickly followed by dissension and quarreling among the victors. It was followed swiftly, too, by the news that Pensacola had fallen to Galvez and that he would soon be on his way to take revenge on the rebels. Many did not wait to see the form his revenge might take. Their flight, in which Hutchins was certainly in the van, had been made a story more tragic even than that of Willing's wanton looting in the area where he had failed as a merchant but left bitter memories as a marauder.

The leaders of the revolt with wives and children, says Claiborne, "struck into the wilderness" in flight. The historian went on: "Fearful of pursuit, fearful of ambush, dogged by famine, tortured by thirst, exposed to every vicissitude of weather, weakened by disease, more than decimated by death, the women and children dying every day, this terrible journey marks the darkest page of our record."

Among the fugitives, he said, were Lymans and Dwights, and "many of the most cultured families of Massachusetts and Connecticut." When, along the path that was to become the Natchez Trace, they reached the Bayou Pierre, the waters were very high. Mrs. Dwight found an old Indian pirogue, or canoe, and led the crossing.

"Christians never despair," Claiborne quoted her as saying like a Pilgrim heroine, "I will proceed onward in the search and not stop as long as my limbs will support me."

Charles Gayarré, in his *History of Louisiana,* wrote even more dramatically and perhaps more romantically of the flight:

The fugitives had to cross an immense wilderness, inhabited by hostile Indians, and, as they were Loyalists, they had to pursue a circuitous route, in order to avoid falling into the hands of the armed bands of Americans who had shaken off the yoke of the mother country. But they were placed between a choice of evils, and they determined for the perils of the journey.

He described the hazards of interminable forests . . . streams, deep and broad . . . steep and lofty mountains, disease and storm. They had to be constantly on the alert, he said, "against the Indian foe, who, they knew, were hovering around them." With Latin emotion, Gayarré surpassed even Claiborne in his story of the frantic flight.

The mother's breast [he wrote] dried up under the parched lips of the plaintive infant, who drooped and fell like a withered leaf; the orphan sat weeping on the mother's grave, which he was soon to leave; the wife's wailings were heard for the husband's loss, and the husband's manly cheeks were seen furrowed by tears near the wife's corpse. The aged father gave his last blessing to his family, and sank to rise no more. Sorrowfully, indeed, journeyed this miserable band, some on horseback, and many, whose horses had died, on foot. The greedy buzzard during the day, and the howling wolf at night, seemed to be instinctively attracted toward them by the hope of anticipated prey.

Somewhere along the way, probably where the Natchez Trace turned more sharply north, the party divided. One group, of which Colonel Hutchins was a member, went by Alabama and Georgia and at the Atlantic Coast "crossed on a raft, the Altamaha at its mouth." They finally arrived at Savannah, then in British control, in the later part of October, after traveling 131 days. The other group, wrote Gayarré, "had the bad luck of falling into the hands of

American insurgents." Their luck was not so bad as he recorded it.

Much history as to what happened to that second band which did not cross Georgia to Savannah and the sea is lost in the wilderness. Still, Gayarré's statement that they had the bad luck of falling into the hands of the American insurgents minimizes the complexity of the company of the rebels. Not all were, like the Hutchinses and the Lymans, "loyal subjects of King George." Some, indeed, were Colonial in their sympathies. Still, as A. W. Putnam, a descendant of the family of Israel and Rufus Putnam, put it in his *History of Middle Tennessee: or the Life and Times of General James Robertson,* they "preferred to be the subjects of the King of England . . . than the compulsory slaves of the King of Spain."

In the wilderness they found a friend and defender in a man whose family were to have much to do with the whole story of the Natchez Trace. His name was James Logan Colbert. He must have been aging in his power then as one of the first of the Scottish and British traders who had been moving westward since the seventeenth century. He had been a man in flight once himself as one of those highlanders who, as adherents of James the Pretender, fomented the Jacobite uprising in 1715.

Apparently Colbert arrived in the Southern colonies in January, 1736, and headed straight for the wilderness. He was only one of many such traders. Some of the first fortunes of South Carolina were based upon trade—and not only trade in deerskins, called "leather," and furs. Also, though the Colonial records are more reticent about it, the traders encouraged the Chickasaws to war on other tribes in order to provide slaves for seaboard planters.

Evidence of the trade is provided in a South Carolina law which prohibited the branding of slaves as "leather" was branded. Some South Carolina aristocratic families based their fortunes on such trade. In that state's Low Country Choctaw slaves were valued as hunters. In return the

Indians who captured men of other tribes as slaves got guns, powder, bullets, flints, war paint, blankets, scarlet cloth, and embroidered serge.

When the Natchez fugitives came toward him up the Trace, Colbert, as Scotchman turned Chickasaw, had already gained the reputation of "pirate," which clung to his name because of raids on Spanish boats and posts on the rivers. Sometimes even stalwart James Robertson, the Tennessee leader, referred to him as a pirate, though only in correspondence with neighboring Spanish officials whom he hoped to placate. It was this "pirate" who became the champion and protector of the Natchez rebels against the Spanish. Having given strong assistance to the British during the siege of Pensacola, he now had hospitality for the refugees and a desire to treat with Spain for the exchange of others who had been captured.

On May 2, 1782, in his capacity as "pirate" he seized a Spanish boat containing 4,500 pesos and—a more important prize—a prominent and voluble Spanish lady, the wife of Francis Cruzat, the Spanish commander at St. Louis. She was a lady whose talkativeness after release contributed much to history. He held her hostage for some of the Natchez rebels in New Orleans.

It is not known exactly where Colbert lived at this time. The main Chickasaw settlement, however, was a few miles north of the present Tupelo, along what became the Natchez Trace. He had a rich lodging, according to Madame Cruzat and other Spanish prisoners, and owned 150 slaves. His sons who were to follow him in eminence along the Trace were born of several Chickasaw wives. The clear fact is that he admitted with some arrogance to Galvez's successor, Governor Estevan Miró, that he had given refuge to Natchez rebels.

"Sir": he wrote, "I Receivd yours of the 29th July this day Wherein you mention as follows Concerning the late Inhabitants of the Notches which you term as Reb[els] & Signifys in your [letter] As I harbourd them Rebles. Now Sir you ought to be the last Person that Should Ever mention Anything of that Nature to me when you Upheld Mr. Willing in Robing & plundering the Inhabitants on the Missisippy, before the war was Ever declared between the Crown of great Brittain & his Catholick majesty notwithstanding I never mein to Uphold Or Harbour Rebles of any kind. for those People that left the notches I do not Look Upon them as Rebles Neither do I emagine they were Ever your subjects therefore I can but look on them as Other Inglish Subjects. . . ."

So the Spanish did not get them. They arrived at the recently established American settlements along the Cumberland River, in 1783, at a time when every white man and white man's gun were needed in the struggle for survival against the Indians. Men were needed where boys like young Jonathan Robertson had to man portholes in stockades. Even then, however, Jonathan's father, Col. James Robertson, was negotiating for peace with the Chickasaws, probably including Colbert. Ironically, perhaps, not the refugees but Colbert soon lost his life in the wilderness. In November, 1784, on a journey to persuade other chiefs that perhaps their best course lay in friendship with the Americans, he was said to have been thrown from his horse and fatally injured. Some thought instead that his Negro slave who brought back the news of the accident had murdered his master.

Claiborne gave a long list, including two Lymans, who escaped to the Cumberland settlements. Putnam listed more. They remained, he said, at the stations in Tennessee for several years, but "they kept a strong desire to return to the Mississippi, avenge themselves, expel the Spaniards, recover their property, and secure their homes and the territory as rightful portions of the United States."

Mr. Putnam's account, written in 1859 when he was president of the Tennessee Historical Society, packed as much opinion and patriotism as fact into that passage. Most of the refugees were glad to go back to live under a lenient

Spain. Coming and going, these men in a real sense began the Natchez Trace as an ever more crowding passage between Natchez and Nashville, first called Nashborough. That place was then scarcely a town. James Robertson, whom Andrew Jackson called the Father of Tennessee, had only come ahead of his settlers to the bluff above the Cumberland River on Christmas Day in 1779.

Then thirty-seven, Robertson was already an old-timer on the frontier. He had visited this west in 1770. He had been with Richard Henderson in 1775 when that great and grasping North Carolina land speculator made what Ida Tarbell, in a study of the westward movement of Abraham Lincoln's ancestors, called a "vicious" trade for a vague title to many thousands of acres of Kentucky lands with some— by no means all—of the Cherokees. It was Henderson who dispatched Boone to Kentucky with early settlers in 1775. Also, Henderson's advertisements of his grandiloquent Transylvania Company scheme to settlers east of the mountains matched the propaganda of John Law in the Mississippi Bubble. From his salesmanship came a folk song surpassing any TV commercial:

> Rise you up, my dear, and present to me your hand,
> And we'll take a social walk to a far and distant land,
> Where the Hawk shot the Buzzard and the Buzzard
>   shot the Crow.
> We'll rally in the canebrake and shoot the Buffalo!
> Shoot the Buffalo! Shoot the Buffalo!
> Rally in the canebrake and shoot the Buffalo!

Nobody along the border knew better than Colonel Robertson that the way to the country along the Cumberland River in Tennessee which he chose would not be "a social walk." He was one of the great men of the frontier. He fought the Indians and won their trust as well. He did more to build the settlement than he did to enrich himself in its lands. The task of the colonel, who later and for poor pay helped make a real road of the Natchez Trace, was to drive a herd of horses, cattle, and sheep overland by the Wilderness Road to the bluffs of the Cumberland. That year the river was frozen so solidly that his cavalcade crossed it on the ice.

The rest of the settlers, including 120 women and children (one a thirteen-year-old girl named Rachel), came with Rachel's father, Col. John Donelson, great-nephew of the first president of Princeton.

On a voyage never undertaken before, Donelson's flagboat, properly named the *Adventure,* led a flotilla of boats down the Holston River to the Tennessee, down the Tennessee to the Ohio, and up the Ohio to the Cumberland and the meeting with Robertson. It was a 985-mile journey through uncharted waters, by shoal and suck and roaring rapids. Shores were infested by Cherokees who still resented the deeper movement into their hunting ground.

With the American Revolution still in progress, there was threat also from Shawnees to the north who had been incited to drive back the Americans "or make wolf-bait of their carcasses." And from the company some carcasses were left by the way. Babies were born and died. British lead thudded into the timbers of the boats. Smallpox broke out among the voyagers. A Negro slave died of frostbite, and all suffered in one of the coldest winters ever known in Tennessee. Food supplies ran low. But Donelson brought his settlers to the cabins Robertson had built on April 24, 1780. That was just a year before the time when the "old soldiers" like Colonel Hutchins at Natchez revolted against Spain. In the American Southwest, settlements at each end gave full reason for the road from Natchez to Nashville called the Natchez Trace.

As Nashville, or the stations of the settlers around it, developed despite the incursions of the Indians and bad white men, too, Natchez revived almost before the refugees from the revolt got through the wilderness. Colonel Hutchins, as he hurried eastward with the group which reached Savannah, had a stalwart wife (and probably Johnny) still in Natchez. When the Spanish first arrived, displaying every evidence of the horrid revenge the rebels feared, Mrs. Hutchins stood her ground. And when Spanish soldiers hung one of her Negro slaves named Tony, she defied them. She cut the rope and saved his life. Also she spoke so sharply to some of the Spanish officers that more timid neighbors were appalled. Her courage was honored by Carlos de Grand-Pré, who had been sent to command the town.

"You did right to permit no seizure of this lady's property," said his superior, Don Pedro Piernas, at New Orleans. "We war not on woman or for plunder. She had already been robbed by American briggands, and our forbearance will contrast honorably with theirs."

And when Colonel Hutchins got back from his flight, which he apparently did not slacken until he went all the way to London, he found his property intact. Indeed, such was the leniency of the Spanish that at length he got from them 4,532 more acres. And Johnny, eight or nine on the colonel's return, was already hunting in the canebrake with the Negro slave for bears. It seems good to assume that this black hunter was the Tony Mrs. Hutchins cut down from the Spaniard's rope. All we know is that this Tony lived to great age, filled with many memories. Johnny, too, as an old man remembered well not only the tumult of angry men but also the bears in the canebrakes when he was a child.

IV: THE DOUBLE-DEALERS

IN POSSESSION of the lands on the east bank of the great river which the British had held, the Spanish were eager and wary, and fearful and gullible, too.

A census taken by Governor Miró in 1788 showed a population of 2,679 people in the Natchez District, 1,000 more than there had been in 1785. This thousand came in with Spain's consent, even its invitation, to accept His Catholic Majesty's rule. All were eager to take the arpents offered on the bayous and the watercourses, depending upon the number of slaves they brought.

By no means all who came for land brought the loyalty Spain hoped to buy. Not all of those welcomed were quite trusted. Miró once told those administering oaths of allegiance to "carefully observe the manner in which they shall receive them, and the expression of their faces. Of this you will give me precise information, every time you send me the original oaths taken."

This was not an undue precaution, and it turned out not to be an adequate one. Col. Anthony Hutchins had brought back unaltered his British sentiments when he was allowed to return to his Spanish properties. Some people who had fled to Tennessee remained ardent Americans, sure that the land was destined to become a part of the young United States.

At high and low levels the wilderness country was a wilderness of loyalties, too. Not only would Colonel Robertson on the Cumberland flatter Miró by naming

Middle Tennessee after him, misspelling it Mero. Afterwards as well, good men like George Rogers Clark and
Senator Blount of Tennessee, Kentucky politicians as well as
Carolina and Georgia land speculators, toyed with such a
transmountain independence as might serve Spain—and
would certainly serve, they thought, the West. Dr. James
O'Fallon, an adventurer and chief agent for great
speculators, told George Washington one story and Miró
another about land settlement plans above Natchez later to
be labeled the Yazoo Frauds.

Even George Washington's great Prussian aide Baron von
Steuben, then settled far north on the Mohawk River, was
involved in such scheming. He proposed that if Spain
would give him 2 million acres of suitable land on the east
bank of the Mississippi, he would establish an armed colony
which would guard Spanish dominions from the
southbound stream of people looking for land.

"The people are all Mississippi Mad," the baron wrote in
1788.

Von Steuben's plans did not materialize. But the madness
he described was full grown when Spain sent to Natchez as
governor the amiable, lenient, ceremonial, hospitable, and
sometimes bumbling Manuel Gayoso de Lemos. He is still
recalled in Natchez as a glittering personage. He seems to
have embodied the Spanish flavor which is still revered in
architecture and recollection in the town on the bluffs above
the big river. In history, however, he seems a sort of
Castilian innocent presiding over a decade of double-
dealing in which the reputed gentility of the times was more
often than not the mask of grasping men, among both
aristocrats and roustabouts.

Gayoso moved about much among the people and was
popular with them. Educated in England, he spoke the
language of the surrounding planters. Later he was to marry
one of their daughters. As ceremonial and extravagant
widower, he made a real capital out of Natchez and
provided its society with a little court. *Bon vivant,* he built a

great and beautiful house called Concord, emblematic of the tranquility he hoped, like Bienville long before him, to establish. He laid out the outlines of the city and provided a square along the bluffs and streets spreading from the river. From it for years in Natchez tradition, gentility looked down with tolerance and scorn upon the squalor and sin of Natchez-under-the-Hill.

In the galleried, flagstoned mansion of Gayoso a frequent visitor was Gen. James Wilkinson. That persuasive personage was always ready to take more than his share of hospitality—or of anything else. Eloquently he paid in companionship and promises for Gayoso's highly convivial hospitality. Once he said he would willingly sacrifice one arm if he might embrace Gayoso with the other. The general was energetic as well as congenial. And it may be that in the very deftness of his perfidy he did more than other men to develop the Natchez Trace both for the West it served and for his own gain. The swift downstream currents of the great river, the slow overland way homeward—as well as the pushing Americans and defensive Spaniards—made an almost perfect design for his activities as trader and traitor, taking a golden profit from both.

He came into the surging West when Kentucky was emerging from its pioneer period and was hunting trade instead of buffalo or bears. Educated as a physician, he had turned to arms in the Revolution. He played a minor but shoddy part in the Conway Cabal against George Washington's leadership, though always loudly insisting upon his honor in the devious conspiracy. He had survived it and secured a post as clothier-general of the colonies. Grave irregularities were found in his accounts in that post.

In Pennsylvania, before he was thirty, he had shown his lasting characteristics as an intriguing, hard-drinking, avaricious man. Nevertheless when he came to Kentucky in 1784, with a Philadelphia Biddle as his wife, his ready pen and handsome person were persuasive. Soon, pushing men

like George Rogers Clark and others aside, he made himself
leader in the expression of discontent with the new
American Confederation.

That government was providing opportunities for him.
John Jay (with the approval of the great Washington) was
about ready to relinquish free navigation of the Mississippi
to Spain. That meant giving the cork to Middle American
trade to Spain which held the river's mouth. It also meant
strangulation of western trade. Many in the West were ready
to secede from the new confederacy. And that created a
situation in which Wilkinson could make himself the
champion of Kentucky (and other western areas, too), the
pensioner of Spain, and convivial recipient of the hospitality
of such charming Castilian gentlemen as Governor Miró
and his Natchez subordinate, Manuel Gayoso de Lemos, at
the same time.

As ex-soldier, new speculator, and politician, Wilkinson
went down the rivers from Kentucky, in 1787, with two
flatboats and a smaller vessel in which he traveled more
comfortably. He was by no means the first such trader.
Indian barterers had traversed the rivers. The first French
had moved on the streams from Canada to the Gulf. As
early as 1760, Jacques Thimoté de Monbruen, whose
grandfather was the first Canadian elevated to the French
nobility, made the same trip with his wife.

As hunter and trader, De Monbruen, who later became a
well-known citizen of Nashville, was on the Cumberland
that year in "a large boat with six or eight hands"—the
precursors of the thousands of flatboatmen and Trace
travelers. Muddy waters pouring from a creek showed him
that a herd of buffalo were crossing the stream or stamping
around a salt lick. Quickly he made a cargo of buffalo hides
and tallow and headed with "freight and boat for New
Orleans." Little more than wilderness was on the shore at
Natchez when he passed it.

General Wilkinson was not the first to make the voyage on
the lower river under the Spanish regime. The first cargo-

laden boat from the increasingly productive West to
Spanish Natchez was officially listed as a "small scow from
Fort Pitt," loaded with flour, which arrived in 1785. Its
arrival was such an event that the Spanish governor there
asked his government in Madrid what to do about it. The
answer was a vacillating policy by the Spaniards who held
the river's mouth. It was also the source of continuing
irritation and intrigue.

Wilkinson made that situation the basis of what later
times would have regarded as his "racket." He still wore,
despite the fact that it was a little tarnished, his revolutionary title of General. Only thirty, "beaming with
intelligence," handsome still and ingratiating, the general
tarried briefly at Natchez on this trip. Floating on down the
river, he not only sold tobacco for which Kentuckians
eagerly desired a market. Also, then with Spanish officials,
he began his long and profitable career as agent and
pensioner of Spain, which hoped transmountain Americans
might prefer Spanish domination to American weakness.

To give Wilkinson all possible credit, he did not seem a
simple scoundrel then—indeed, there was seldom anything
simple about his rascality. He was a civilian—merchant,
farmer, and promoter at the time. In the young West he was
by no means the only fortune hunter. Indeed, when he
drifted with his flatboats down the rivers, his trading
journey seemed a good, bold enterprise to Westerners.
They were growing more and more impatient with the
apparent unconcern with their problems shown by the weak
American republic on the settled and satisfied Atlantic
seaboard.

The West did not know or very much care, in 1787, that
on this trip Wilkinson sold to Spain, for a price and a
pension, not only his tobacco but also his loyalty, upon
which no country, his own or any other, or anybody could
really depend. At the gracious suggestion of Governor Miró,
who would not be content to have a district misspelled in his
honor in Tennessee, Wilkinson took a secret oath of

allegiance to Spain. He became, as belatedly opened archives showed, Spanish Agent No. 13. And after this trip, with plenty of money from "tobacco," he took the sea route to Philadelphia. From there he traveled over the mountains to Fort Pitt, where the Monongahela and Allegheny rivers meet to form the Ohio, and thence down to the Bluegrass country.

Three years after Wilkinson made his profitable voyage, at least 60 flatboats stopped at Natchez with the crops and goods of Kentucky, Pennsylvania, Ohio, Tennessee, and Virginia. And as early as that year, 1790, Spanish authorities there reported at least 250 men returning northward over the Natchez Trace. Spanish bureaucrats kept multitudinous records.

"Dios guarde a Vs. muchos anos," Gayoso's predecessor, Governor Carlos de Grand-Pré, regularly saluted Governor Miró, at a time when Miró knew he was increasingly going to need the protection of God from the tide of Americans pouring down by land and water toward his outpost at Natchez. Certainly nothing would long or effectually stop the traders who came by the river to return by the Trace. They came in a variety of boats. There were canoes after the Hiawatha northern, birchbark fashion. There were others, called pirogues, hollowed from the trunks of big trees and fastened together with heavy planks. There were bateaux, light, flat-bottomed boats tapering toward the ends, and skiffs, light enough to be rowed. More important were the keelboats and barges. Most significant of all were the great flatboats. They were called arks, Kentucky boats, New Orleans boats, and, most often, broadhorns. Their only means of propulsion was human muscle and the current of the river. They varied greatly in size, from 20 to 60 feet in length and 10 to 20 feet in width. They cost about three or four dollars for each foot in length and were generally sold for lumber at their downstream destination. Some of them had pens for cattle, horses, and swine.

In Grand-Pré's reports, which have a quaint quality now,

he translated the first names of the boat owners and crews into their Spanish equivalents. There was a Juan Williams who came, with 25 Negroes, to settle. Guillermo Thompson arrived from Kentucky with 150,095 pounds of tobacco and 70 barrels of flour. Another gentleman came with three saddles and 80 gallons of whiskey.

Both were already essential items in the hard-riding, hard-drinking neighborhood. Monongahela rye was a favorite in the trade. It was also an intoxicating symbol of the sentiments of men in western Pennsylvania, as well as in Kentucky, who felt themselves neglected or mistreated by the seaboard states. George Washington had to send troops to quell the rebellious distillers in western Pennsylvania after Congress, in 1791, levied a tax of four cents a gallon on such spirits. Kentucky bourbon came down the river later. Also, there were stills in many of the cargoes. Already there were some who, according to an early Mississippi saying, considered "a barrel of whiskey a week but a small allowance for a large family without any cow."

Alexander Wilson, the famous ornithologist, wrote of the "Kentucky boats, loaded with what it must be acknowledged are the most valuable commodities of a country; viz., men, women and children, horses and ploughs, millstones, etc." Other arks came loaded with skins of otter, beaver, fox, and wildcat, butter, linseed, unbleached linen, carriages, candles, tallow, wagons, lard, iron bars, all the products of the central United States. And all the boats which came, including most of those owned by men who planned to settle, carried crews which went back home through the wilderness. They were not only men from Fort Pitt, Tennesseans, and Kaintucks. This Kaintuck label was also often applied to Buckeyes from Ohio and Hoosiers from Indiana—to all boatmen from the North.

Perhaps in fixing the southern terminus of the Trace the most significant flatboats which arrived, in 1790, were those of William and Theophilus Minor. They brought along 200 barrels of flour, 500 pounds of bacon, 5 pairs of millstones,

5 barrels of cider, and 15 barrels of whiskey. These Minors were undoubtedly relatives of Stephen Minor, who had come to the region earlier from Pennsylvania. Now in Spanish service, he was known as Don Estevan Minor in his capacity as Spanish officer and adjutant at Natchez. These new Minors, coming to take up plantations, were lucky to have such a relative. Stephen (or Estevan) was a man who could ease every path, particularly his own.

Natchez itself was still only a village for such men's trade. Already, however, as grace grew with wealth on the plantations around it, there were signs of the liveliness which was to mark Natchez as more and more boatmen pranced or staggered home through it. As wickedness is generally romanticized most by the pious, a preacher-historian wrote that "perhaps as early as 1790, if not earlier" a race track on the flats under-the-hill served "dissipation and irreligion."

The rich settlers, says Claiborne, brought to Natchez in this period "culture, social position, enterprise and considerable wealth and these elements controlled and characterized the community. At no period since has there been better order and fewer crimes." Maj. George Willey, a revolutionary veteran who arrived on Christmas Day, 1787, agreed.

"The commission of crime was not greater than in the frontier settlements of our own countrymen," he said, "and, indeed, all the bad reputations which Natchez ever acquired was after it came into the hands of Americans."

Perhaps in mellowing recollection he gave the early town too little credit for the violence which was part of its vitality. Even he recalled that "the well-known disposition of the Spaniard to use the knife in all their quarrels" caused the governor to forbid the carrying of any weapon made of steel. "But the Spaniards evaded it by making a kind of stilletto of hardened wood with which they managed . . . to kill one another." Even more troublesome were the Indians, who, like flatboatmen after them, came into town to get drunk.

They could only be controlled by "an old Frenchman, named Baptiste, their interpreter," who quieted their most disorderly outbreaks with his whip.

"It is curious," this reminiscer mused, "that the Indian who seems to have no fear of a gun or a knife, has a great dread of a whip."

Apparently, however, amiable Spanish officials and the unusually tolerant Spanish priests contrived to create a period of serenity. Sternness was accompanied by forgiveness. For many crimes the privilege of sanctuary was allowed, and often in the early mornings a Spaniard who knew he needed it would be seen with "his finger in the keyhole of the church."

General Wilkinson never needed such sanctuary. He strutted to the finest houses. And often, undoubtedly, he brought with him a young, able, and adventurous assistant. His name was Philip Nolan, whom the general once called "a child of my own raising." In such society the handsome, reticent Nolan became the brother-in-law of the Spanish adjutant, Don Estevan Minor. That young Spanish official had married Katherine, a daughter of the rich, proud merchant Bernard Lintot. Minor, already acquiring the lands on which he would breed the best race horses, was regarded as a good match for Katherine. For decades in Natchez she would be called "The Yellow Duchess" by those she scorned. Always her clothes, her furniture, even her carriage had to be the color of gold.

Nolan had seemed a less likely suitor. Though vouched for by his popular patron Wilkinson, dark rumors hung around his activities. There seemed a difference, too, between the fine horses Minor rode and those Philip sold. Nevertheless, though less willingly, he was accepted by the elegant Lintots as the husband of Katherine's passionate and less punctilious sister, Fannie.

Horse racer and horse dealer, the Lintot sons-in-law were certainly two of the most romantic figures of the age of double-dealing which marked the American West from

Natchez northward. Minor later acquired Gayoso's great house and grew rich as an American planter in the years when cotton made Natchez the capital of its kingdom. Nolan became much better known in fiction than in fact. He has come down in the American story as "The Man Without a Country." In such distortion, he is a familiar figure. What happened was that years after he was dead, during the Civil War, when loyalty to Union was a crusade, Edward Everett Hale used Nolan's name for his parable of the tragedy of treason.

"Damn the United States!" this fictitious Nolan cried. "I wish I may never hear of the United States again!"

And as most ex-schoolboys remember, author Hale had the court-martial turn this Nolan demand into his punishment. In actual fact, in the Natchez District in his time, he was only one of many men who seemed inconstant as to country. Their loyalties sometimes seemed of a hop, skip, and jump variety, depending upon personal safety or private profit.

The likenesses and differences in the brothers-in-law Nolan and Minor are dramatic. Both were adventurous and decorative. Both, of course, loved horses. Minor's rich descendants became leading breeders and racers of thoroughbreds in the Natchez region. Indeed, there is a document which shows that Minor won $450 on a horse race in 1783 from a man who lost so much on the horses that he ran off and left his debts to be settled by the sale of his wife's slaves.

A friend advised Nolan to "attend to your business and think not of horse racing." Nevertheless, Nolan was probably the greater gambler with horses—not at the track but on the plains. He was one of the most famous wild horse hunters in the country west of the Mississippi. He went as far as San Antonio after the roving herds said to be the descendants of animals brought over by the Spaniards in their first conquests. Though he was supposed to sell them only to the Spanish cavalry, officials winked for a while when he shared the profits of the trade. These tough, wiry horses became a familiar aspect of travel on the Trace.

"To catch them," wrote a French traveler, "they make use of tame horses that run much swifter, and with which they approach them near enough to halter them. They take them to New Orleans and Natchez, where they fetch about $50. The crews, belonging to the boats, that return by land to Kentucky frequently purchase some of them. The two that I saw and made a treat of were roan colored and of middling size, the head large, and not proportionate with the neck, the limbs thick, and mane rather full and handsome. These are capricious, difficult to govern, and frequently throw the rider and take flight."

There was a difference, like that between Nolan's Opelousas horses and the fine breeds Minor rode, in the men themselves. Sometimes it seemed almost like that of the much romanticized split personality of old Natchez, between the town on the bluffs and Natchez-under-the-Hill. A good deal of romanticism has attended the contrast between the sin and squalor on the shore and "the tranquil streets—the elegance of the wind-swept heights" on the bluffs. In Natchez history there were houses of prostitution and gambling houses, too, on the hill as well as under it. Planters sometimes engaged in brawls as rough as any on the shore below.

Actually the hill and river flats did not flourish so coincidently that a romantic could always look at one time from genteel heights to a bawdy bottom. Undoubtedly Nolan came down from the plantations, where he was accepted because of Wilkinson and his wife, to recruit for his horse hunts tough customers who gathered on the shore. On his trips with such men he was much more than a rough adventurer. Thomas Jefferson himself, as a man interested in everything and especially every aspect of the West, wrote Nolan for information about the "large herds of horses in a wild state, in the country west of the Mississippi."

"You will render to natural history a very acceptable

service," Jefferson wrote, "if you will enable our Philosophical Society to add so interesting a chapter to the history of this animal."

Undoubtedly Nolan had more business on the Trace than the sale of Opelousas horses. Dark as he was, he might have been the unidentified "Spaniard or Frenchman" who came up to Natchez about this time leading from New Orleans two stout packmules with saddles of Spanish make. They carried heavily laden leather bags which clinked. It was in this manner that Spanish pieces of eight were transported, and $3,000 worth was the standard mule load. Indeed, for 20 years after this time, the circulating medium of the territory was chiefly Spanish coin—out of the mints of fearfully guarded Mexico—doubloons, dollars, halfs, quarters, pistareens, and picayunes.

The dark gentleman in Natchez employed a man named Ballinger to take his burdened mules up the Trace. Perhaps Ballinger's first name was Joseph, though that may have been his brother's name. What is known is that the first Ballinger made it to Nashville, and there succumbed to the sickness which often overtook travelers on the road. So the first Ballinger got his brother to complete the journey to Frankfort, Kentucky. In Frankfort, which General Wilkinson had begun to develop a few years before on lands which he had bought for $433, the second Ballinger put up at a tavern and asked the general's whereabouts. He apparently made no secret about the clinking bags. He admitted he had $6,000 for the general. Already there were suspicions about the general's secret services to Spain. But that worthy's explanation of the bags of silver as "tobacco money" sufficed to protect him and to arouse the hopes of other Kentuckians, too.

As assistant to Governor Gayoso, Minor also had business on the Natchez Trace. For all his gaiety and leniency to his increasing number of American subjects, and his conviviality with men like Wilkinson, Gayoso came to Natchez with serious work to do. His duty was to further the

Spanish policy of inducing Americans to settle on Spanish lands and to hold others back by pushing Spanish domination northward. In both tasks he had work for the amiable but hard-riding Stephen Minor. Minor's journal of a trip he took up the Natchez Trace not only described part of that path but nakedly exposed the double-dealing self-interest, involving the Americans, Spaniards, and the not-so-innocent Indians, which marked the unspoiled wilderness at the time.

In the service of Gayoso, Minor, resplendent in his Spanish uniform, rode up the Path to the Choctaw Nation. From the journal he left, historians have concluded that his lack of comment on the character of the trail indicates that it was already a way familiar to travelers. As Minor reported it, it was a rough way still. The Trace crossed the lovely Bayou Pierre at a place called Grindstone Ford. The rains had so swollen the waters there that Minor had to swim the bayou and two of its branches, transporting his provisions and equipment on rafts. The way was beaten smoother at the southern end of the Trace. Some well-traveled parts of the trail were sunk deep in the soft soil, and the sides were matted with roots and vines. There were more streams, rougher ground, more hills ahead.

Minor found the Choctaws grumbling that the British had never paid them, as they had agreed to do in 1777, for the lands Spain was now assuring to settlers in possession. One of the chief Choctaw complaints, however, rose from the protest against the Spanish push of its claims to trade along the river up to Walnut Hills (now Vicksburg) and beyond, toward Chickasaw Bluffs (now Memphis). This grumble came chiefly from the white traders who had settled among the Choctaws, married Indian women, and produced a growing race of half-breeds. Some were tough customers, as the Spanish learned, by no means friendly to His Catholic Majesty's government. Among them were men who had "participated in crimes punishable by hanging."

In the early 1790s, there were already at least 500 of them along the trail.

Minor listened to the Indians and the truculent traders. Then a principal chief, Franchimastabe (which in Choctaw means "he took a Frenchman and killed him"), found an opportunity to be alone with Minor. The Spanish lieutenant made the most of it.

"The Governor of Natchez observes justly," Minor quoted himself as saying to him, "that you are the Head of a great Nation and your expenses and efforts in holding Meetings and making Speeches certainly must be very considerable, and that you now can repay yourself all this providing yourself with the major part of the Gifts which are destined for the Chiefs, and if this were agreed, it would remain the most profound secret."

Minor put in his journal Franchimastabe's answer.

"I always thought," the old chief said, "that in the end you would find the sure road to my heart."

The chief was ready to provide a packhorse to bring back the gifts. Specifically he wanted: "a Saddle, bridle and spurs, four kegs of Whiskey, an Ax, some Sugar and Coffee, some tweezers to remove the beard, and two dozen combs for his children and grandchildren."

That would not be all, Minor was sure. It was a bargain. Not all trade on the Natchez Trace, then or later, was either so complex or so simple. Still, the "sure road" which Minor found to Franchimastabe's heart ran to that of many others, too. Double-dealers were not always after special gifts. Sometimes grudge as well as treasure was negotiable along the Trace. So was the increasing American push, which seemed patriotism before anyone coined the phrase "manifest destiny." The problem was not as simple as General Wilkinson counting his money in Frankfort, where he never seemed to have enough.

V: WEDDING JOURNEY

THE LIBERTY they had won seemed very lean to many of the soldiers in the seaboard states who had fought for American independence. The years of war left them restless. Conservative politicians who took over government in many states seemed to them ungrateful for their services. Hard times set in. And North and South the stream of men and families, carts, and scrawny stock thickened in the mountain gaps. They were welcomed as strengthening such settlements as those on the Cumberland. Some first settlers, however, scowled at the more pretentious of the newcomers.

"We used to think we had the devil to pay (and a heavy debt, too, running on long installments) before the doctors and the lawyers came," said Captain John Rains, one of the Long Hunters who had entered Tennessee before the Robertson-Donelson settlers, "but the doctors introduced diseases, and the lawyers instituted suits, and now we have all to pay."

Such a man as Colonel Donelson, however, who had led the flotilla of settlers down the rivers in 1780, rejoiced at the arrivals who would fill their lands and serve their speculations. Though Donelson did not live to see the full flood of this movement, he found wealth in Tennessee. It was characteristic of the still-dangerous country that he found not only prosperity but death there, too. He did not live to see his daughter Rachel's disgrace.

The colonel was ambushed while surveying more of the land which became steadily more valuable as more settlers crowded into the West. Rachel always believed white marauders killed him. She did not think the Indian lived who could surprise and murder her father. Child of a dangerous land, she had been a charmer, too, even when she came to the Cumberland in her father's flotilla on the rivers. She was at the time of her arrival, said a historian who wrote during the lifetime of people who remembered her, black-eyed and black-haired and "as gay, bold and handsome a lass as ever danced on the deck of a flatboat, or took the helm while her father took a shot at the Indians."

Four years later, in 1784, her cousin, Mary Donelson Wilcox, reported that with her "lustrous dark eyes . . . she was irresistible to men." Many suitors came. And trouble came with them. Of the three men most associated with her story, two were gentlemen who left high reputations behind them. One, according to the verdict of most historians, was what the West already called a son-of-a-bitch. Rachel's story on the Natchez Trace rises from the fact that she married the son-of-a-bitch when she was seventeen. His name was Lewis Robards. There is some evidence that he was a slave trader. Certainly a man by the same name was a big slave trader in Kentucky a quarter of a century later. In Mercer County, Kentucky, where Rachel met him when she visited one of her brothers who had moved there, Robards' family occupied the finest house in the neighborhood. Rachel apparently had chosen well when she married him in 1785.

And Robards had married not only beauty but wealth, too. Despite troubles with land titles and Indians, Colonel Donelson, according to James Parton, the historian, took root in the new Cumberland country and "flourished greatly." Land, Negroes, cattle, horses, whatever was wealth in the settlement, Parton said, "he had in greater abundance than any other man." He left much property when, after many fights and escapes, he was found murdered in the woods.

Yet, on such a frontier there was frolic and dancing as well as fighting and death. The good fighter was honored, and sometimes, to the delight of his neighbors, he made tall tales about his powers. One of the noted Castlemans, hunters and traders, declared: "Castleman fired, girdled an oak, nicked the epidermis of an Indian's back, knocked over a catamount, brought down a flock of turkeys from the tree-tops, laid out a buffalo, blazed a section of lands, split enough boards to cover a shanty, and if I had fired once more, you may say I wasted time and ammunition."

As lively as such exaggeration was the music of the fiddlers, and men with the box and the bow were as necessary to the frontier as riflemen. The most famous fiddler in Middle Tennessee in these early days was James Gamble, who moved about carrying his fiddle and his bow in a sack of doeskin. Whenever there was to be an entertainment girls like Rachel Donelson demanded his presence.

"Oh, get Gamble! Do get Gamble. We know he will come!"

And Gamble came, making such music as the young people swore you could still feel and hear, not only in all-night dancing, but next day, too. Once, in the 1790s, Indians attacked Gamble as he hurried to a dance. Badly wounded, he saved his fiddle and made his way to a station where his wounds were dressed. Then "with perfect cheerfulness he lay on his back for some weeks, 'all the time a-fiddling,' trying to make his instrument imitate the surprise, the firing, the screaming, the race, the escape, his bandaged condition, and his hopes for the future." It must have been a symphony of American settlement.

All accounts suggest that young Rachel was the natural belle of such a land of danger and dancing. Indeed, the gay Mrs. Robards, says Parton, was not only the best storyteller and the most dashing horsewoman in the western country, she was the best dancer as well. Men did not stop noticing her when she married Robards, and three years after her marriage another man entered her story.

Peyton Short, a young attorney, came to board at the

Robards' house. In Kentucky, as down on the Cumberland settlements in those days, young male boarders were welcome as additional protectors against Indian and outlaw raids. Short was no ordinary fellow. His brother, William Short, was already the *élève* and secretary of Thomas Jefferson, and was then about to accompany the future President as diplomat to France. Possibly, as another able young man of the household, John Overton, said later, Peyton Short paid pretty Mrs. Robards "perhaps a little more than ordinary politeness." Robards saw more than that in their relationship. Though his mother took Rachel's side, Robards ordered her "never to show her face in his house again" and sent word to the Donelsons back on the Cumberland to come and get her.

In most accounts of Rachel's story, Mr. Short is dismissed at this point. Years later, however, he vowed to a friend that so far as he knew and believed Rachel "was as pure and virtuous as an angel." He added also that when Robards came to him "uttering threats and vengeance against him" he found that the jealous husband was willing to accept $1,000 in appeasement of his suspicions.

Short's later marriage indicates his position on the frontier. His wife was Maria, daughter of John Cleves Symmes of New Jersey, first judge of the new Northwest Territory. Symmes was a sometimes careless speculator in land grants along the Ohio, opposite Kentucky, where Cincinnati and Dayton were to grow. Still, his settlers, on lands where Indians met the retaliation of Kentuckians, helped increase the traffic which went down the rivers and back across the Trace.

Another of Symmes's daughters married William Henry Harrison, a Virginian who came West to become the aide-de-camp to "Mad" Anthony Wayne, and later returned to the East as President of the United States. Young lawyer Short made other important connections, not all so advantageous. He was for a while—to his loss—partner in a store in Frankfort with General Wilkinson, whose various enterprises and speculations required all the gold he could get, and by any means.

The discarded Rachel, no longer dancing, lived with her widowed mother in what was called her "block-house" though it was "somewhat more commodious than any other dwelling in the place." At that house, 10 miles from Nashville, another young boarder came into Rachel's life. His story has not been neglected. His name was Andrew Jackson. He was twenty-one and already in a hurry to make a fortune. Indeed, back in the Carolinas from which he came, says Marquis James, some "feared that he gambled not always as a sportsman who can afford to lose, but as an adventurer who has to win."

He had fought a duel and left a wild reputation behind him when he came over the just-opened Cumberland Road in 1788. He brought along his law books and a Negro slave girl he had bought for $200. On the way his alertness averted an attack by a Cherokee war party. He shot a panther and tomahawked that beast's cub when the animals tried to kill a colt. On his way he had been noticed in Jonesboro as a prancing young man riding a fine horse and leading another, with saddlebags, gun, pistols, and foxhounds.

When Rachel first saw him he must have appeared as an old sweetheart in Salisbury, North Carolina, remembered him, in "a new suit, with broad-cloth coat . . . ruffled shirt . . . his abundant suit of dark red-hair combed carefully back . . . and, I suspect, made to lay down with bear's oil. He was full six feet tall and very slender, but . . . graceful . . . His eyes *were* handsome . . . a kind of steel blue. I have talked with him a great many times and never saw him avert his eyes from me for an instant."

Undoubtedly he looked so at Rachel. And when the jealous Lewis Robards came to the Cumberland asking her forgiveness, it was not long before his jealousy was aroused again. This time he was not dealing with one who would make an inquiry as to whether he wanted blood or money.

Jackson had been polite, as all men were to the lovely Rachel, but when word reached him that Robards was accusing her in his name he met Captain Robards "near the orchard fence."

There Jackson, his friend and partner John Overton later reported, "began mildly to remonstrate" with Robards about his unwarranted jealousy. Mildness never lasted long, however, when Jackson remonstrated. And, as reported, "Robards became violently angry and abusive." Jackson proposed pistols, but no duel ensued. Dutifully Rachel went back to Kentucky with her husband but was not there long before they quarreled again. Then in July, 1790, at the request of her family, Jackson went to Kentucky to bring her back to her sister's house near Nashville. Though Robards later legally labeled this an "elopement," in the same month or the following one he was back in Tennessee seeking another reconciliation and was quickly furiously jealous again.

"I'm a mind to cut off your ears," Jackson is reported to have said on this occasion.

Robards sought to place Jackson under bond to keep the peace. But patience with the Kentuckian was growing thin on the Cumberland. Already Rachel's friends were saying that Robards "was in the habit of leaving his wife's bed & spending the night with the negro women." On the other hand, the precise and proper Overton, who had moved to the Cumberland, wrote that "during our attendance on wilderness courts, whilst other young men were indulging in familiarities with females of unlaxed morals, no suspicion of this kind of the world's censure ever fell to Jackson's share."

Cuckold or knave, Robards went back to Kentucky but left Rachel fearful that he would be back to "haunt her." So a decision was made that she would go for peace and safety to the Natchez country. Dangerous river passages, of course, were not new to Rachel. Memories of her coming to the Cumberland settlements with her father must have been in her pretty head when she prepared to sail with the flotilla of flatboats of elderly Col. John Stark, an American-born Spanish subject, "in the winter or spring" of 1791.

This voyage was no unique trading enterprise. As boatman and merchant, old Colonel Stark had often before made the trip with the currents down the twisting and connecting Cumberland, Ohio, and Mississippi rivers between 2,000 miles of shores filled with lurking Indians— and often with white outlaws, too.

The Cumberland poured into the Ohio 50 miles below Cave-in-Rock on the Illinois shore, where the worst of the outlaws on the river and the Trace were soon to set up their station for the murder and loot of flatboatmen. Already on the river shores and in the woods of this West there were men as "destitute of moral principles as they were destitute of property." The rivers themselves were treacherous with shoals, sucks, snags, and sawyers, as submerged trees were called.

Turbulently the blue Ohio converged with the tawny Mississippi. Often between green and clay banks the sky was low and gray over stormy water. Many voyagers found the trip monotonous. Sir Charles Lyell, the geologist, wrote that he became tired of seeing only caving banks on one side and advancing sand bars, covered with willows and poplars, on the other. In a March sailing he noticed that on a downriver course the willows became greener and the gray moss hung more abundantly from the trees.

Others found change and excitement enough. Men like Colonel Stark loved the rivers as others love the sea. And like some sea-going men, Colonel Stark did not feel too happy with a woman like Rachel Robards as his passenger. The familiar story is that Rachel asked the old Colonel to take her along on his expedition to Natchez. According to this version Jackson made the trip only at the Colonel's "urgent entreaties." The probability is that it was Jackson who planned the trip.

He was already well established in the country to which

Rachel fled. He had been one of the first to take advantage of the uneasy overtures which the Spanish and the settlers of the back country of the feeble and divided new American States made to each other. Trade was important to both. Also, Colonel Robertson, as the leader of the Cumberland settlements, was anxious to stop the Spanish-incited raids on his people by the Creek Indians of Georgia and Alabama.

Robertson may have felt sometimes that the protection of the stationers by the Spanish was that which vultures gave to lambs. Still he had made amiable overtures to the Spanish governor he feared. The colonel did not object when men in his settlements took the land grants Miró offered in hopes of securing their allegiance to Spain rather than to the precarious young American republic on the Atlantic seaboard. Jackson was one of the first to respond to this guileful generosity. There is no evidence, however, that he swapped loyalties for land.

Four months after he reached Nashville, he was already interested in trade with Natchez. Then in May, 1790, before he had been on the Cumberland a year, Colonel Robertson used Jackson as an agent in his efforts to placate the Spaniards. He was returning a runaway slave from the Spanish country, he wrote Manuel Gayoso de Lemos, the affable governor of Natchez, by "Mr. Andrew Jackson, a Gentleman of Character and Consideration, very much respected in this Country and generally esteemed." And in July, 1790, Col. J. C. Montflorence thanked Jackson "for the little venture in Swann skins which you were so obliging as to take down to the Natchez for me." In Nashville, "Swann skins" seems as odd an item in trade as Colonel Montflorence was as a man. French teacher, soldier, smuggler, and diplomat, his association with the prominent Blount family had brought him to Tennessee. There a native historian said he could "grace an assembly and flirt with the belles of Paris; could sit on a stool or dance with the pioneer women on a dirt floor in log cabins on the

Cumberland." He lost his money and went back to Paris where no less a personage than General Lafayette reported his death to Tennessee friends.

Undoubtedly swan skins were used as a part of Indian ceremonial costumes. More prosaically, they were useful as a rain repellent. The phrase as used by Colonel Montflorence could have been a euphemism for black slaves, since Jackson was already dealing in that human commodity.

Few other letters to or from Jackson in this period survive. Perhaps the most important document shows that by July, 1790 (before he sailed with Rachel) he had already run up a bill for $234.01 with Melling Woolley, Natchez merchant, chiefly for liquor. Before that, of course, he had well established himself in Natchez. When he first visited that growing community on the Mississippi he enjoyed the hospitality of the leading residents of the area, including Thomas Marston Green, Jr., and Abner Green, at whose fine plantation house Rachel was to stay. Marquis James, in his story of Jackson's young manhood, said that Abner Green had acquired the house from Governor Gayoso. Fine as the house was, that seems improbable, since Gayoso did not come as governor until 1789. Thomas had built him a splendid house nearby. James wrote that there were few such splendid homes in "that far world."

Undoubtedly the Greens were part of the social world in which Gayoso and his handsome adjutant Minor moved. Despite occasional clashes with Spanish policy, they acquired and held huge land holdings around old Greenville. It was then an important center on the Natchez Trace, 28 miles northeast of Natchez. Abner Green married into the even wealthier family of Col. Anthony Hutchins. Jackson arranged to sell slaves to the Green brothers. Obviously he obtained their friendship, though the son-in-law of Abner Green said later that Jackson then was "a restless and enterprising man . . . embarking in many schemes for the accumulation of fortune, not usually resorted to by professional men."

The tangible evidence of his enterprise in Natchez is that he acquired a tract of fine land near the Green mansion, Springfield, 25 miles up the Trace toward Nashville, where the Mississippi meets the Bayou Pierre. On his property near Bruinsburg Jackson built a log house, talked of construction of a race track, and planned other improvements. Also, then or later he became a business partner of the Greens. At the time of his first visit they needed the new amiability of the Spaniards as much as he did. A few years before, when the state of Georgia undertook to extend its boundary westward to the Mississippi, to include Spanish lands, one Green had landed in the Spanish jail for his zeal in that lost cause. It was to the Greens that Rachel went in refuge.

The river journey, however romantic, was uneventful. Perhaps Captain Stark brought his cargo of lovers to the flats beneath Natchez Bluffs. Maybe he put in at the Bayou Pierre instead, which was nearer their destination at the house of Abner Green, a day's journey up the Trace even for such a horseman as Lt. Estevan Minor. There was sanctuary for Rachel. And in security there was hospitality in plenty in the houses of other planters flourishing under the Spanish regime. She blossomed again in their company. Undoubtedly she danced again. Still she was lonely and fearful when, after seeing to her safety and happiness, Andrew rode up the Trace to Nashville.

He was an angry man soon after he arrived. As it turned out, Rachel need not have fled down the rivers. Instead of returning to Nashville to "haunt" her, Robards went to Richmond, capital of a Virginia which still contained Kentucky. There, on December 20, 1790, probably while Andrew and Rachel were together on the rivers, he secured a bill from the legislature permitting him to seek a divorce before a jury. It did not, as was legislative custom in those days, grant him a divorce. But in the bill Robards alleged adultery. Jackson first impulsively proposed to go after Robards with his pistol and force him to retract his charges. Instead, believing Rachel divorced, he asked old Mrs. Donelson's permission "to offer his hand and heart to her daughter."

"Mr. Jackson," she said, "would you sacrifice your life to save my poor child's good name?"

"Ten thousand lives, madame, if I had them."

And promptly he was on his horse posting southward on the Natchez Trace. He took Rachel both the news and his love. She paled at Robards' charges.

"I expected him to kill me but this is worse," she said.

As daughter of an often tough-talking frontier she must have understood then that enemies of her husband might later suggest that in Natchez she was the creature of a code "whereby if a man should fancy his neighbor's 'pretty wife' . . . he has nothing to do but to take a pistol in one hand and a horsewhip in another and . . . possess . . . her." Jackson could not have been unaware that even from men like John Sevier, Tennessee's first governor, might later come in quarrel the charge that "I know of no great service you have rendered the country except taking a trip to Natchez with another man's wife." Jackson had told old Mrs. Donelson that he was ready with his life for Rachel, and his pistols were already cocked for the consequences.

Still, the steel in his blue eyes met Rachel's dark ones. In August, 1791, she and the tall young lawyer and trader were married, as tradition says, in the house of Thomas Marston Green, Jr. Some historians doubt that house was the still-standing mansion, Springfield, with its wide upper and lower galleries, recessed doorways, and rooms rich with hand-carved woodwork in a lacy design. It also seems doubtful that the tradition is true that she was married by Green in his capacity as magistrate. His authority in that office had lapsed with the pretensions of Georgia that its Bourbon County extended to the Mississippi. In this

Catholic-Spanish country the probability is that the
Jacksons were married by one of the Irish Catholic priests
who had been brought in in the hope of converting the
increasing number of American settlers. As remembered,
one of those good priests might have added to the gaiety of
the wedding.

In this region where only the Catholic religion was
tolerated, old Major Willey left vivid and affectionate
memories of these young Irish clerics.

"I remember well Father Brady," he wrote, " . . . the best
shot, the best rider, and the best judge of horses in the district. And Father Malone, with a wink and a joke, and a
blessing and an almo for everyone—welcome at every
wedding, every frolic and every dinner—most exemplary in
the discharge of every duty, but with a slight weakness for
his national beverage on St. Patrick's Day, when his
patriotism would prove stronger than his head. However, in
those days, and for years after, the clergy of all denominations took their morning nip and their midday toddy, and
were always considered the best judges of Madeira."

Afterward, for a little happy while, the young couple
stayed in Jackson's own log house at Bruinsburg. In a
clearing on the bluff looking down on both the Mississippi
and the Bayou Pierre, they were at last safe together. They
entertained the friends who had been so kind to Rachel.
One such visitor, a gay bachelor, wrote later a note of thanks
to Rachel: "I cannot lose the remembrance of the agreeable
hours . . . at Bayou Pierre."

VI: RETURN AND REVENGE

EVEN the days immediately after Andrew Jackson's marriage were not filled merely with "agreeable hours." Energetic as he was ardent, he already moved in the drive for fortune which sometimes saddened Rachel. Marriage did not mean that he neglected his business at Bruinsburg. Up the Trace law practice and land deals required his attention in Nashville. So a month after their marriage they set out homeward over the already crowding road.

We know much and little about that journey. Jackson's friend John Overton carefully collected all the facts he could about the trip. His work, however, was done a third of a century later as a sort of lawyer's brief. It was designed to meet and refute political smears about both Andrew and Rachel in furious Presidential politics. Much had been forgotten when Overton wrote. Witnesses were dead. Documents had disappeared. Still much was explained about the journey after the "agreeable hours" which was distorted into a relentless scandal designed to destroy a politician regardless of its effect upon a woman's heart.

The Jacksons rode, Overton said, with a company of 100 persons when they left Bayou Pierre in September, 1791. Travel in such large companies was a customary precaution on the Trace. The groups were composed of a variety of people pulled together only by the common denominator of their wish for safety. And what a cavalcade this one must have been! Yet only the names of three of its members are known: Andrew and Rachel, and a dangerous, swashbuckling, Virginia-born Kentuckian, one Hugh McGary. The Jacksons had no reason to fear him. McGary's brother had married Jackson's cousin.

Many of the others, we know from the composition of similar companies, were undoubtedly returning boatmen, rough men, but generally good company on a dangerous road. Some others were disappointed settlers or speculators. Some peddlers or traders moved in such bodies, their packhorses loaded with everything from powder and bullets to flowered calico, red girdles, vermilion, linen shirts, and even small looking glasses. Often beside them were men traveling in the West merely for adventure. Such travel seemed to have a peculiar fascination for bolder European visitors, some of whom went home and wrote popular and often imaginative books about it.

Also in such groups, as the outlaws quickly learned, were not only men with money in their belts but others leading horses "laden wholly with dollars the proceeds of the cargo . . . taken down the river." Others, who had spent their hard-muscled earnings in tough good times, came home penniless and sick. Some, even as they started, announced that they were so poor and thin that they "had to lean up agin a saplin' to cuss." A fastidious traveler down the Trace once described such men as he passed them, headed northward.

"These were dirty as Hottentots," he said, "their dress a shirt and trousers of canvas, black greasy and sometimes in tatters; their skin burnt wherever exposed to the sun; each with a budget wrapt up in an old blanket; their beards eighteen days old added to the singularity of their appearance, which was altogether savage. These people came from various tributary streams of the Ohio, hired at forty or fifty dollars a trip, to return back at their own expense."

Obviously the Jacksons made no such appearance. Undoubtedly, also, there were others in the company in which they traveled who, by the standards of the times, were richly equipped. Partisanship went into Albert Gallatin's description of Jackson in Congress a few years later as an "uncouth-looking personage . . . his manners and deportment those of a rough backwoodsman." No one who described Rachel in her youth was so uncomplimentary. The realism which attended the reports of her appearance as she aged gives credence to the stories of her good looks in her dark-haired youth. Both she and Jackson were twenty-four years old. Both were excellent riders accustomed to the wilderness. Certainly Jackson carried a pair of pistols in holsters for ready use if necessary. But whatever his reputation for hotheadedness may have been, on this trip he was less ready to use them quickly than was Hugh McGary.

Considering Jackson's position as a lawyer, trader, and slave dealer, it is safe to assume that he and Rachel were accompanied by black servants on the trip, which generally required twenty-one days. Along the way such slaves handled the baggage and prepared the meals. Perhaps the Jacksons had better fare than ordinary travelers. From the journals of others we know that most people headed northward had as their principal provisions dried beef and a special kind of hard biscuit. They carried one powder of roasted Indian corn and another called Conte, made from the root of the China briar. Travelers high and low praised fritters made of this powder when sweetened with honey and fried in bear oil.

The servants hobbled the horses with leathern thongs or chains at night, packed them in the morning, kindled the fires, and pitched the tent for the Jacksons. Certainly neither of the Jacksons rode tough Opelousas horses such as Philip Nolan caught and sold. Their mounts were the kinds of horses implicitly described by Stephen Minor in his report of his gallop up the Trace. While some of the boatmen in the company shared one of the wiry Western ponies, the

Jacksons may have had such animals for their baggage and slaves.

Such a traveler as Jackson knew and loved horses. For such a journey he probably chose either the highly regarded Chickasaw horses or the Kentucky horses, which Alexander Wilson, the ornithologist, described as "the hardiest in the world." They were ridden, he said, "through roads and sloughs that would become the graves of any common animal, with a fury and celerity incomprehensible by you folks on the other side of the Allegheny." From Kentucky, Hugh McGary probably rode such a horse. And he was not the kind of man who would want younger Andrew Jackson to ride ahead of him.

None of the stands set up later for the accommodation of travelers existed when the Jacksons headed homeward. Yet Turner Brashears, of Maryland, who later kept such a "House of Entertainment," was already living on the Trace. Perhaps it was a cleaner wilderness for the lack of them. An English traveler over the road a few years later described one such accommodation.

The house, he said, consisted of only one room. It was filled "with bridles, saddles and baggage of our party, as well as other lumber belonging to the family. In this our supper (consisting merely of mush and milk) is to be cooked; and in this (after that was over) we are to take up our abode for the night. For my part, rather than be poisoned by the effluvia of living, I walked on the banks of the river till supper-time; and that over, I spread my blanket out on a grassplat in the garden, and there laid me down till morning; yet even for this rough fare, they had the impertinence to charge us a quarter of a dollar apiece."

The Jacksons were undoubtedly more content in their tent beneath the stars. Andrew kept no journal of his trip He was not a journal-keeping man. He faced the hazards other travelers met. Starting in late summer he and Rachel did not find the swollen streams Minor reported. Yet the

Jackson party, like others, had to skirt the swamps and swim the wider streams, transporting their provisions and equipment on rafts.

The southern end of the Trace was at this season thick with dust. Still, some of the streams were difficult of passage. Even little creeks could be deceptive. Some which looked as if they might be taken at a good horse jump turned out to be unfordable. Luckily, earlier travelers sometimes had felled large trees across such streams on which, with tottering step, later travelers could cross carrying their baggage.

Andrew and Rachel met such hazards. The path grew worse beyond the Natchez District. Every day's journey brought a more gravelly soil. They passed an area of open woods and prairie which an English traveler felt might more properly be called "Barrens." There, he said, the openness of the woods and the deficiency of timber arose "more from a natural unfruitfulness than too great a luxuriance of soil." Steadily the path became rougher, more broken, more bushy. The hills steepened south of the Tennessee River. From the thickets and swamps the mosquitoes and gnats swarmed.

The Tennessee River was the tremendous obstacle. Within its cane-lined shores, the best crossing point travelers found was where the river was "above a quarter of a mile wide, and flowed with so rapid a stream that it was with difficulty that a person (breast high) could stand against it." Jackson, his early biographer Parton was sure, had crossed it many times before, "as he did other rivers too wide to ford or swim." He had never had Rachel with him in crossing the river, which "appeared to glide in silent dignity, with its surface smooth and unruffled, and its body dark and clear, at once proclaiming the depth and importance of the current." Rafts sufficed where no ferry was yet provided. Occasionally the rafts were "borne irresistibly down the river—a river twelve hundred miles long, its banks peopled with doubtful Indians."

There were still some such Indians. Also, when Rachel

and Andrew rode, murder was already established as a vocation on the Trace. Often only circling buzzards called attention to such crime. Judge John Haywood, one of Tennessee's first historians, kept a long catalogue of early Trace murders, however. The accuracy of his catalogue apparently irked one of the worst of those killers, who described the Judge's method of composition. Haywood did his writing while lying on a bull's hide under a tree, and the complaining bandit said, "he's so fat it takes three niggers dragging at the tail to haul him into the shade." This historian noted murder in the year the Jacksons came home on their wedding journey.

"In June, 1791," he wrote, "three travelers from Natchez to Nashville were found dead on the Trace near the mouth of the Duck River; there were eight in company, and only two came in."

Either Indians or white outlaws could have been the murderers in this case, though the Indians already were less menacing, and the more famous outlaws had not yet begun to operate. Menace to the happiness of the Jacksons came from a member of their own party. He was that Hugh McGary, the third known member of the group with which they rode. On the way through the wilderness, Overton wrote of the journey in his careful defense of the Jacksons from calumny later, McGary maturated his venom against the Jacksons.

"Circumstances then occurred," Overton wrote, "calculated to excite in M'Gary a strong feeling of dislike toward General Jackson, which it is unnecessary to detail as they related solely to a meditated attack by the Indians."

Perhaps "meditated attack by the Indians" was so familiar a matter that Overton felt it "unnecessary to detail" this one. Still, after treaties in 1786 in Hopewell, South Carolina, and at Nashville in 1783, peaceful relations had existed with the Choctaws and Chickasaws along the Trace. Indeed, in the intrigues involving Spain and the United States during and prior to this period, one historian has said that these tribes were "courted as a beautiful maiden by these rival suitors."

Still the irreconcilable Creeks often swept westward in raids. Also there were sometimes gangs of often drunken Indians as well as orderly tribes. Sometimes they were roused by white outlaws. Often they were merely stirred by the liquor which white men brought in. Even among the more peaceful Indians there was begging and pilfering. Harmless Indians, a traveler said, "think it no crime to steal *privately* whatever comes in their way." Sometimes it was suspected that red men let travelers' horses loose in order to get rewards for helping find them.

Several years after the Jacksons' journey, a young man who rode up the Trace told of meeting a party of about forty war-painted warriors just returning from a fight on the west side of the Mississippi.

"As soon as they saw us," he wrote, "they set up a rude hallo, and ran to meet us, holding in their hands the scalps they had taken from their enemies, and grinning with a degree of self-satisfaction at this mark of their prowess in the field of battle. Turning from this disgusting scene, we entered that part of their encampment where they were cooking their victuals which consisted of the body of a deer which they had lately killed in the woods. They welcomed us in their rough manner, by shaking hands and offering us the pipe of peace; which we were obliged to accept; otherwise we should have affronted them."

The Jacksons suffered no greater harm from any Indians they met. Indeed, the circumstances of any Indian danger they may have faced are unknown. What is known is that Jackson differed over the course of action to be taken in connection with the Indians' "meditated attack" with Hugh McGary. The Indian danger, if any, disappeared. Jackson, who was to be as rough an Indian fighter as ever lived, understood more diplomatic dealings, too. Also, probably as protective bridegroom, he urged the course of greatest safety. In the process he made a bitter enemy, who was to help poison Rachel's whole life.

In his biography of Jackson as a border captain, Marquis James described McGary as a famous "frontier soldier and Indian fighter." Undoubtedly McGary felt then that he was Jackson's superior in any conflict with the savages. Indeed, Andrew Jackson never fought any body of Indians until 1813, after he became a general. Still, McGary, who was older than Jackson, was one of the most notorious blowhards and bravos in the early West.

Nine years before he rode up the Trace with the Jacksons, McGary had a similar argument with Daniel Boone about an Indian fight in Kentucky. Then Kentuckians were pursuing a body of Indians and Canadians who had struck at Bryant's Station, 6 miles northeast of Lexington, on August 15, 1782. Boone did not like the looks of the trail they followed. He counseled that they were being led into an ambush by the British and the Indians. McGary, then a major, met Boone's wilderness-wise counsel with a whoop of scorn. (Nearly two centuries later a historian of the Ohio River country, perhaps with some regional bias, presumed that McGary's cry was a "rudimentary form of the rebel yell of the sixties," which "would still be the glory and the nemesis of his type of Southerner in the days of the Confederacy.")

"Let all who are not cowards follow me," McGary shouted.

Many did. And in the Battle of Blue Licks, August 19, 1782, one of the bloodiest battles ever fought on the frontier, many died, too, under the withering hidden fire Boone had feared from ravines along the limestone road. Even before that McGary had quarreled with James Harrod over an Indian attack. Harrod had preceded Boone in establishing Harrodsburg (where Rachel's domestic troubles began) as the first settlement in Kentucky. Boone and Harrod were not men to be pushed aside in Kentucky.

Perhaps because Kentuckians had had enough of this loud braggart McGary, and because of his reputation for rashness, he was arrested at Haggins' Race Path near Harrodsburg for betting a mare worth £12.

Though the Calvinists then probably outnumbered the Cavaliers, this seems a strange charge in such a state of hard riding and high stakes as Kentucky. Betting on a horse would not have seemed a crime to Andrew Jackson, then or later—nor to many Kentuckians. The existence of the track in Harrodsburg indicated interest in the turf. The court there must have felt it had special reasons in McGary's case. It declared him to be "an infamous gambler . . . not to be eligible to any office of trust or honor within this State."

On the Trace, Jackson was not putting Rachel at stake on McGary's counsel. Nobody knew better than this steel-eyed Southerner (a type quite as common as the war-whoop Southerner) that fools were often more to be feared than rogues on the frontier. There may have been some of both in McGary. Apparently he was ready to stack the cards for future play after Jackson declined to permit the kind of folly for which, as boastful frontier fool, McGary became most famous.

Without further incident the newlywed Jacksons arrived in the Cumberland settlements in October, 1791, "amid the joyous congratulations of her relatives and a large circle of mutual friends." A big and happy party was given for them. Jackson bought the Poplar Grove plantation as a home suited to his bride. In Nashville, according to Overton, they were "beloved and esteemed by all classes." Some idea of the esteem is marked by the fact that at this time Jackson was elected a trustee of Davidson Academy, the cultural pride of the frontier town.

Then, two years later, in December, 1793, Jackson learned that the act of the Virginia Legislature in December, 1790, had not granted Robards a divorce. Instead, just two months before, in September, 1793, after waiting two years, Robards had brought an action under the act and put the ready and willing Hugh McGary on the witness stand. McGary testified that Andrew and Rachel had "slept under the same blanket."

And the jury, "being duly sworn well and truly to inquire into the allegation in the plaintiff's declaration . . . do say, that the defendant, Rachel Robards, hath deserted the plaintiff, Lewis Robards, and hath, and doth, still live in adultery with another man."

Jackson's friends later were at much pains to prove that McGary had only seen the Jacksons on the trip up the Trace after they believed they were legally married. Upon that marriage Jackson at first wanted to insist. He swore that, damn it, he would not consider a second marriage, since Rachel was his wife before God and in "the understanding of every person in the country." Overton's counsel prevailed, however, and a second ceremony was performed on January 17, 1794. Perhaps Overton spoke as much about the roads, such as the Natchez Trace, as in the Jacksons' defense when he said in explanation later:

"The slowness and inaccuracy with which information was received in West Tennessee at that time will not be surprising, when we consider its insulated and dangerous situation, surrounded on every side by the wilderness, and by hostile Indians, and that there was no mail established till about 1797, as well as I recollect."

Not all the roads then were so rough and dangerous as the Natchez Trace. Still, Nashville was an uncertain way even from Kentucky, and a vastly longer way from the central government in Philadelphia. And Natchez, toward which Americans were looking as to land which should be their own, was 600 more wilderness miles beyond Nashville from the capital of the republic. Yet travelers on the Trace multiplied. Rachel was to ride it again in a carriage at a time of triumph. She even danced again in Natchez. But in her full story, that first wedding journey over the Trace was to become at last her journey to heartbreak, humiliation, and death as well. From that not even Andrew Jackson's ready pistols could protect her. Others, some years later, would fortunately get their mail and the news essential to their happiness at a faster rate—except where murder intervened.

VII: PATHS OF GLORY

THE INDIGO vats stank. They attracted great swarms of flies. The preparation of the blue dye was believed to shorten the lives and reduce the value of slaves.

Other regions were better suited than the Natchez area for the production of tobacco, sugar cane, and corn. Cotton had been grown early in the Natchez District as well as at the other end of the Trace, near Nashville. Soon after the settlers arrived on the Cumberland the sad news was recorded that Colonel Robertson's younger brother, John, was killed by Indians while picking cotton at Clover Bottom, where Andrew Jackson and others later laid out a race track.

Still, it was the combination of the coming of cotton as the great fleecy crop and the arrival of the American flag which hastened the turning of the Trace from a pathway into something approximating a road. In less time than it took the Jacksons after their marriage to learn that Rachel had not been divorced when her new vows were spoken, planters in Natchez were already informed about and reproducing and improving the cotton gin which the Connecticut Yankee, Eli Whitney, had devised in 1793 on the coast of Georgia.

Indeed, the golden age of Natchez and the Trace which ran to it began in Manchester, England, and Madrid, Spain. Steam power in the manufacture of cotton goods, which greatly increased the demand for the fiber, had been introduced in England in 1785. And ten years later the first cotton gin was brought to Natchez. That same year, on

October 27, 1795, the United States and Spain signed the Treaty of San Lorenzo el Real. It opened the Mississippi to American trade and fixed the United States border at the 31st parallel, 40 miles below Natchez—or was supposed to do so.

Still, other things, besides the indigo vats, stank. As far off as Philadelphia, George Washington, as he prepared to retire from the Presidency, did not like the smell of some of the things in the Old Southwest. For one thing he did not like the way Spain was stalling after signing the treaty. He dispatched to Natchez, at the head of an American force, a queer Quaker named Andrew Ellicott to see about that. And he suggested that Ellicott turn a watchful eye on the operations of the ubiquitous General Wilkinson.

The bootless bribes that personage had received from Spain had not sufficed for his extravagances and speculations. One of the general's businesses was a store in Kentucky. To it, says James Parton, Andrew Jackson's first major biographer, settlers from the Cumberland rode for the purpose of "procuring some article not obtainable at their own scantily supplied repositories." One such rider, this historian was sure, was Jackson. It is certain that Wilkinson's partner in the store was Rachel's friend Peyton Short. He lost in Wilkinson's failure. The agile, if fattening, Wilkinson found the way to save himself. With magnificent gall and with the smell of Spanish gold still on his hands, the general in 1791 had gone back into the United States Army, though without severing his amiable relations with Spain.

Short had no such way to restore his fortunes. Yet he was not left entirely unavenged in his losses. By an unnoticed irony in history, it was Short's brother William, the protégé of Jefferson, who conducted most of the long negotiations that resulted in the treaty which opened the Mississippi River and fixed the border below Natchez. That agreement threatened to destroy forever the pattern of international rivalry which provided for Wilkinson's perfidy and profit. It did not. If he left Short with losses, Wilkinson had other aides.

Still, Wilkinson knew that rumors about him had reached even the President. His quarrels with his army superior, Gen. "Mad" Anthony Wayne, had created more enemies for him. Their bitterness did not diminish when Wayne's death made Wilkinson the ranking officer of the army. Wilkinson took his Spanish pension but dodged a meeting in Detroit, where he had his headquarters, with an emissary of the Spanish governor of vast Louisiana— Francisco Luis Hector, Baron de Carondelet.

Far from withdrawing in terms of the treaty, Carondelet, still hoping for a secession of the Western states from the American republic, called on Wilkinson to make himself "the Washington of the West." Wilkinson was more aware of the Washington in the East. The general called Carondelet's belated proposal a "chimerical project." He was taking no chances, but he wanted his money. So, in 1796, the year in which Washington asked Ellicott to go West, Wilkinson sent the baron a letter in cipher by his faithful young agent Nolan. In it he reported that by "great treachery" or robbery he was being deprived of money due him from Spain. Also, he indicated his almost apoplectic agitation.

"For the love of God and friendship," the general wrote, "enjoin great secrecy and caution in all our concerns. Never suffer my name to be written or spoken."

He could not have chosen a better messenger than Nolan. Then only twenty-five, no one moved down the river and up the Trace, too, with greater celerity. He also moved often into Spanish territory in the far southwest, where he captured the wild Opelousas horses which were so essential to travel on the Trace. Probably no man in those years provided more propulsive power to travelers on the old path than Nolan did with his strong, wiry horses. Men expected to see him when he appeared from anywhere—or everywhere. It may have been only an accident that, as

Ellicott came down the rivers from Pittsburgh in 1797, Nolan joined him.

He appeared as a young man anxious to obtain instruction from Ellicott, famed surveyor and mathematician. He accompanied the American commissioner as far as Natchez. And it is possible that on the trip he learned more than surveying. He assured Ellicott that Wilkinson's connection with the Spaniards had been purely commercial. Indeed, Nolan told the Quaker surveyor that "a deceptive policy was necessary in dealing with the Spanish Government" and that Wilkinson "had a plan to save the nation, if attacked by Spain, by seizing Carondelet and carrying him to the people of the country." Ellicott listened. He was not entirely reassured.

The American boundary commissioners under the treaty met no welcome from the Spanish as they floated down the stream. Efforts were made at various points to persuade them to delay. The Quaker commander pushed on. In February, 1797, he arrived at the same locality on Bayou Pierre to which Jackson had taken Rachel. He received equal welcome from the Greens and their neighbors. Their prosperity under Spain had not reduced their American patriotism. He was also met in this area by Governor Gayoso, who, with his smiling adjutant Minor beside him, did not attempt to hide his annoyance. He was being prodded from down the river by Carondelet.

Indeed, apparently Nolan, not lingering long with his beloved Fannie Lintot, left Ellicott at Natchez to go to confer with the baron. Ostensibly he had set out with surveying instruments and a passport from Gayoso to explore and map the North Texas region for the Natchez governor. Evidently Carondelet received him with the same trust he had given him the year before when Nolan had brought Wilkinson's letter. That proud Don was a short, plump gentleman, "somewhat choleric in his disposition, but not destitute of good humor," according to the historian Gayarré. Now he was angry. Spanish officials later dealt with

Nolan as a "bandido Americano." In 1797, however, Carondelet, in a rage, confided in him.

"I am," he declared of Natchez and the little American force approaching it, "going to give the Americans lead and the inhabitants hemp."

It did not seem that simple to his unhappy subordinate, Gayoso, at Natchez. With much local support, Ellicott with his small company moved near the town. The Quaker raised the American flag. Gayoso ordered him to pull it down. Ellicott stood his ground. In general, the collision of the Quaker and the Spaniard was a war of talk, but it was attended by much turbulence, too. Gayoso arrested one of the Greens. This Green escaped from jail, said the governor, "conscious of his criminality." It seems doubtful that this Green was troubled by his conscience. He and others took sides firmly. Military companies were formed. And between the Americans and the small Spanish garrison Gayoso commanded, suddenly that indestructible Tory, Colonel Hutchins, appeared.

Apparently as British and irascible as ever at eighty, Hutchins had picked up a rumor, probably from reports the Spanish were spreading to serve subterfuge and delay, that a British invading force was coming down from Canada. He was prepared to raise the Cross of Saint George to greet them. Americans, including Ellicott, then talked as roughly to the old man as some were talking to the Spanish. Some of them produced a doggerel description of him:

"Squeaking Tony, lean and bony."

In the middle of the turbulence in Spanish Catholic Natchez, Ellicott arranged for an itinerant Protestant evangelist named Hannah to preach. Parson Hannah took his gospel into the Irish section of Natchez. There he got contusions instead of converts. The Spanish sent drunken Indians whooping around Ellicott's camp. A larger group of Americans locked up the Spanish garrison in the fort. Some spasmodic collisions occurred. A few shots were fired by a Spanish patrol. Spanish artillery was aimed at Ellicott's tent.

Few if any casualties occurred. Apparently, however, if
Ellicott was getting little support from soldiers under
General Wilkinson, Gayoso was getting even less from the
bold Carondelet.

Finally, in late June, 1797, Gayoso, who had taken refuge
in the fort, made his way in great trepidation to a conference
with Ellicott at the plantation of the affable Captain Minor,
who had somehow gracefully moved from the position of
adjutant to that of mediator. "By a circuitous route," says
the historian, John W. Monette, Gayoso "made his way
through the thickets and canebrakes to the rear or north side
of Minor's plantation and thence through a cornfield to the
back of the house, and entered the parlor undiscovered." In
humiliation, he accepted the rule of a Committee of Safety
including inhabitants and invaders—without giving them
either lead or hemp.

It was an uneasy peace, attended by more than international conflicts and private finagling. In July, yellow fever
came in its mysterious way up the river. Nobody then
understood this "Stranger's Fever." It seemed generally to
come up from Natchez-under-the-Hill. In one raging
epidemic a doctor reported that while people who could
fled from Natchez and those who remained died untended
in its houses, he found not a sign of it on the route from
Natchez to Nashville. Still, in that summer of 1797, a fourth
of Ellicott's party died of the disease, marked at its termina-
tion by vomit black from the admixture of blood.

Ellicott himself recovered in seven days to continue his
troubles with the lingering Spaniards. More and more,
however, there was mention of "Major Minor, Mr. Ellicott's
friend" and "Stephen Minor, in whom Ellicott had
confidence." Finally and peacefully, due apparently to
Minor's smooth mediations, the last Spanish troops left the
Natchez fort late in March, 1798. The American flag flew,
never to come down.

The Spanish governor and the Quaker commander who
fought this comic-opera war were contrasting characters.

Both certainly had their virtues. Gayoso, dark and debonair, seems still almost the symbol of the best of Spanish Natchez. One modern historian says that he "enjoyed the reputation rare among Spanish colonial officials, of never using his office for personal gain. He died in bankruptcy." Certainly he added much to the appearance of Natchez, notably in his own house, Concord, which Minor got after he was gone.

Physically, Ellicott was Gayoso's exact opposite. His figure was bulbous. His eyes were pale blue, his mouth more pursed than smiling. He was, however, a very belligerent member of the Quaker sect. Certainly he was a surveyor of note. He had made the first accurate measurements of Niagara Falls. He had helped survey the new Federal City of Washington, though he quarreled bitterly with his associates on that job. Perhaps, as was said by a sympathetic biographer, he "had a happier hand with the theodolite than with the pen"—or with his tongue. Still, both he and Gayoso seem hardly to have deserved all the harsh things that were said of them by men supposedly on their own sides.

Gayoso was charged with drinking too much. It was reported that he died, two years after these tumultous days in Natchez, following a drinking bout with General Wilkinson in New Orleans. He was also charged with the greatest extravagance. Other men in the Natchez District were to suffer from that fault in building houses, dispensing hospitality, riding fine horses. Yet a contemporary Spanish associate was sharp when he assigned reasons other than honesty for the fact that Gayoso died bankrupt.

"The Governor's natural disposition," wrote the Spanish intendant Juan Ventura Morales to his government, "is to waste what he owns as well as what he borrows."

Even worse things were said of Ellicott. Many of them came from Wilkinson, about whom the Quaker had sent reports to his government. Perhaps the boundary surveyor was too quick to quarrel with the officer of the force which

Wilkinson sent in his own good time behind the boundary commission to the Natchez scene. Not intimidated even by his own country's military, Ellicott called Wilkinson's officer, Capt. Isaac Guion, "a violent and overbearing man."

The charges flung by Ellicott at his countryman in arms were declared to be unjustified by historian Claiborne, who had no good word for anybody who spoke disrespectfully of his grandfather Colonel Hutchins. In his history of the period he preserved the charges brought out by Wilkinson against Ellicott.

The historian elaborated: Ellicott was far from temperate or frugal. He used the powers under his commission for personal profit. When at last time came to establish the boundary line, the Quaker commissioner and his "gang," so Claiborne recorded, dawdled, eating salt pork and guzzling whiskey. Also, the famous surveyor, his enemies reported, had brought a woman along who went insane and later had to be "chained in a mad house."

Indeed, years afterwards Wilkinson produced an affidavit from one of Ellicott's associates on this mission that this woman was called Betsy and always sat at Mr. Ellicott's table. Though her position was that of washerwoman to the party, "her character was that of a prostitute and of the lowest grade." Ellicott introduced her to Gayoso, this story went, on his arrival in Natchez, though it was believed that Ellicott, his nineteen-year-old son, and Betsy all three "slept in the same bed at the same time." And, it was added, others were invited to the mattress.

"This is the man," Claiborne burst forth about the Quaker, "that some partisan writers have held up as a model gentleman, patriot and saint."

It was not a saintly time. Ellicott himself, with some hyperbole, said that "a large proportion of the inhabitants of the Mississippi Territory were a set of the most abandoned, malicious, deceitful, plundering, horse-thieving rascals on the continent." Also, many of the

Spanish shared the view of Don Luis de Pañalvert y Cardenas, bishop of Louisiana, that "the emigration from the western part of the United States and the toleration of our government have introduced into this colony a gang of adventurers who have no religion and acknowledge no God, and they have made much worse the morals of our people by their coming in contact with them in their trading pursuits."

The good bishop spoke of their "pernicious maxims . . . their own restless and ambitious temper . . . many of the inhabitants live almost publicly with colored concubines, and they do not blush at carrying the illegitimate issue they have by them to be recorded in the parochial registries as their *natural children.*" Perhaps, however, what worried the bishop and other Spanish dignitaries most of all was that these adventurers patted their own robust boys on the shoulders saying, "You will be the man to go to Mexico."

Venom and glory were mixed in the drawing of the boundary line. One who took part in the work of cutting a wide path through the swampy region said that the muddy surface squirmed with all sorts of creatures, "not of those kinds which invite and delight the view of the inquisitive naturalist, but of the most disgusting and noxious kinds."

"A few were serpents of the waters," he wrote, "frequently entwined in clusters to the number of several hundreds, a vast variety of toads, frogs, including the bull-frog, and the thundering crocodile, all of hideous forms."

The heat reached 120 degrees as the sweating men cut and piled the cane, the brush, and the trees. Then they set the great mass afire.

"It was a most astonishing line of fire," this observer recorded, "the flames ascending to the tops of the highest trees and spreading for miles. . . . The continual explosions of rarified air from the hollow cane resembled the re-echoed discharges of innumerable platoons of musketry and mocked every idea that could be formed of the effect produced by the conflict of the most formidable armies.

The scene was truly grand, aweful and majestic."

This labor and fireworks along the 31st parallel made a boundary that would not long be needed. Afterwards, nature proved that it could heal and cover even such a wound as this. Still it was a labor which might have made a road like that which men only hoped the Natchez Trace might become. Beside it, unable to delay the process, Gayoso bowed with grace. Indeed, as Ellicott reported it, Gayoso saluted the American at the line with an embrace and kiss. The Quaker did not care for the gesture.

"I had not been shaved for two days," he wrote. "Men's kissing, I think a most abominable custom."

Possibly, considering Ellicott's stubble at the time, Gayoso agreed. Certainly it could not have been a pleasant occasion for him. The American flag flew over all of modern Mississippi except the Gulf Coast. A thickening stream of Americans who would never even pretend to be lieges of Spain were traveling the Natchez Trace. Ellicott's efforts were not unrewarded. He spent his last days as a respected professor of mathematics at West Point.

The burning of the boundary must have provided unequaled fireworks in the southwest. It certainly surpassed by far the first triumphant American Fourth of July which Ellicott celebrated in Natchez. Important as was that occasion, it did not seem worth waiting for to one of the most famous chroniclers of the Trace, who headed north upon it at the time of tumult which led to final American occupation. Indeed, Francis Baily hardly noticed the melodramatic collision of the Americans and the Spaniards when he came through Natchez, overland, in 1797. He was irritated by the fussiness of a Spanish official about his documents. He had trouble getting biscuits made for the trip ahead, since the best biscuitmaker was a Spaniard who was "obliged to do it clandestinely."

Baily, then a young man of twenty-three who was to become a founder of the Royal Astronomical Society, moved northward in company with more significant travelers. Indeed, in terms of their recognition of the difficulties of the way north and the need to do something about it, few men were more important than these companions. They were five sad Dutchmen who had attempted to apply ingenuity to northward travel in Middle America, which the Mississippi's currents then made impossible by boat. Their failure symbolized the necessity of the Trace.

Full of high hopes, these Dutchmen had come floating down the rivers in a queer craft they had built near Pittsburgh. It was equipped for upstream travel with two large paddle wheels on its sides, "like a water wheel of a mill." The wheels were turned by eight horses on a treadmill below deck. But the horses broke down. It is not known what breed of animal they used. Certainly they could have been the Opelousas horses, more of which Nolan was then off seeking. It is known only that the Dutchmen "sold the boat and horses at a very great loss, and proceeded homeward in disgust through the wilderness." Steam might be turning the spinning mills in Manchester which called for more and more cotton. It was yet to be applied to boats and rivers—certainly to the relentlessly flowing Mississippi.

The Dutchmen were not only poor. Two of them were not well when they headed north from Natchez. Sickness was not unusual on the Trace. Indeed, three years after the pathetic Dutchmen took the pathway, Joseph Bullen, a Presbyterian missionary to the Choctaw Indians stationed near present Tupelo, spoke of many sick men among the travelers. They suffered from exhaustion and summer fevers, sometimes from prodigious and prolonged hangovers from final debauches indulged in before hitting the trail. Those were less likely to be sick, he thought, who headed homeward before the twentieth of June.

So, in July, time did not seem to be on the side of the unsuccessful Dutch inventors. Nothing did. Certainly fortune was not smiling on them. Indians stole two of their horses. This "fresh misfortune coming upon them when they were so ill-prepared to bear it, seemed to overcome them." A third of the five became ill. Thus, twelve days after they had started, they gave up. Other members of the party were reluctant to leave them. Yet if they tarried, provisions for all would be exhausted. The Dutchmen understood. They offered no reproaches. All they asked was that, as the party went on, it try to send back some Indian who understood the use of medicinal herbs. Baily did send back such an Indian. However, history does not record whether or not the Indian reached them, or what happened to them. Many sick and lonely men died beside the path.

The companions of the apparently doomed Dutchmen made their trip successfully. Even when ferries were provided, however, some felt it necessary to fortify themselves for the river passages, particularly that of the Tennessee. A Virginia gentleman, returning with a party after a visit to inspect possible Mississippi investments, gave lively recollections of stimulants more certain in their results than Indian herbs. He wrote:

Got to Colberts at the ferry about 8 o'clock; got 7 quarts of whiskey at 1 Doll per quart & 4 dried fish at 6 pce apiece; Cross't the River; J. Green broke one of the bottles of whiskey; went 3 or 4 miles; sto'pt; Sam'ls horse broke another bottle of whiskey; we then determined to drink the balance to save it; went about 10 miles to a good run of water; Bill lost his coat from behind him.

Young Baily apparently required no such stimulation. He was, nevertheless, almost intoxicated with joy when he reached the outskirts of Nashville. There he reported meeting "two coaches fitted up in all the style of Philadelphia or New York, besides other carriages, which plainly indicated that a spirit of refinement and luxury had made its way into this settlement." Nevertheless, Francis Baily found that the best tavern, kept by a Major Lewis, was one in which the sleeping quarters were "open at all hours of the night for the reception of any rude rabble that had a mind to put up at the house."

Still, beneath the lofty oaks and maples around the station of Founder Robertson, Indians gathered, more peaceful now. They were also a little less impressive in their beads and tinkling bells. The population of their hunting grounds was thickening and the quantity of their game thinning. The next census would show 105,602 people in Tennessee, and even 8,850 down the Trace in the new Mississippi Territory. They were a long way from the seat of the national government, which no longer believed that it could remain unconcerned about this American southwest. Natchez was the nation's ultimate outpost.

"You will see," wrote Timothy Pickering, ardent Federalist and Secretary of State, in 1799, "that the passage of letters from Natchez is as tedious as from Europe, when westerly winds prevail. . . ."

Washington, who had wanted Wilkinson watched, had retired to Mount Vernon. John Adams gave the general his confidence and maintained him in the southwest. And Thomas Jefferson, still only a citizen at Monticello, turned with interest and confidence to Philip Nolan. As natural scientist, Jefferson, in June, 1798, wrote that dark young man asking about the western herds of horses. Nolan apparently was off after more such horses at the time.

The letter came into the hands of Daniel Clark. Clark was a rich and romantic Irishman who owned properties near Natchez and in Spanish Louisiana, too. Together with an even richer uncle, he had had business and social connections with General Wilkinson since 1787, when he was a twenty-one-year-old newcomer. Soon, says the always colorful Claiborne, "His equippage was princely; his charities ostentatious; his gallantries notorious." When he wrote Jefferson, Clark was a flashing blade just over thirty. Also, he was a close friend of Nolan's.

When Clark replied to Jefferson for his absent friend, he said of Nolan that "that extraordinary and enterprising Man is now and has been for some years past employed in the

Countries bordering on the Kingdom of New Mexico either in catching or purchasing horses." He was expected "on the Banks of the Mississippi at the Fall of the Waters with a thousand Head which he will in all probability drive into the U.S. . . . You judge right in supposing him to be the only person capable of fulfilling you [sic] Views as no Person possessed of his talents has ever visited that Country to unite information with projects of utility." Clark added that Quaker Ellicott was, when he wrote, a guest in his house and had been given much information on the subject by the absent dark young man.

The rich Irishman also enjoined Jefferson, for Nolan's sake, to keep the information to himself, "as the slightest Hint would point out the Channel from whence it flowed and might probably be attended with the most fatal consequences to a man, who will at all times have it in his Power to render important services to the U.S., and whom nature seems to have formed for Enterprises of which the rest of Mankind are incapable."

For further information in the meantime, he recommended to Jefferson William Dunbar, of Natchez, whom Clark and Nolan often visited. Dunbar, said Clark, was a man who "for Science, Probity, & general information is the first Character in this part of the World." There seems much basis for that opinion. This gentleman was called by courtesy "Sir William," because, though a pioneer American planter, he was the youngest son of the holder of an ancient Scottish earldom. As a young man in his twenties, he had come down the river in the early 1770s to the same sort of misfortunes which so many other settlers then encountered. Some of his most valuable slaves were lost in a black insurrection. Then he was plundered by Patriot Willing. Next, his plantation was raided by Spanish soldiers under Galvez. He was forty-three when he established another plantation, called The Forest, 9 miles from Natchez. Now he was one of those who was doing most to improve the culture and processing of cotton. Also, as a wealthy older man he had as young friends such men as Clark and Nolan and Minor. Minor he called "a lively, agreeable man." He spoke with far greater admiration of Nolan.

Dunbar gave Jefferson information he had from Nolan about the horses, about fossil bones of "great magnitude" in New Mexico which Nolan had reported to him, of strange lake monsters there which the Indians thought were the ghosts of the first Spaniards and Dunbar conjectured might be hippopotamuses, and on strange prismatic sun spectacles on clear evenings in Natchez.

Clark also wrote Jefferson again from Natchez, on November 12, 1799. While he had been at Dunbar's house, he said, Nolan had arrived from Mexico bringing with him "1000 head of horses." He had been lucky, he explained. General Wilkinson's friend, Governor Gayoso, had written the governor of Texas "to arrest Nolan as a Person who from the Knowledge he had acquired of the interior parts of New Mexico, might one day be of injury to the Spanish Monarchy." By chance that letter was unopened, "and during this interval Nolan who was unconscious of the machinations of his Enemies passed thro' the Province, was treated as usual with the utmost attention, and only learned the circumstances from me a few days ago when preparing to go to the Frontier of Texas to bring in a small drove of Horses which he had still remaining there."

Clark did not connect the name of Nolan's enemies with the "machinations" he mentioned. Only tradition reports the efforts of Nolan's wife, born Fannie Lintot, to persuade him not to return to the Spanish trans-Mississippi country. Another Dunbar letter to Jefferson told the sad news and the end of the story. It leaves more mysterious still the relationships of adventurers, men of intrigue—or agents of elegant double-dealers along the frontier.

Sir William wrote Jefferson that his source of information had been "cut off . . . by the imprudence of Mr. Nolan who persisted in hunting wild horses without a regular permission." He had, of course, gone West again. This time, Dunbar told Jefferson, "a party being sent against him, he was the only man of his company who was killed by a random shot." He is commemorated only by the name of Nolan River, near Waco, Texas, beside which he was killed.

"I am concerned for the loss of this man," Dunbar wrote the Sage of Monticello. "Altho' his eccentricities were many and great, yet he was not destitute of romantic principles of honor united to the highest personal courage, with energy of mind not sufficiently cultivated by education, but which under the guidance of a little more prudence might have conducted him to enterprises of the first magnitude."

So died "The Man Without a Country," just as his country was pressing southward and, as the Spanish always feared, eying the West beyond the river. He helped satisfy Jefferson's curiosity and tie diverse characters together. It is not regarded as significant in history that his wife, Fannie Lintot, sister-in-law of the prospering and always agile Minor, died of a broken heart. It has seemed even less significant that the order to Spanish soldiers to go after Nolan came from Gayoso after he had moved to New Orleans, still the friend and drinking companion of General Wilkinson.

Gayoso died, reputedly after a lively night with Wilkinson, before his order resulted in Nolan's death. Nolan was killed in 1801. Undoubtedly in both cases General Wilkinson grieved ostentatiously. With the stars of his American rank on his tunic, he remained ostentatiously convivial as well.

VIII: THE DEVIL'S BACKBONE

NATCHEZ was hot and beautiful on August 6, 1798, after the boundary had been cut below it and the United States was in undisputed possession. Its mixture of American and Spanish character seemed as rich and strange as the black shade and bright flowers in the town on the bluff whose streets were bordered by chinaberry trees. Winthrop Sargent, who that day came as first governor of the new Mississippi Territory, did not like it. He did not conceal his feeling. He was sick and scornful.

As a stiff-backed Massachusetts Yankee, Sargent was under orders to conciliate the people of this new American outpost. He found them a company as complex as the town, which was marked by its Spanish architecture and customs but already boisterous with the push of Americans. Natchez was easygoing and quick-tempered. And the hot sun splashed the streets like the gold everybody was after. That gold was cotton-soft and hard-minted.

Sargent was no newcomer to the West. Then forty-five and a widower, he had been one of the disillusioned revolutionary veterans who in the Bunch of Grapes Tavern in Boston organized the Ohio company to settle the northwest. There, he said, "the veteran soldier and honest man should find a retreat from ingratitude" and "never more . . . visit the Atlantic shores." He kept his seaboard prejudices, however. And the far from prim customs, which remained in Natchez after Gayoso was gone, offended him. Diffused over the territory, he reported, "are aliens of various characters, among them the most abandoned villains who have escaped from the chains and prisons of Spain, and been convicted of the blackest crimes."

"Natchez," he added, "from the perverseness of some of the people, the inebriety of the negroes and Indians on Sundays, has become a most abominable place."

Already, too, in addition to Spaniards, Negroes, and Indians, the tumultuous trade of the Americans was creating down on the shore below the bluffs, and so farther from Sargent's sniffing nose, a more "abominable place" still. Some students have insisted that it was not until the Americans grew in numbers under their own government, floating down the river and returning by the Trace, that wicked Natchez-under-the-Hill began to attain its reputation as the wildest hellhole on the river.

Certainly not all the Americans who came were Puritans like Sargent. Some of the most cultivated among them, who came to buy plantations, practice professions, and go into trade, were lively and lusty men. Still the American push was provided by men who developed vast muscles from poling and rowing on the river and tramping homeward through the woods. There were classes among them. All keelboat men, who propelled their pointed boats with pole and oar, felt superior to those rafters who merely floated downstream.

But all the rivermen, generally called flatboatmen regardless of the craft upon which they labored, declined to use their great muscles ashore for anything but brawling, mayhem, and occasional murder, for the fun of it. They said they were half horses and half alligators. And perhaps their crows for combat like those of fighting cocks from dunghills, were best reported by the river's great chronicler. After their passing, with obviously admiring remembrance and some literary flourishes, Mark Twain in his *Life on the Mississippi* recorded a typical sample of their battle cries:

Look at me! I'm the man they call Sudden Death and General Desolation! Sired by a hurricane, dam'd by an earthquake, half-brother to the cholera, nearly related to the smallpox on the mother's side! Look at me! I take nineteen alligators and a bar'l of whiskey for breakfast when I'm in robust health, and a bushel of rattlesnakes and a dead body when I'm ailing. I split the everlasting rocks with my glance, and I quench the thunder when I speak! Whoo-oop! Stand back and give me room according to my strength! Blood's my natural drink, and the wails of the dying is music to my ear. Cast your eye on me, gentlemen! and lay low and hold your breath, for I'm about to turn myself loose!

Others reported variants of these whoops. One such was: "I'm the man that, single-handed, towed the broadhorn over the sand-bar—the identical infant who girdled a hickory by smiling at the bark, and if anyone denies it, let him make his will and pay the expenses of a funeral . . . I'm spiling for some one to whip me—if there's a creeter in this diggin' that wants to be disappointed in trying to do it, let him yell—whoop-hurra!"

The cry was intended not merely to announce in a tavern that its shouter could lick anybody in the room, but to inform those on the shore he could lick anybody on the river. And with bone-breaking and eye-gouging, the challengers went about the business of proving it. One man's challenge often resulted in the melees of whole mobs. The tallest of such tales attend the folklore of Mike Fink, "the King of the Keelboatmen," who hailed from Pennsylvania. He could, his mythology maintains, outwork, outdrink, and outfight any human on earth.

As man, or as a combination of legends, he was the cock-a-doodle-doo of the rivermen. No portrait of him is available, but the impression that remains is that the man did not live who could have gouged out Mike's eye, bitten off his ear, or even cauliflowered it. His precision with the rifle was as proverbial as his effectiveness with his bare-knuckled fists. For a man like Fink, cutting off a wild turkey's head with a musket ball at 100 yards, while the bird was in full flight, was not regarded as remarkable. At 40 paces he could drive a nail home, to its head.

Natchezeans like to think that Fink came to his end on the shoddy shores below their bluffs. So do the folklorists of a good many other places. The general agreement seems to be that after a quarrel with a friend, one Carpenter, Mike was to be allowed, as demonstration of good will, to put a bullet through a tin cup full of whiskey, William Tell fashion, on the friend's head. All knew that, as the proclaimed best shot on the river, Mike could do it. Instead the bullet apparently went below the cup through Carpenter's skull.

"Why, Carpenter, you've spilt the whiskey," Fink said.

Before he could say more, another "friend" of Carpenter's killed Fink. Only then was it discovered that the accurate Fink had shot between cup and skull to knock Carpenter out temporarily but only with a crease through his scalp.

Yet despite their insistent idleness and animal contests on shore, the Finks, to use the term for all, had their code, and their memory has not always been maligned. Indeed, one Bill McCoy is as much a symbol of the flatboatmen's rude code of honor as was Fink the traditional figure of the roisterer. Patience perhaps was growing thin when in a brawl Bill drew blood and aroused indignation. A recessing court called for bail which he could not hope to provide. Then, according to Natchez tradition, Col. James C. Wilkins, businessman and planter, despite the protest of his friends, provided $10,000 bond for Bill's appearance at his trial months ahead.

McCoy set out homeward up the Trace, and the prevalent prediction was that he would never be seen again. The morning of the trial arrived—and no Bill. All were sure that the colonel had lost the money he had foolishly put up. Time had almost come for the court to adjourn and the bond to be forfeited when a cry swept through the courthouse crowd. In came McCoy, unshaven and dirty, his hands torn, his eyes haggard, and sunburnt almost to a crisp. He had started from Louisville as a hand on a boat, but low water so delayed it that he realized he could not make Natchez on time. With his own hands he shaped a canoe from a fallen tree. He had rowed and paddled 1,300 miles almost without stopping. And almost half-dead he had met his obligation. The Colonel embraced him. His quick acquittal was a celebration of Natchez huzzaing approval.

Mark Twain described both the good and the bad boatmen as "rough and hardy men; rude, uneducated, brave, suffering terrific hardships with sailor-like stoicism; heavy drinkers, coarse frolickers in moral sties like the Natchez-under-the-Hill of that day, heavy fighters, reckless fellows, everyone, elephantinely jolly, foul-witted, profane, prodigal of their money, bankrupt at the end of the trip, fond of barbaric finery, prodigious braggarts yet, in the main, honest, trustworthy, faithful to promises and duty, and often picturesquely magnanimous."

Such rivermen, who were horsemen and trampers, too, on the Trace, finally received their anthem in a song written by Samuel Woodworth, who also wrote "The Old Oaken Bucket." It ran:

> We are a hardy, freeborn race,
> Each man to fear a stranger;
> What e'er the game, we join the chase,
> Despising toil and danger;
> And if a daring foe annoys,
> No matter what his force is,
> We'll show him that Kentucky boys
> Are alligator horses.

Such men required facilities for fight and frolic. And Natchez, which thrived on the trade they brought and the money they left behind them, provided it. Natchez-under-the-Hill, a mile-long flat below the bluffs, was sternly described as "a stale sordid sodden place." Still, with a vividness which sometimes reflected fascination through indignation, travelers reported its congregation of "whores, boatmen, gamblers, bruisers" frequenting "barrooms and gambling hells" and brothels reeking with the smell of dirty men and women, of garbage and river muck.

No such kind words as the flatboatmen sometimes got were spoken of the fashionably dressed young men smoking or lounging as gamblers, sharpers, and pimps on the river shore. But they as well as boatmen crowded "the low, broken half sunken sidewalks," together with the "tawdrily arrayed, highly rouged females . . . negroes, mulattoes, pigs, dogs and dirty children." In the midst of such squalor, Natchez-under-the-Hill was romanticized, nevertheless, in terms of such elegant houses as that of Madame Aivoges, "the paragon of prostitutes."

Perhaps in her carpeted, curtained house, as tradition says, she was the red-curled and green-eyed madame of delectable white and octoroon whores. Wine in her perfumed precincts may have taken the place of Monongahela whiskey—or even rawer local brands. Maybe her dark and golden girls played the spinet for a clientele sternly selected through a peephole in the door. Perhaps, indeed, the legend is true that the madame was killed by a son, maintained on her lecherous earnings at an expensive Eastern school. He discovered her business only when he came as a customer while visiting aristocratic friends at a plantation on the hill.

Certainly there were black, yellow, and white sluts hanging half-naked out of hovels and seeking to lure to rumpled beds any roughneck flatboatmen with the cash. Quality varied as much as color, from kinky heads to tow ones, from fragile beauties to one Annie Christmas. Operating a floating house of prostitution, she was reported to be 6 feet 8 inches tall and able to handle in a fight or a bawdy frolic the toughest flatboatmen on the river.

Generally gentlemen, even governors, on the high bluffs could disregard the rowdy sinning on the shore. It helped business and did not intrude upon plantation society, though that society's later story suggests that some of the down-the-hill violence may have been contagious up-the-hill, too. Perhaps the decorum and serenity on the bluffs have always been exaggerated. Still, there was a cloistered charm in the houses with doors and windows tall and wide to admit the breezes from the river. Old high Natchez took its grace from the tiered galleries about such houses, the iron grillwork and vaulted corridors of the chief buildings the Spaniards had left. Though some neater visitors objected, there was color, too, in the way the merchants turned their stores "inside out every morning to adorn their fronts and create zigzags on the sidewalks."

Not all merchants, of course, were peddlers who spread their goods on the streets. Some were men as proud as any in the place. Bernard Lintot had stressed his social rank and position in the community when he first objected to the marriage of his daughter to Philip Nolan. Now under Sargent, the new American governor, two merchants, Abijah Hunt and Anthony Glass, were to mark the Trace, one with his efforts and the other with his crimes. Hunt, though perhaps a little arrogant in his conservative views, was to be the man who tried to build the Trace as a dependable route of communication. Glass, gleaming with the pretensions of respectability, was to be a sinister figure in its crimes. Hunt, with Sargent, was eager to improve the path. Glass (or Gass, as his name is sometimes given) was ready to help rob and bleed it.

Governor Sargent's poor opinion of the Natchez to which he came was to be returned in terms of local opinion of him. Claiborne wrote that he was "incompatible in tone, sentiments and manners with the people he was sent to." Still, some, notably Hunt as another Federalist, shared his strong antidemocratic views in a region in which by no means all of the inhabitants were rich men or great landowners. Those who had come first and taken up the rich alluvial river bottoms were followed by others who pushed back eastward from the river lands. There they met a third wave of settlers, the overflow of the seaboard poor who crowded into the unfertile pine-barrens.

Unpopular as Governor Sargent quickly became, he made some brusque sense. He shaped laws, even if he sometimes seemed to enforce them too legalistically. He dealt with a wild confusion of land titles secured under various regimes. He had been in Natchez less than two months when he suggested to Timothy Pickering, then Secretary of State and an equally furious Federalist, the construction of a post road southward from Nashville in the older part of the United States to the Natchez District. Even later officials of the national government knew that the Natchez Trace was still "no other than an Indian footpath very devious & narrow."

Officials in Philadelphia were slow to move. So, within a year after Sargent's arrival in Natchez and apparently with his approval, Hunt set out through the wilderness to report the need and the facts directly to the Postmaster General. Hunt was no young adventurer. When he rode he was a gray, stooped, busy man who had built his own business as a merchant, selling everything from boxes and barrels of goods to children's shoes. He was to become one of the richest men in the region.

Hunt was persuasive in Philadelphia. Though no road was ordered built, the Postmaster General did make a contract for the carrying of mail once a month from Natchez to Nashville over the ancient Trace. To accomplish this, Hunt was appointed the first postmaster at Natchez, at a salary of $2,400 a year. Hunt was also given the contract to carry the mail from Natchez to McIntoshville, halfway to Nashville. Sometimes called Tocshish Stand, it was near present Tupelo, and had been established earlier by a man named John McIntosh, who had, like many other Scotsmen, "embibed the habits of the Indians." The contract from Nashville to McIntoshville was given to Col. Matthew Lyon, of Nashville. One of the first and most articulate mail riders on this route was John L. Swaney, who, in his old age, left romantic reminiscences of it, including stories of hard-riding outlaws and murder.

Quite naturally the activities of merchant Glass were not documented then or later by Post Office Department documents or anything else. He was considered an honest merchant and citizen in Natchez. In his store he offered a good stock of dry goods, hardware, and general merchandise. He seemed to be doing well, and was well liked. He was more convivial than the serious Hunt. A good mixer, he was often at the King's Tavern, from which men set out for the wilderness and to which tired men arrived after traversing the Trace.

Actually, Glass was the fence and informer of bandits. He got rid of not easily negotiable loot in his store. More important, he spotted for his associates with horse and gun those travelers setting out with the richest loads. Apparently he did well in the business and survived it. Nevertheless, there were occasions when some eyebrows were lifted. Once Glass rode north along the Trace with a rich Kentuckian, Campbell by name, whose body, robbed and mutilated, was found a few days later in a swamp. Only the coincidence of their departures connected Glass with the matter. Still, many wondered.

Undoubtedly in his business informer Glass had subordinate informers, too—whores Under-the-Hill, gamblers, Negro servants in the taverns and inns. Nobody, of course, knows all the bandits with whom he worked. The history of bandits on the Trace is as old as the frontier itself. Before Glass's time it was already known as the Devil's Backbone. Certainly while Glass served as a sort of agent for outlaws, it deserved that name.

One of the most notorious of those who helped build the path's dark and bloody reputation was Joseph Thompson Hare. He came up the Trace from New Orleans, while the Mason gang and others came southward along it from Kentucky and Tennessee. Hare was a country boy, born near Philadelphia. He had been city-sharpened there, and in New York and Baltimore, before he came south. There he learned of the rich pickings possible on the road through the wilderness for a man ready to murder for money. Hare was ready. For him that was a professional step upward from picking pockets and rolling drunks.

In many ways he became the model of the romantic highwayman. He was literate, which was something of a distinction among the rougher elements on the road he traveled. In a weird, mystic, perhaps manic way he was religious, too. Sometimes as highwayman he seemed to himself almost like a horseman of the apocalypse. To great physical powers he added occasional sentimental sensibility. There were lines of behavior which he drew for others if not for himself.

One member of Hare's gang had good looks as well as great muscles. At first the bandit chief took no exception to this young bandit's little side line in roguery. The young man married young girls and left them after he had gotten their dowries. Hare did not object until the fellow showed up with a fragile young Spanish girl out of a nunnery. When Hare protested, the young fellow both kept the girl and stole Hare's wallet as well. Furthermore, a few days later when Hare met him in a tavern, the fellow was boasting that he could "whip any man in town." The big young man had asked for it, and Hare gave it to him: "Everytime I caught hold of him he bellowed for help. He was like a wolf caught in a sharp trap."

Hare was no mere bruiser, however, though the historians' favorite modern word for him seems to be "hoodlum." As a boy he had been apprenticed to a tailor. And ever after when he had the money he was the model of elegance and the figure of fashion. With his loot he bought the finest clothes for wear on his recurrent debauches in New Orleans, Nashville, and Natchez. Indeed, years later when he wrote of his arrest for the crime for which he was hanged, he noted in his diary: "I had bought one plaid coat, lined with crimson silk at the price of $35, and one coat in the style of an officer's, at the price of $75, very dashy, when two men whom the owner of the shop had sent for, entered and apprehended us. . . ."

He did not always appear so gaudily attired on the Trace. There, he and his companions in crime painted their faces with berry juice and bark stains like Indians on the warpath. This not only provided disguise but increased the helpless fear of their victims. Still, he needed tips on money-laden travelers, and it is possible that he was one of Glass's clients. He began his career as a highwayman when he saw companies starting toward the wilderness, "and was told that they carried a great deal of money with them through the Choctaw and Chickasaw Nations to get to Kentucky, Tennessee. . . ."

He rode to the Trace. He was not impressed by its beauty. For him only hiding or surprise was served by the woods of the "black-willow, the black-ash, water maple, pecan, pawpaw, cypress, sweet-bay, magnolia, catalpa, persimmon, locust, dogwood, wild-plum, tulip-tree . . . broom pine, buck-eye, wild cherry . . . the beech, the chestnut, the chincopin." The cane was for cover. The sumac and the trumpet flower were only vines which veiled the road. In the richness of bloom and foliage, Hare and his gang, perhaps with the help of informers, found such a company as they sought just beyond the Natchez District in the Choctaw country.

"We took three hundred doubloons, 74 pieces of different sizes and a large quantity of gold in bars, six inches in length and eight square—thirty-weight of it," he said of the first man he surprised. "With the others, I found 700 doubloons and five silver dollars, and four hundred French guineas, and 67 pieces the value of which I could not tell until I weighed them. I got twelve or thirteen thousand dollars altogether from the company, all in gold."

One of the men robbed by Hare told him that he had fought for his money on a privateer but that he could not fight in the silent wilderness. Perhaps even then Hare, as a man accustomed to the clamor of cities, shared the feeling about the whispering wilderness which later filled his diary with moods and fears. He gave the man back several gold pieces and his watch.

"He looked as thankful as if I had done him a favor, instead of robbing him," Hare said.

They pushed on to a hideaway in the Chickasaw country just below the Tennessee line, where, in the midst of a canebrake, an overhanging rock "made a sort of cave, that we could easily make safe from every savage that walked the wild wilderness." Savages did not trouble them. Indeed, one Indian became their scout. They themselves were the savages in a land of largely harmless Indians. And Hare, as diarist, made himself seem less savage than the men he led.

A few days later, he said, he had trouble keeping his followers from killing four men they held up. Leaving his men in the brush behind him Hare rode up to the traveler "that had holsters before him." He told him that he had twelve highwaymen behind him, and the dry crackling cane seemed to prove his words. Hare felt gloomy, too, as the cane crackled under a dull sky. For a moment the men he threatened hesitated in fear. Hare's men muttered angrily.

"Shoot them and have done with it," one of them shouted.

Then one of the older men, a merchant, began shaking and crying, "For God's sake . . . for God's sake. . . ."

All promised that they would never identify the highwaymen, and Hare called one of his men up to take $7,000 from them.

Occasionally Hare was careless. One incident which showed this failing took place when he halted a slave trader riding from Natchez. Such men often carried much money. The route over the Trace to the labor-hungry Natchez District, planting its wealth in cotton, was cheaper than the route by sea from the seaboard slave pens. Another traveler

on the road described such "a long procession" of slaves
going down the Trace "like a troop of wearied pilgrims."
The slow pace, the fatigued air, and their tattered garments
"gave to the whole train a sad and funereal appearance."

"First," this chronicler said, "came half a dozen boys and
girls, with fragments of blankets and ragged pantaloons and
frocks, hanging upon but not covering their glossy limbs.
They passed along in high spirits . . . capering and
practicing jokes upon each other, while their even rows of
teeth, and the whites of their eyes—the most expressive features in the African physiognomy—were displayed in
striking contrast to their ebony skins."

These were followed by "a tall mullato, with high cheek
bones, with lean and hungry looks, making rapid inroads
into a huge loaf of bread, whose twin brother was secured
under his left arm." There were yellow women, too, and a
"woman very black very short breathing like a porpoise."

Hare watched such dark trains from his hiding place in
the woods. The slave stealers would come later. His
business was with slave dealers who came back up the road
with their Negroes left behind and the price they had
brought in their leather saddlebags. This time he was too
eager. He had left his men at the cave, and he had only one
pistol with him.

"I rode up to his left side, and told him to deliver his
money, for I was the devil, and would take him to hell in a
second if he did not drop that gun off his shoulder, and his
pistols, too, if he had any."

This time the slaver decided to take a chance. As he
dropped the gun from its holder, he pulled the trigger,
firing straight toward Hare's face. Blinded by the smoke
Hare's answering shot missed. Also, the highwayman saw
two other men not far up the Trace. The slaver galloped
away. Calmly, Hare said, he dismounted to recover his hat.
He reloaded his gun and waited for the two strangers.

They halted, looking at him quizzically.

One drawled, "Seen any deer hereabouts?"

Hare allowed that he had.

"I suppose that was one ye fired at just now? Why didn't ye kill him?"

"A man will sometimes miss a thing," said the highwayman.

The men jogged off, and when they had gone a little way Hare heard their loud laughter in the silent woods.

Rich with loot, Hare and his band rode on to Nashville. They found good rooms in "a very good house, kept by a widow lady." Hare, the dandy, bought himself "a black boy, and two horses and a gig." Then, spending their money freely as they went, they drove to Louisville and floated down the river past Natchez to New Orleans. Gambling, whoring, and being blackmailed, too, they soon needed the replenishment of the loot available on the Trace. As a precaution this time, they secured Spanish passports so that, if they got into trouble on the American side of the Mississippi, they could cross the river to the Spanish domain west of it.

Hare was already growing more moody as they camped in a cave north of Natchez. No man had ever visited the place, he wrote, "since the flood." In its gloomy silence, he was troubled by the noise of the "very large" alligators, which sometimes "cried like a young child." Still, he went about his bold business. He and his companions relieved Trace travelers of enough to go to revel in New Orleans, then give a big ball in Pensacola. Arrested there as American spies, their dancing friends came to their rescue. Then, riding back toward the Trace, Hare read to his followers from John Wesley's magazine. The great Methodist evangelist did not convert him from his ways, however.

"We raked the woods from the Southwest Point to the Choctaw line."

About actual murder Hare was a little reticent in his diary. Somewhere along the way, however, he murdered a rich Virginia gentleman who had converted his property into money for a move to Mississippi. He was the father of

Madeline Price, "a miracle of beauty," for whom Aaron Burr tarried too long in his escape from the Natchez neighborhood a few years later. How many others Hare killed only the buzzards could count.

His time on the Trace was drawing to an end. Perhaps his mistake was not murdering a drover whom Hare, working alone, had robbed of a small sum of money. He took his money but spared his life. Then this cattle dealer hurriedly organized a posse. More than angry citizens seemed on Hare's trail.

"As I was riding along very rapidly," Hare wrote, "to get out of reach of pursuit, I saw standing right across the road, a beautiful white horse, as white as snow; his ears stood straight forward and his figure was very beautiful. When I approached him, and got within six feet of him, he disappeared in an instant, which made me very uneasy, and made me stop and stay at a house near there, all night."

Some years later when he was waiting for the gallows for another crime, he interpreted this vision: "I think this white horse was Christ and that he came to warn me of my sins, and to make me fear and repent."

The vision of the horse served a more useful purpose that night. Hare only repented of his sins on paper. At this time his halt at the house gave the posse time to catch him in bed. He was sent to jail for five years. He came out and left the country unreformed. Years after that, caught buying his gaudy coat, he was hanged in Maryland, in 1818, for a $16,900 holdup of a night mail coach.

The capture of Hare did not bring safety to the Trace. Indeed, the days of his desperate activities and those of others like him are difficult to separate or arrange in time. Certainly, on August 14, 1801, Col. Joshua Baker, a merchant and planter of Hardin County, Kentucky, according to *The Kentucky Gazette* was robbed on the north side of the "Big Biopiere River" (probably the Bayou Pierre). The colonel and three companions were returning with the proceeds from his flatboats full of crops they had taken down the rivers. As they halted at a small stream, four men appeared with blacked faces and demanded their money. They took the horses, traveling utensils, and about $2,300 in cash. Fortunately one frightened packhorse, loaded with a considerable sum of money, ran away and was later recovered by the colonel and his friends.

It was not much later that merchant Glass was attentive to visitors in Natchez. They were Samuel Mason and his son. Mason, born in Virginia around 1750, was a man with a good record as a patriot in the Revolution. He was a fine-looking man, according to the historian of old times in Tennessee, Josephus Conn Guild. Weighing about two hundred pounds, he was "rather modest and unassuming and had nothing of the raw-head and bloody-bones appearance." Only later did people give special note to one physical flaw as giving him a wolfish appearance. He had a "tooth which projected forwards, and could only be covered with his lip by an effort." It did not seem a fang when he first appeared in Natchez. There, Glass got the Masons quarters at Walton's Tavern. He introduced Mason as an upcountry planter, and suggested that he had plenty of money to spend. Mason was well dressed. Like all gentlemen in this horsy country, he carried a riding crop. His boots were brightly shined. He seemed a highly acceptable visitor until one day one of Baker's companions, who had returned to Natchez, recognized him.

"That's the man!" he shouted. "The man that robbed Baker!"

Maj. George Willey, in his recollections as a Natchez old-timer, described the result. His memory was that the robbery took place in Hinds County "where the road crosses the creek still known as Baker's Creek." Apparently there were other witnesses. Baker and his friends had stopped for dinner the day before the robbery with a Mrs. Watkins. While she was preparing the meal, Mason rode up.

"I noticed him," she said, "as he passed the saddle bags of

the travelers, which were placed on the gallery. He managed
to give each of them a push with his foot as if to feel their
weight. After apparently satisfying himself that the saddle
bags were filled with specie, he bade me good day and rode
off."

The Bakers, she said, were robbed the next day. However,
the Masons displayed outrage at the outcry in Natchez
against them. They were defended, Willey said, by a
distinguished lawyer named Wallace, who "went to work to
get up a public feeling in favor of his clients, and succeeded
so well, that although the Masons were convicted, the
general sentiment was that they were unjustly punished."

Also, this lawyer got them off with a sentence of thirty-
nine lashes and exposure in the pillory. At this time, for
lesser crimes, such as merely stealing Baker's horses, they
might have been branded with an "H" on one cheek and a
"T" on the other, or had their ears nailed to the pillory and
cut off. Still, this first public punishment of the Masons, as
Major Willey described it, must have been a spectacle in the
river town.

"I witnessed the flogging," he said, "and shall never
forget their cries of 'Innocent' at every blow of the cowhide
which tore the flesh from their quivering limbs, and until
the last lash was given they shrieked the same despairing cry
of 'Innocent, Innocent.'

"After they were released the older Mason said to the
surrounding crowd, 'You have witnessed our punishment
for a crime we never committed; some of you may see me
punished again but it shall be for something worthy of
punishment.'

"He and his son then, shaving their heads and stripping
themselves naked, mounted their horses and yelling like
Indians, rode through and out of the town."

Postmaster Abijah Hunt, who was concerned for the
safety of the trail over which he dispatched the mails, may
have been present on that occasion at the Old Natchez Jail
at the corner of Franklin and Union streets. He continued to

move the mails. Also, then or soon after, he had in partner-
ship as merchant with him his nephew, David Hunt, who
was ultimately to have 1,700 slaves and own 25 separate
plantations. Still, in eccentricity or thrift this younger Hunt
always deducted a penny from every bill he paid.
Sometimes, out of his hearing, he was called King David.
Less awed or envious people referred to him as "the model
planter of Mississippi."

Others prospered, too. Governor Sargent found more
than "abandoned villains" in the Natchez District. Thomas
Jefferson did not reappoint him as governor because, as that
anti-Federalist President put it, Sargent had "not been so
fortunate as to bring the harmony and mutual attachment"
that the new territory required. However, on a breeze-swept
plantation gallery, with a glass in his hand and the moon
rising over the magnolias, the stern Yankee did find
"harmony and attachment" Before he sent Abijah Hunt
northward through the wilderness to petition the government for a road, he acquired the heart and hand of the well-
connected, plantation-owning Widow Maria Williams. As
an ex-official he never long left the "abominable place" to
which he had come. He belonged to Natchez for the rest of
his life. He named the early, beautiful plantation house he
built there Gloucester, after the seaport in which he was
born in Massachusetts and from which he had once felt that
veterans and patriots had to move West to escape Eastern
ingratitude.

It seems doubtful that Anthony Glass was present at the
flogging of the Masons. On such a violent occasion,
attracting the diverse populace, he would have been
ostentatiously busy with his barrels and boxes, his
hardware, dry goods, and general merchandise. Still, he
undoubtedly showed himself in confident respectability at
such convivial places as King's Tavern or Monsieur Ude's
pleasant café. The town had been excited, but some men
shrugged. There were whispers about Glass, as there had
been earlier. However, no evidence, adequate in a

courthouse, was ever brought against him. Apparently he was a judge of values in suspicion as in everything else. He moved quietly. After most of his trigger men were dead he was living, respectable-seeming still, in Walnut Hills (now Vicksburg).

There, as property owner, he gave Thomas Rodney, who Jefferson as President sent as an anti-Federalist judge to the Mississippi Territory, "a pre-emption claim to 370 acres." Judge Rodney, who later sternly held Aaron Burr in bail, collected fossils, wrote poetry, and organized dancing societies, had not paid for the lands when he died.

IX: MASON'S HEAD

JOHN Swaney the mail rider set out from Nashville on Saturday night. He carried a few newspapers, "letters and government dispatches" in his oil-dressed deerskin mail pouch, and a "half bushel of corn for his horse, provisions for himself, an overcoat or blanket, and a tin trumpet." Riding hard, by midnight he reached the cabin of Tom Davis in the Big Branch of the Harpeth River. Less than 25 miles from Nashville, this was the last white man's house. Beyond lay the wilderness.

On Sunday morning he reached the Duck River. There John Gordon, first postmaster at Nashville as Abijah Hunt was in Natchez, operated a ferry. Here man and horse ate breakfast before starting on the 80 miles to the Tennessee River. Already at that wide stream the Chickasaw Colberts, who had harbored the Natchez refugees from the Spanish nearly twenty years before, took travelers across.

"The Indians were contrary," the mail rider remembered in his old age. They would not come across the river for him if he failed to get to the landing before bedtime.

The Colberts were more than contrary. They were shrewd, strong, and had a Midas touch for making money. And sometimes they seemed not too particular as to how they made it. Before Colonel Robertson, the Cumberland founder, made a treaty with them which lasted long and well, he called them "pirates." Certainly the Spanish held to that idea. From the beginning, however, these Scotch-

Chickasaws were careful to avoid crude banditry. One story was that always they were traders with skins and meat to offer for coffee, cloth, powder, and guns. Still in this trading "it was an easy process from chaffering to disputing, from angry words to blows, from robbery to murder."

Certainly such charges were unjustified when Swaney crossed the river to spend the night with George Colbert. This Colbert then had been petted not only in Nashville. He had been to Philadelphia and seen George Washington. While Swaney rode, George Colbert was to help make the treaty for a better road over the Trace—and get a good cut for himself in the process. A few years later an informed traveler wrote that this Colbert's house looked "like a country palace with its abundance of glass in doors and windows." It was probably less pretentious when Swaney came. The mail rider apparently got along well with George Colbert, whose Indian name was Tootemastubbe. He was "an enemy of education, missions and whiskey," which apparently he put together as menaces to the Indians.

From this Colbert's house Swaney rode 120 miles to the chief villages of the Chickasaws. On the way not a house or even an Indian hut interrupted the wilderness. Making a fire with his tinder-box, Swaney spent one night camping in the woods or canebrakes. At the end of this wilderness ride was the house of another Colbert. Whatever may have been its comforts or discomforts, Swaney always remembered the pretty half-breed—or even eighth-breed—daughters of the household. So did others. Tired and dirty boatmen and well-accoutered gentlemen, too, stopped sometimes just to stare at girls who were described by turns as "the prettiest woman in Mississippi" or even as "the most beautiful woman on the continent."

Here Swaney made his first exchange of horses. In old-age recollection he exaggerated distances. Still it was 80 miles from the Colbert Ferry to the Chickasaw settlements near Tupelo. The Trace did not pass through the chief

Choctaw settlements, but he rode through their nation toward the smoother path to Natchez. The whole distance was about 500 miles.

Apparently Swaney seldom rode alone. Going and returning, on that lonely path other men fell in with him for company and protection. No man wanted to face the wilderness dark, the cries of animals, and the crackling of the cane alone. Lurking anywhere beside it might be the Masons or other bandits. One such man who joined Swaney was John B. Craighead of Nashville, perhaps a relative of the clergyman supposed to have performed Andrew Jackson's second wedding ceremony. Craighead had brought boats of produce to Natchez and was now on his way home.

Setting out on a cloudy early evening, they had not gone far when they realized that they were being followed by two armed men. Friendly Indians whom they encountered slipped back in the dark but brought back more fearful word that the men were apparently waiting for the moment to attack. Swaney figured this was the best time to run for it. So they struck into the woods, paralleling the Trace in the darkness. Back upon it they put spurs to their horses. Craighead and Swaney got to Nashville safely. Not all whom Swaney encountered on his hard rides were so fortunate.

Once when he slept in the woods, he heard voices at daybreak. Hoping they came from a company of returning boatmen, Swaney blew loud on his horn and galloped toward the sounds. And as he came toward the scene he heard the robber's word.

"Surrender!"

A mounted gentleman with still-smoking empty pistols in his hands was cursing helplessly. A bandit with painted face covered him with his musket. The robber fired, and the gentleman fell forward across his saddle horn. Swaney's horse shied and reared. Suddenly the Trace was empty except for the dead traveler sprawling beside his horse. Hurrying down the Trace the mail rider caught up with the companions of the dead man. One was his teen-age son.

They had come from Carolina with the idea of purchasing a plantation in Mississippi.

Swaney guided them to a nearby Indian village, called Pigeon Roost, in the Choctaw country to get assistance. When they got back the robbers had been before them. The dead man's body had been stripped to his underwear. His horse had been taken. However, the robbers apparently had been nervous, too. They had failed to find the money belt which the traveler wore next to his skin.

The dead man's boy cut a slab from a tree. With his knife he carved an inscription for the shallow grave they dug:

ROBERT MCALPIN

MURDERED & KILLED

HERE JULY 31

In his old age Swaney thought the year was 1800. He could not be sure. And even then no one could be sure, as was afterwards suspected, that this was the work of Mason and his gang. Still Swaney, who knew them best, seemed to think so. He had known Mason and members of his gang earlier. All had worked in other places and on other roads before, like Hare, they recognized the easy pickings on the Trace. One of them was Wiley Harpe—"Little Harpe," so called when he was not using an alias. He and his brother Micajah, "Big Harpe," had been the "terrible Harpes" of Tennessee and Kentucky.

These brothers were born in North Carolina, sons of a Tory who had fought with the British against his neighbors. Afterwards he had to run West to save his neck. Perhaps pushed by the same fury behind them, "the terrible Harpes," then in their late twenties, had come West in 1795. Some felt that "their tawny appearance and dark curly hair betrayed a tinge of African blood." Two sisters, Susan and Betsy Roberts, came West with them. Susan, who claimed to be Big Harpe's wife, was "rather tall, raw-boned . . . and rather ugly." Her younger sister, Betsy, was a gay, blonde "perfect contrast with her sister." In Knoxville Little Harpe, adding to the female contingent, was married to pretty Betsy Rice by her preacher father. All three women seemed available to both men—and all seemed perpetually pregnant.

Swaney knew the Harpes, he said, when he was a race rider in Knoxville. He rode, he related, when a horse of the Harpes' was "beaten by one belonging to Sam Gibson and party."

"The Harpes," he recalled, "had bet everything they owned, and having lost were completely broken up. The night after the race the two Harpes killed and robbed an old man two miles west of Knoxville, and ran away into Kentucky, when they entered upon a career of robbery and murder."

Others give the Harpes less excuse for entering upon a career of crime. They had been suspected of hog stealing and other minor depredations before. Now, however, they began to leave behind them a bloody trail. They not only robbed their victims. They also added torture and mutilation to murder. They were early practitioners of a special art in disposal of the bodies of those they killed. They ripped open their bellies, removed the entrails, and filled the cavities with stones. Then they sank them in swamps or streams.

Wandering, killing, robbing, once they lived in a cavern—perhaps Mammoth Cave. Big Harpe said when he was dying that the only thing he was sorry for was that he had there smashed out the brains of one of the Harpe infants on the wall of the cave. No other smashed heads or splattered brains disturbed his conscience, if he had one.

At Cave-in-Rock in the river bluffs along the Ohio River in Illinois, the savagery of the Harpes was too much even for the other desperadoes who lay in wait for flatboats there. Ordinary murder did not trouble them. Still, they were not pleased when the Harpes made a sport of it. Once, as a joke, the Harpes tied one of their victims to a horse. They whipped the neighing, galloping animal with his screaming rider over the cliffs. For that the other robbers ran them out. Not long after, in the loft of a house where they slept, Big Harpe tomahawked a fellow lodger because he snored too loudly. Then, for good or evil measure, he came down the ladder from the loft and killed the woman of the cabin and her baby. A furious posse came on the Harpes and their women and children just as they were about to rob another stranger.

Little Harpe rode into a thicket and disappeared. But the riders found Big Harpe. The man whose wife and child he had killed put a bullet into his spine. Big Harpe was too slow dying. So while he lingered paralyzed, the widower began cutting his head off with a butcher knife. He cut round the flesh, then down to the bone. At last he twisted the head off as he might have done in slaughtering a pig.

"You're a God Damned rough butcher," said Big Harpe as the decapitating began, "but cut on and be damned."

Big Harpe's head was nailed to a fork in a tree in northwest Kentucky, not far from the present town of Henderson, and the rain-whitened skull grinned down at travelers for years. People in Kentucky stopped wondering where Little Harpe had gone. The women they left behind all married subsequently and lived respectable lives. Sometimes the distance between respectability and roguery was short on the frontier.

Little Harpe had first known Mason, who had been so soundly whipped in Natchez, as the reputed founder or operator of the "Liquor Vault and House of Entertainment" at Cave-in-Rock. Others give credit for the establishment of this den of thieves to a man named Wilson. Mason certainly spent evil time there. He had turned bandit late. In the early 1790s he was a respectable citizen and justice of the peace who had bravely fought both the British and the Indians. His turn to crime was not credited to losses on horse racing but to a daughter who slipped her lover into the house at night wrapped in her petticoats and out the same way next morning.

Then, though Mason had warned the man, one Kuykendall, to stay away, his daughter ran away and married him. Perhaps the respectable justice of the peace was shamed by this affair. Certainly Kuykendall was no prize bridegroom. He, too, had run away from Carolina on account of crimes. He was reputed always to carry in his waistcoat pocket "devil's claws," apparently instruments superior to "brass knucks," which he could slip on his fingers and at one swipe take off the whole side of an opponent's face.

Feigning forgiveness, Mason invited the couple to an "infare" with plenty of fiddle music, whiskey, dancing, stomping, and hilarity. In the midst of it Kuykendall went out into the darkness and to his death as planned by old man Mason. The old man, his sons, and companions fled in confusion and on the way committed a second murder when they shot a pursuing officer. With Mason was Samuel Mays and his sister, a clubfooted girl. This Mays, together with Little Harpe, was working with Mason on the Trace when mail-rider Swaney rode it. They were to be with the old robber until his end.

Little Wiley Harpe, who escaped the fate of Big Harpe, was also luckier than Kuykendall. One story about him is that he met a young Tennessee farmer named Bass riding north along the Trace with his sister. Bass was not well. Little Harpe very helpfully rode home with them. When Wiley left, the Bass girl with all her few belongings went with him as his bride. Not long after he came back with a sad story that his wife had been thrown from her horse and killed. He was gone by the time suspicion led the Bass family to find and open the girl's grave. No autopsy was necessary to show that she had been beaten to death and her body hideously mutilated.

Swaney reported much of the bloody story of the Mason gang. Killings and robberies increased after Mason's public whipping in Natchez. The body of the rich Kentuckian, who had ridden up the Trace with Anthony Glass, was found, robbed and mutilated, in the cane. Beside it a crude legend was marked on a tree, "Done by Mason of the Woods." It was soon after that that Glass discreetly moved to Walnut Hills. Still the robberies continued. Swaney came upon a group of terrified boatmen who had camped "in what was called Gum Springs, in the Choctaw Nation." The night before, while they were putting out pickets for safety, one of them unintentionally had stepped on a bandit hidden in the dark brush. He rose yelling and shooting. The terrified boatmen went headlong into hiding in the woods. And when Swaney found them all their firearms and money had been taken and they were "the worst scared, worst looking set of men [I] ever saw, some of them having but little clothing on, and one big fellow had only a shirt."

Apparently with Swaney's appearance the boldness of the boatmen revived. Armed with sticks, a big Kentuckian, who had lost his pants, led the pursuit. He found his pants with some doubloons still sewed in the waistband and quickly lost his eagerness for pursuit in the process. Soon afterwards they came upon Mason and his gang. They were behind trees with their guns ready.

"Clear out!" the bandits shouted. "We'll kill every one of ye!"

And the big Kentuckian, now with his pants on, led the flight of all the rest. Not all of Swaney's meetings with Mason were so uproarious.

"He frequently encountered me and other mail riders on the route," Swaney said, "and was always anxious to hear what was said of him. He often told me not to be afraid of him as he was after money and not letters."

And Swaney added: "On one of my return trips from Natchez, I fell in with the wife of young Tom Mason, carrying a baby and a sack of provisions in her arms. She was making for the Choctaw Agency, to go thence to her friends. She begged me to help her on her way, which I did by placing her on my horse. I did this for a day and made up for lost time by traveling all night. Mrs. Mason told me they were all safe and out of reach."

As their crimes continued and pursuit was pressed, they undertook to get out of reach. Mason's men not only robbed on the Trace but on the river, though they preferred the money coming back in the wilderness to the produce going down on the streams. Like Hare before him, Mason had secured a Spanish passport which permitted him to cross the river, thus escaping American authority. There, however, the Spanish surprised him, tried him, and sent him and his men as prisoners to New Orleans. At their trial the ever-protesting Mason tried to put the blame on one John Setton, which was the alias then worn by Little Harpe. New Orleans authorities decided to turn them all over to the Americans at Natchez. Then, on March 26, 1803, in a storm on the Mississippi, the robbers escaped.

The determination to catch them was growing like the trade on the river and the Trace. President Jefferson had replaced the rigid Federalist Sargent with the sometimes irresolute but far more conciliatory Governor William C. C. Claiborne. His younger relative, historian Claiborne, quoted him as writing optimistically to James Madison soon after he arrived in Natchez.

"The river front here is thronged with boats from the west," he reported, meaning only the still sparsely settled trans-Appalachian country. "Great quantities of flour and produce continually pass. Cotton, the staple of this Territory, has been very productive and remunerative. I have heard it suggested by our business men that the aggregate sales this season will exceed $700,000; a large revenue for a people whose numbers are about 9,000 of all ages and colors. Labor is more valuable here than elsewhere in the United States, and industrious people soon amass wealth. . . ."

That meant more boatmen, more settlers, and other travelers on the Trace. The governor tightened the noose around the killing and hiding Mason. He called on Federal soldiers at both ends of the Trace for assistance in catching the highwaymen. He was determined on order and safety in a growing territory. When he arrived he had found the country "wholly defenseless," he wrote.

"Bordering on a foreign power," he added, "separated from the nearest state by a wilderness of 600 miles—with numerous savage tribes enveloping our settlements, and a servile population nearly equal to the whites—an armed militia is essential to both safety and tranquility."

Meantime he put the necessary bait in the trap for Mason and his men. He offered a $2,000 reward for Mason—dead or alive. After their escape from the Spaniards, the gang's robberies continued. When Swaney came upon Mason, the old man's vanity about public reaction to his activities seemed to be growing, too. For seven months he ranged like an all too tangible ghost along the wilderness road. Then in October two strangers, who had been in and out of Natchez, came back to town. Their names were supposed to be James Mays, he of the clubfooted sister, and John Setton, man of tawny appearance and dark, curly hair. They brought a strange burden. It was a big lump of blue clay. Inside the clay, used to prevent decay, was the head of Samuel Mason.

The two men reported that they had found Mason at a hiding place in the swampy region around Lake Concordia, near the town. There, while he slept, they had tomahawked him and cut off his head. They presented their grisly prize at the Circuit Court then in session in the old town of Greenville, on the Trace just north of Natchez. Before the judge, they made their affidavit to get a certificate to the governor for the reward. Among those invited to identify the head was Swaney, who, according to the historian, Guild, had his doubts about it. Others seemed to think it was old Mason's head, all right. The wolf fang should have made identification easy. While the question was being resolved, a Captain Stump from Kentucky came into the courtroom. He stared at Setton. When he had alighted at the tavern, he spotted in the stable the horses of Setton and Mays. They had been stolen from him in a robbery in which a companion had been murdered on the Trace two months before. To the courtroom, he proclaimed one of the reward seekers as one of the thieves.

"Why, that man's Wiley Harpe," he cried.

Still, Stump hesitated before Setton's vigorous denial. Several boatmen appeared.

"That's Harpe all right," they said.

The clincher was provided by a man named John Bowman, from Knoxville, where the Harpes had begun their predatory parade.

"If he's Little Harpe," he told the court, "he'll have a scar under the left nipple of his breast, because I cut him there in a difficulty we had, one night in Knoxville."

Harpe's shirt was torn off. The scar was there.

One version is that this scene occurred in Natchez and that the robbers, now deprived of Mason's head, briefly escaped. The established fact is that on February 8, 1804, they were hanged in "Gallows-Field" in old Greenville. Afterwards their own heads were cut off, too. Along the Trace, Harpe's was put on a pole north of the town, Mays's at the south. Like Big Harpe's skull in Kentucky, they grinned, rotting and rain-washed, at travelers on the more and more crowded road. Furthermore, if the head they had had was not Mason's, nobody ever heard of Mason again. It is not in the record what happened to that skull in its ball of blue clay.

Undoubtedly, however, the "safety and tranquility" which Governor Claiborne sought had been served. Men rode with more confidence up the Trace, which was still "very devious & narrow." Plans were already being pushed to make it more than an Indian footpath. When Samuel Mason's severed head was rolled in the clay, George Colbert, the Scotch-sired Chickasaw, and General Wilkinson—and General Wilkinson and the Choctaws, too—had already agreed on a treaty. It would give to the perilous passage through the wilderness at least the semblance of a road. Planters, politicians, and promoters at both ends were elated.

"What," wrote an enthusiast in Nashville to a newspaper in the new national capital at Washington, "could tend more to the welfare of the western country than thus to connect our infant western settlements, and promote our commercial intercourse?"

The answer seemed obvious. Still, the uncertainties which covered it were as thick as the clay plastered around Mason's severed head.

X: EVERYBODY'S BARGAIN

IN OCTOBER, 1801, only a few American soldiers at
Chickasaw Bluffs guarded the strategic heights from the
Spaniards across the wide river. It was still Chickasaw
country, though Jackson's partner, John Overton, had a
trading post there. Twenty years later Jackson and Overton,
as real-estate promoters, called the site Memphis "on the
American Nile." Even at that time it was a remote place.
Perhaps that made it more comfortable for Marcus
Winchester, younger partner of Jackson and Overton. That
young man, son of Gen. James Winchester, had married the
octoroon mistress of United States Senator Thomas Hart
Benton.

Colors were often richly mixed on this frontier. They
were in this autumn of 1801, when Americans and
Chickasaws met on the bluffs to discuss a better road from
Nashville to Natchez, through the Indian nations. From the
wide, tawny river, the gold and crimson woods stretched
back toward Nashville, then almost the point of an
arrowhead-shaped mass of half a million trans-Appalachian
Americans. As chief negotiators, Gen. James Wilkinson met
George Colbert. Chief general in the small American army,
Wilkinson was already purpling from his bouts with the
bottle. Colbert, spokesman for the Chickasaw chiefs, had
the features of an Indian but the paler skin of his Scotch
father. Other darker Indians listened when he spoke.

Colbert was younger than Wilkinson. He and his three
brothers held leadership in their tribe. At the conference he

was "tall and slender with straight black hair" which "came well down to his shoulders." Then, as always, he wore the dress or uniform of white men of his time. He was, Governor Claiborne of Mississippi learned, a man "possessed of a very great address, and in business has a perfect command of his passions." Others, in the vernacular, called him "a cunning Indian." Soon after this conference, Dr. Rush Nutt, as an observant visitor among the Chickasaws on the Natchez Trace, described him as "an artful designing man more for his own interest than that of his Nation."

Men were already saying much the same thing of General Wilkinson. And both men had much to gain from this meeting on the bluff above the river. Both loved money. And Wilkinson wished to down the persisting rumors that he had received much from Spain. He had been aware of George Washington's suspicions when that President sent Ellicott west. He knew that some still remembered his apparently delicate consideration for the Spanish when Ellicott was establishing the line of American territory below Natchez.

Now Wilkinson wanted the confidence of the new President, Thomas Jefferson. That chief magistrate was reputed to have a prejudice against all soldiers. He might develop a special one against Wilkinson. In the White House as Presidential secretary now was Meriwether Lewis. At the time of Ellicott's little war, Lewis had been on duty at Chickasaw Bluffs, and Wilkinson had written that the young Virginian headed "a select corps of incomparable rascals." Lewis might return the compliment at Jefferson's ear.

The general was as adept a courtier as he was a traitor. Sniffing the political winds with his ruddy nose, a year before Jefferson's election, Wilkinson had written that he was sending him two Italian busts by Philip Nolan, in whose expeditions Jefferson had been interested. There is no evidence that Nolan saw Jefferson. He was killed the month the great Virginian was inaugurated. Wilkinson also turned to his old friend Aaron Burr. He seemed an unlikely source of help. Jefferson had only become President after a Federalist plot, then possible under the Constitution, had collapsed. It was to put Burr, as Jefferson's vice-presidential running mate, into the White House in his stead. The new President apparently felt that Burr did not scorn these Federalist shenanigans so quickly and unequivocally as he should have done. Still Burr helped keep Wilkinson's place in the army. Jefferson commissioned the general to deal with the Choctaws and the Chickasaws about the Trace.

There is more evidence that Wilkinson was eager to please Jefferson. On April 30, 1801, less than a week before the great Democrat's inauguration, the general issued a General Order "regulating the cutting of the hair." It directed that all officers and men cut off their queues. Wilkinson knew that such proudly worn queues had come to be almost the badge of anti-Jeffersonian, Federalist gentlemen, and as such, offensive to plainer Jeffersonians. In simple fashion the order would show where he stood—or at least where at the moment he pretended to stand. He wore no queue when he talked to Colbert and the other Chickasaw chiefs.

"Brothers," he called them. Then he went on: "On the part of your white brethren we have to represent to you, that the path from the settlement of Natchez (through your Nation) to those of Cumberland, is an uncomfortable one, and very inconvenient to them in its present unimproved condition; and we are directed to stipulate with you, to make it suitable to the accommodation of those who may use it, and at the same time beneficial to yourselves. We are your friends and representatives of your father, the President."

Specifically, the government, having decided to improve the Trace, wanted Indian permission to open the road from the Indian boundary line south of Nashville to a point on the Tennessee River below Muscle Shoals, then to the Choctaw boundary. In addition it wanted consent to place some white families along the road to maintain accommodations for post riders and travelers. Similar requests were to be made to the Choctaws for the southern section of the road.

Colbert and the other Chickasaw chiefs listened impassively. They, of course, had known of the plan in advance. Within the frame of his dark hair, Colbert's Indian features showed no flicker of his feeling. Undoubtedly, as did others, he enjoyed the resonant fluency of the gilded general. Still, as indicated by word sent back to the War Department, he expressed his fears that the opening of such a road would mean that the Indians' "cattle and horses will travel too far from home in such roads, and be driven away and stolen by the white people."

The Americans did not dismiss this argument about a road from which the loudest complaints of robbery usually came from the whites. The United States government was willing to agree "that no white people shall be allowed to travel on the road to Natchez, except such as shall have procured passes from our agents at Tennessee and at Natchez . . . and that gates shall be erected at some of the bridges on that road, and maintained by the United States, to prevent the horses and the cattle of the Indians from straying far from home. . . ."

Finally, and probably with sufficient show of reluctance to serve his bargaining position, Colbert gave the Chickasaws' decision. Undoubtedly most Indians were as eager for a better road as white men were, though some felt that white travel across their lands only brought evil. The Nation agreed to the cutting of the road through its land, "but does not consent to the erection of houses for the accommodation of travellers."

"We leave that subject to further consideration," said Colbert, "in order that time may enable our people to ascertain the advantages to be derived from it. In the meantime, travellers will always find provisions in the nation sufficient to carry them through."

Son of his Scotch father, Major Colbert had already carefully figured the advantages for himself. There were gifts for all the chiefs after the conference: powder, lead, gun flints, "50 gallons whiskey at 50 cents," 200 pounds of tobacco, "two dozen scalping knives." Colbert took his share, and got more. He claimed later that at the conference the commissioners had not only assured him of the monopoly of the Tennessee River ferry, but had also promised to build a house for him to entertain travelers, and "a good large ferry boat." In addition, he said, Wilkinson promised him that cabins, including kitchens, storehouses, and stables, would be built for him at his ferry landing.

Wilkinson's men went to work building the road—or at least widening and straightening the Trace, providing some fords, ferries, and bridges. As early as March of the year Wilkinson made the treaty with Colbert, Postmaster General Joseph Habersham had suggested that the use of soldiers on such a task would preserve the health and morale of the troops. Lt. Edmund Pendleton Gaines, who was later to arrest Aaron Burr, was actively engaged in working on the road. So was Col. Thomas Butler. And that aristocratic revolutionary veteran and ardent Federalist was to show Wilkinson that cutting the road was not much more troublesome a business than cutting hair. He let it be known that order or no order, he did not mean to cut his queue.

Not all historians have agreed that Wilkinson's order was a democratic gesture. Claiborne wrote that the general had issued the order for another reason. At a "rather merry" party of officers at Fort Adams near Natchez, he said, "the Gen. by some accident got his queue singed off." So, like the fox that lost its tail, Wilkinson set the queueless style for all. Butler refused to obey. Some of the colonel's friends insisted that he was persecuted for this because he had expressed belief in the reports that his commander was a Spanish agent. Undoubtedly Wilkinson was quick to condemn some of his officers—notably those who voiced suspicions of him. (Less than a decade later Winfield Scott, who would become commander of the American Army and a candidate for the Presidency, got such treatment from Wilkinson. Scott had said candidly that he thought Wilkinson was a traitor. The result was that the general hailed Scott before a court for ungentlemanly conduct and on trumped up charges of fraud. Scott was suspended from the army for a year.)

Other officers spoke their suspicions of their commander more guardedly. Still under Wilkinson, who never lacked energy, soldiers moved to the road-clearing job. All sections on which they worked led, of course, by Colbert's ferry on the Tennessee. Travelers passed the soldiers as they labored. Clearly not even the reservation of stands on the Trace for the Indians would long protect the red men from the white encroachment which had begun years before.

Colbert himself was the product of such encroachment by his Scottish trader father. More and more half-breeds of varying shades lived along the old pathway. Some were blacker than the Choctaws and Chickasaws had originally been. The African slave among them left a mark. But many, like Colbert himself, were much paler than their Indian ancestors had been. There was, for instance, Peggy Allen, the great-granddaughter of the original James Logan Colbert, who lived and had her troubles while Wilkinson was mapping and surveying the road.

The general employed "two confidential Indians," as he described them, and Samuel Mitchell "to mark a guide line" through the Chickasaw country. Mitchell had been named the first United States Agent to the tribe in 1797. Some regarded him as "one of the most conscientious" of these agents. They reported that when he was dismissed seven years later, his loss was felt by both Indians and travelers. Certainly, however, his story on the Trace was brightly colored by his unreturned love for Peggy Allen. She was the daughter of Susie Colbert and James Allen, a well-educated North Carolinian, who like some other men of the time (Sam Houston for instance) turned from civilization to life with the Indians.

One story is that Allen had gone broke in Nashville. In 1797, however, he sold a "drove of beef cattle" to Wilkinson's soldiers, who had just arrived in the territory. Still, a few years later, Allen was in trouble, apparently as a result of the passion of Mitchell for his Peggy. The agent looked at her as other white men had done as they traveled the Trace. In Mitchell's case, however, it was no mere passing delight at the sight of a beautiful girl. He proposed and was promptly turned down. He carried his suit to her grandmother, a dominating dowager Colbert. The old lady considered it an excellent match. Pre-emptorily she sent Peggy off to the agency where Mitchell presided with a string of well-loaded packhorses and ten Negro slaves as her dowry.

The lovely Peggy, whose mother had been only one-eighth part Indian, was as determined as her grandmother. She made the trip to Mitchell's house. That was as far as she would go. She stubbornly refused him, saying, according to Claiborne, that she "would never marry a drinking man white or Indian."

Apparently Allen sided with his daughter. He may have played a part when a handsome young fellow, Simon Burney, from the neighborhood of Natchez, turned up and fell in love with Peggy, too. At any rate, Claiborne reported on the basis of the recollections of mail-rider Swaney, "they were married and immediately left the Nation." Peggy's opposition to drinking men did not carry her all the way to Puritanism. One of her husband's relatives, Capt. David Burney, was called the first breeder of fast horses and gamecocks in the territory.

A pious traveler, Jacob Young, reported in his *Autobiography of a Pioneer* that when he came preaching down the Trace he found Allen under a "great terror of mind." He had quarreled with one of the Colberts, presumably his father-in-law, "who had ordered him to leave the nation, and threatened his life if he did not." Allen, Young said, was determined not to be driven away. Young prayed with him and left him in the hands of his "faithful Creator and kind preserver."

Though the stories about Allen and his beautiful wife and daughter come down to us in somewhat conflicting and confused fashion, apparently the prayers were answered. Claiborne reports that one of the granddaughters of Allen "was the most beautiful woman in Mississippi." She married a Scottish trader named McAuley, but she did not leave the Nation. When her people were pushed out of Mississippi by the relentless, land-hungry whites she went, despite her scant Indian blood, with her tribe to the West.

Perhaps more things than Mitchell's drinking prejudiced Peggy against him. General Wilkinson's wish to get permission to have white families maintained on the Trace, in order that travelers might have decent facilities, does not seem to have been emphasized in the quarters Mitchell maintained at the agency. This agent may have been as kind to travelers, particularly sick ones, as he constantly reported himself to be. He said he spent more than he could afford caring for them. His agency was described by Dr. Nutt after his visit to the Chickasaws. His report does not make it certain that stands maintained by Indians and half-breeds could have been much worse than some operated by whites.

"Although the agency house is in a fine & elevated situation," Dr. Nutt wrote, "free from stagnant & noxious poisons from marshes and standing water, & having good water is yet very sickly this is on account of the carelessness of the attendants. It arises from many skins of cattle left on the yard fence, exposed to the action of the sun &c. They emit a very disagreeable sent [sic]. Add to this the careless attention of the sick to cleanliness. They seldom get many paces from the door in time of operation of physic."

It is not difficult to understand pretty Peggy's reluctance to be mistress of that house. Still not merely romance and sanitation, but other difficulties slowed the opening of the road. Before the agreement with the Chickasaws and the

Choctaws, Wilkinson had acted. He reported to the Secretary of War that he had "issued the necessary orders to Colonel Butler, and have ordered eight companies of the 2nd regiment, to ascend the Tennessee, as soon as watercraft can be provided." They reached the area of Colbert's ferry and went to work along lines laid out by Mitchell. Colbert helped them find a better crossing of the Tennessee and so a better ferry landing for himself.

In the woods and the heat and in the wilderness cold, too, they labored on the road between the Tennessee and the Duck rivers. That section was cut despite some difficulties with the authorities of new Williamson County. The problem there was often repeated in American road-building history. Local politicians declined to approve the most direct route because it missed the county seat. Also some soldiers were detached from the work to provide protection for travelers on the Trace. The most famous bandits like Hare and Mason did not monopolize that business. Soldiers as well as others were concerned with a robber-killer named Tranium, described as "tall, knock-kneed, cropped on left ear, and yellow-haired." There were others.

Still, high hopes for safety and convenience on the road were lifted by Wilkinson's soldiers. A year after he made the treaty while his men were working on ridges and beside swamps, an eminent French observer, François A. Michaux, wrote in enthusiasm about progress on the trail. The "path that serpentined those boundless forests," he said would soon be one of the finest roads in the United States on which a man could cross the southwestern country "in a carriage." His Gallic enthusiasm was not justified.

The army was not qualified to build any real road. Mr. Jefferson had no desire to lavish public funds upon any large military establishment. Also, it is possible that he was not too much impressed with the poor path through the wilderness. Roads were far from perfect, even in the settled

East. In the year he had Wilkinson negotiate about the Trace, Jefferson wrote his Attorney General from Monticello.

"Of eight rivers between here and Washington," he said, "five have neither bridges nor boats."

Furthermore, the quality of accommodations for Trace travelers was not vastly worse than those in parts of the East. Wilson, the ornithologist who traveled the Trace, had no harsher word for its accommodations than those he used about a tavern in North Carolina. There he said the very sight of the supper offered was "sufficient to deaden the most eager appetite."

"You are surrounded," wrote this scientist, "by half a dozen, half-naked blacks, male and female, whom any man of common scent might smell a quarter of a mile off."

Yet as late as September, 1802, Wilkinson wrote that "the business of opening the road from Tennessee to Natchez is progressing but slowly." Indeed, it was moving far less rapidly than the people who continued to pour over it beside the soldiers working in the wet wilderness. Then orders were issued to Wilkinson that owing to the reduction in the army, it would be necessary to stop the work. On January 12, 1803, Colonel Butler was ordered to Fort Adams, below Natchez. This terminated his activity on the northern end of the Trace. Some trees had been chopped. Brush had been cut and some causeways built. Near its terminal cities the road was fairly good. Still, nearly 200 miles in the middle of the way was "entirely in a wilderness state."

There were good military reasons for the dispatch to Natchez of Colonel Butler, still wearing his queue. Also, the need for the road as a means of carrying American strength in terms of soldiers, or even armed frontiersmen, was suddenly emphasized. On October 12, 1802, "the right of deposit of American produce" was suspended by the Spanish government at New Orleans. That closed the port to American Mississippi trade. Once more the West was ready to explode. Once more General Wilkinson was at the center of explosion.

That suspension, supposedly at the inspiration of Napoleon, who had secured a treaty for the return of Louisiana to France, clamped the cork back into the bottle of the expanding West. In 1797, New Orleans purchased 8,600 barrels of up-river flour. By 1803, this had increased to 14,500 barrels. In 1801, $1,095,412 worth of American produce passed Natchez. Furthermore, in that area the cotton fields, calling for more and more black hands, were already spreading. The United States had sent abroad a cotton crop of 200,000 pounds in 1791. That export grew to 20 million pounds in 1801, and doubled that in 1803. Obviously this traffic emphasized the need for the efforts to improve the Trace, which led northward and homeward.

Americans interpreted the closing of the port as an evidence of Spanish pique. They were even more angry when the news came that France was taking over under Napoleon, who seemed ready to consume the whole world. Actually, as Thomas D. Clark, a perceptive historian of the frontier, has pointed out, there were American provocations. Not without reason did the Spanish call the men who came down from Mississippi, Tennessee, Ohio, Pennsylvania, and Kentucky "barbarians." At the end of their journeys they "caroused, played practical jokes, swarmed into bordelloes, gawked in the churches, cluttered up the already filthy city with their rubbish, blustered through crowds shouting lusty oaths, and in general disrupted life."

At a time of such crisis, when Westerners with their long rifles were ready at a moment's signal to pour down the Trace toward New Orleans, Colonel Butler's still insubordinate queue may have seemed certainly a trivial item. His defiance, however, and perhaps his suspicions of his superior's loyalty, were no small things in Wilkinson's eyes. Furthermore, Butler had pronounced the queue-cutting order as "an arbitrary infraction of my natural rights and a non-compliance on my part not cognizable by the articles of war." Even at a time of national crisis, Wilkinson ordered his arrest and trial.

How long this matter of military discipline continued is not clear. It lasted long enough for irascible Andrew Jackson to describe it as persecution in a blast about it to Thomas Jefferson. Jackson had not always agreed with Colonel Butler. Washington had first sent the colonel to Tennessee to move squatters from Indian lands. Jackson was after land himself, and not always with perfect titles or complete consideration for the Indians. Nevertheless he recognized the good sense and courage of Butler as that soldier performed an unpopular duty.

Butler had many other friends. They were disturbed when he became ill while Wilkinson pressed his charges. Soon the colonel was informed by his doctor that he could not live. Thereupon Colonel Butler made his will and gave directions for his burial, which he knew would be attended by the whole command.

"Bore a hole," he said, "through the bottom of my coffin, right under my head, and let my queue hang through it, that the damned rascal may see that, even when dead, I refuse to obey his orders."

Apparently the colonel's death and the escape of America from the crisis created by closing the port at New Orleans coincided. The realistic Bonaparte was no such fighter of lost causes as Colonel Butler. He had revised his first plan for an empire in America as well as Europe. Slave uprisings and yellow fever in the West Indies had reduced his enthusiasm for an American adventure.

Black and mulatto revolt and insurrection on the French islands had been attended by the most horrible cruelties inflicted by whites on blacks, and blacks on whites. Sadism had run through all its phases and colors. Fever and treachery had swallowed whole French armies. Generals in the hot and bloody tropics asked for more men. Napoleon had had enough. If America wanted such possibilities in wide Louisiana into which more and more slaves were pouring, he wanted no more of a distant empire which seemed only a fever swamp of hate, lust, murder, and fear. Also, he needed funds for his widening conquest of Europe. Suddenly, while Jefferson's agents were seeking to buy the "isle of New Orleans," the great Corsican threw the whole of Louisiana, from New Orleans to Montana and Oregon, on the negotiation table at a bargain. Napoleon accepted 15 million dollars for nearly a million square miles.

At the news, Andrew Jackson in Nashville both cheered and raved. He put the Louisiana Purchase and Butler's queue together in one letter to Thomas Jefferson, on August 7, 1803. By his sale of the vast territory Napoleon had cut himself off from American adventures exactly two years after the date of Wilkinson's hair-cutting order. Jackson wrote Jefferson two years and four months after Wilkinson's abrupt banning of queues.

"Sir, . . . The golden moment . . . when all the Western Hemisphere rejoices at the Joyfull news of the cession of Louisiana . . . we hope will not be . . . [marred] by the scene of an aged and meritorious officer . . . before a court martial for the disobedience of an order to deprive him of the gift of nature . . . worn by him both for ornament and convenience. . . .

"Sir the removal of such an officer for . . . his well known attachment to his locks . . . gray in the service of his country, opens the door for the greatest tyranny."

Jackson was in a fighting mood. In the month in which Congress ratified the Louisiana Purchase he had been ready with his pistols against John Sevier, affectionately called Nolichucky Jack. That old land speculator and Indian fighter had served three terms as the first governor of Tennessee. Then Jackson, who had little military experience, defeated him by one vote for the post of General of the Tennessee Militia. In rough words between them, Sevier flung Rachel's name into the argument. The fight which followed was a fiasco, but Jackson's temper was ready for quick flame. He was ready for arms, too. He and other Western men feared that the Purchase might be attended by a Napoleonic trick or by more Spanish intrigue. He directed his militia "to be in order at a moment's warning to march."

It did move, but not under Jackson's command. Col. George Doherty, an experienced soldier and revolutionary veteran, was put in charge of the first detachment of Tennessee Volunteers. They set out south, on December 1, 1803, to be ready in the event that Spain might not peacefully accept the transfer of Louisiana. Their movement over the still far from finished road was attended by suffering in the winter weather and lack of supplies for themselves and their horses. They arrived at Grindstone Ford "destitute of food." There the army contractor refused to supply them, saying he had no orders.

As it turned out the march was unnecessary. At Natchez, Doherty wrote to Sevier, who had been re-elected governor of Tennessee for the fourth time, that he "was met with halting Orders from General Wilkinson & to recruit ourselves & horse & return to the State from whence we were drawn."

"I had not a verry agreable march thro' the Wilderness," he wrote, "owing to the weather being so verry wet and the road being so excessively bad . . . I verry much dread our return. I am doubtful of being well supplied in the Nation."

His forebodings were well founded. The return was as onerous as the way down, and unattended by the patriotic fervor of advance. Men who had moved as rapidly as they could with their long rifles ready on the way south, dragged their guns and themselves as they moved north. They brought home no good words for the Trace upon which soldiers had been hacking at a wilderness which grew thick again behind their axes and their knives.

Only Colbert profited from the march. He put in a claim

for ferrying the soldiers which stunned the penny-pinching bureaucrats in the new, muddy capital at Washington. Payment of Colbert's boat bill was at first withheld by the government. He admitted that his charges were high in comparison with those in more settled sections of the country. He insisted, however, that the trouble was that the government had not helped him as it had promised. The house it had agreed to build for him at the landing was only half-finished, and he had to spend much money completing it. Also, the ferryboat they had built for him had been made of green wood and had rotted within a year. The river was wide, and he had to go far upstream in order not to be swept past the landing on the opposite side. The hire of boat crews was costly.

The government grumbled for two years before it paid the bill. Even then it paid it only after sending General Robertson, Tennessee's founder, and Return J. Meigs, an Indian agent, to investigate. They recommended that $100 be deducted from the claim in addition to the $300 the Secretary of War had already cut from it. Still, they recommended that the United States pay the chief $500 on a house and $50 for a new ferryboat. The government settled. This was not the last time it would pay Colbert well. Government fees suited him best, but Colbert took what he could get from a traveler, trader, boatman—maybe even bandit.

The same year the Volunteers passed, Lorenzo Dow, the eccentric evangelist, came to the river, on his way proclaiming his threats of hell and hopes of paradise. Colbert put the penniless, long-haired preacher across, taking as toll Dow's last possessions, a penknife and a few pennies, though the regular rate was 50 cents for a man and $1 for horse and rider. Colbert felt very charitable about that. Also, he had respect for pennies and penknives as well as for dollars. All went to put windows in Colbert's "country palace" on the river shore. The family had graduated from piracy to plutocracy.

Down the Trace General Wilkinson did very well, too. He was present at the peaceful transfer of Louisiana to the United States at the Cabildo in New Orleans on December 20, 1803. The departing French prefect, Pierre Clément Laussat, reported to Paris about the pompous general. He was, said the Frenchman, "already known here in a bad way, is a flighty and rattleheaded fellow, often drunk, who has committed a hundred impertinent follies."

Pique may have prompted such a description. Undoubtedly Wilkinson glittered in resplendent uniform as he moved through the ceremonies, looking lordly even without a queue. All things looked good for the general. His friend Burr was momentarily in favor. Jefferson hoped the retiring Vice-President, as presiding officer over a senatorial court of impeachment, might play a sympathetic role in the President's efforts to get rid of a federal judge.

One observer wrote that at the time Jefferson paid Burr more attention and invited him to his house more often than ever before. More important to Wilkinson in this process of courting Burr, Jefferson made the general the governor of Upper Louisiana with headquarters at St. Louis. Also in the bargain Burr's brother-in-law, Dr. Joseph Browne, was made secretary of that territory, and Burr's stepson, John Prevost, a judge in New Orleans.

As it turned out, Burr did not serve Jefferson's wish to remove the judge from the bench. He presided with "meticulous dignity" and "impressive impartiality." The judge was acquitted. Still, in the West, as he retired from the national scene, insolvent and debt-ridden, hated by Federalists and rejected by Democrats, Burr seemed to have stout friends upon whose gratitude he could always depend.

XI: THE DEVIL'S ADVERSARIES

CHIEF Colbert at his Tennessee ferry may have been acting against his better judgment when he took the penknife and other last possessions of Lorenzo Dow to put that evangelist across the river. Preachers were traveling the Trace as well as soldiers, bandits, and settlers. Colbert apparently had no great preference for the men of the Book over those of the gun, the bottle, the plow, and the knife.

One of those riding for the Lord, the Reverend Jacob Young, reported that ferryman Colbert was not too enthusiastic when Young told him that he was headed as a good Methodist down the path to preach at Natchez.

"Ah," said the shrewd ferry owner, "Natchez people great for preach, but they be poor, lazy, thieving bad people."

Colbert was even less pleased with the information that Young was from Kentucky.

"Kentuckian bad people, and white man worse than Indian everywhere, though they have much more preach and learn much. Indians never know how to steal till white man learn them. We don't want any preaching in this country. We are free and we intend to keep so."

Even then freedom was a word variously interpreted by those who wished to be free to press into the wilderness and those who wished to keep the wild lands the free range of their fathers. Some white men as well as Indians, however, shared Colbert's views about preachers and preach. Yet even more determined on the road than those out to steal money-filled saddlebags were other men, many deeply devout, some fanatic, who came to save men's souls. Even before the Spanish arrived to insist (not always too firmly) that only Catholicism would be permitted, the Reverend Samuel Swayze, Congregationalist, had come in from New Jersey to take up lands near Natchez and to plant and preach at the same time. Sometimes under the Spanish regime Protestants preached secretly in naves made of moss-hung trees in the woods. A Baptist preacher had come to the Mississippi country in 1781. There were other excellent ministers, too numerous to mention, of various denominations. They included Adam Cloud, Joseph Bullen, Richard Curtis. They came to teach and help as well as preach. The push of the Methodists began in 1799.

In January of that year, Bishop Francis Asbury, who had himself ridden some of the longest and roughest American roads, appointed young Tobias Gibson, of South Carolina, to preach in the Old Southwest. Gibson came westward by horseback over the mountains and the trails to the Cumberland settlements. Near present Nashville he sold his horse and bought a canoe. Floating down the Cumberland, the Tennessee, the Ohio, and the Mississippi, he reached Natchez. From there he rode up the Trace. Dow, as the most colorful of the religious riders, wrote in the journal of a journey on the Trace that he came to "Biopeer, and Big Black, and preached the funeral sermon of a niece of the Rev. Tobias Gibson; and the Lord was with us."

"I left my horse," Dow wrote, "with brother Gibson, and took a Spanish race horse, which he was to be responsible for, and I was to remit him the money by post . . . in November."

Dow broke down horses in his rides on the Trace and other trails. Coming to the Trace first, in 1804, when he was twenty-seven years old, he was close behind the politicians and explorers who, after the Louisiana Purchase, were looking more intently across the Mississippi River. Louisiana, Dow said, had long been a "refuge for scape-gallows." He himself visited it to get himself a horse on a small-scale Philip Nolan pattern. He had no swift, tame horses with which to catch wild ones. He caught one Indian pony "by climbing a tree and dropping a noose over the head." In addition to the much-needed animal, he found in Louisiana other things for which to praise Providence. That power, he said, had saved the land from the Inquisition.

Other men may have saved more souls along the Natchez Trace than Dow did, but none left a more lively journal of the riding of the preachers upon it. He called himself the "Cosmopolite," because of his wide and speedy travels. Some other people with less charity labeled him "Crazy Dow." A Connecticut Yankee, Dow was lean and melancholy. He never cut his hair or shaved his beard. Generally, unless he had to swap it along with his few other possessions for survival or a ferry fee, he wore a long black cloak. There was a fanatic light in his eyes, but an unexpected shrewdness in his head.

Out to pour his message into willing or unwilling ears, he attracted attention by trick and trumpeting. He seemed especially to enjoy riots which he roused in the Lord's name among the settlers. Some of them wanted no churches or preaching to stop their horse racing, cockfighting, dancing, fiddling, and Sunday fun. Sometimes Dow tricked them into conversion. Always he went about his mission in the wilderness with a speed which deserved the respect even of the post riders. He made engagements far ahead, and despite high water or hell—which was very real to him—managed to keep them.

"Sinners," he cried in his asthmatic voice, "you are making a beeline from time to eternity."

Dow did not think the Lord required decorum in devotions. He preached in log churches, in open fields, in any hall he could get, even in grogshops in Nashville or Natchez. Often he had trouble getting places for his meetings. When he held them, some of the unregenerate asked if God was deaf that Dow and his congregation had to make so much noise. His critics made more, he replied, when they were drinking toasts.

"We had a cry and a shout, and it was a weeping, tender time," he wrote of one of his meetings. Some other times of "cry and shout" almost resulted in riots. Once, preaching on "Judgment Day," he put a little Negro boy in the top of a pine tree. There, at the cue from Dow, he was to blow loudly on a horn. When Dow had worked his listeners to the proper fervor and spoke of Gabriel trumpeting the world's end, the little black boy dutifully let loose a resounding blast. Panic ensued. Then when the hoax was discovered, the indignant started to mob the preacher. Dow was equal to the occasion.

"And now, Brethren," he shouted over the tumult, "if a little Negro boy blowing on a tin horn can make you feel so, how will you feel when the last day really comes?"

Dow did not underestimate his powers. And the publishers of his *History of Cosmopolite,* which went into many editions, added some stories, "believed to be genuine," which emphasized the lively legends left behind his preaching. One tall tale, which seems more Rabelaisian than Methodist in its flavor, had to do with the notion spread that the swift-moving Cosmopolite could summon the Devil for his vituperation.

Once, this story said, he sought lodging for the night at a cabin. The woman of the place, saying her husband was away, was reluctant to receive him. However, when she found out he was Preacher Dow she gave him a place to sleep in a back room. He had not been there long when another visitor came. Dow in the next room heard the man and woman joke and frolic. Suddenly there was a banging on the cabin door. The woman's husband had come staggering home from a tavern. As quickly as she could the woman of the cabin hid her friend in a bag of cotton. Her husband was furious at her delay in unlatching the door.

"Hush, my dear, hush," the woman whispered. "Lorenzo Dow is in the house."

"O blood and tobacco!" muttered the husband. Then he asked, "The man who raises the Devil?"

"Sure it is, and why don't you be still?"

Loudly the befuddled spouse insisted on seeing the spectacle. So Dow was brought out. Requiring that, if he raised Satan, the man of the cabin only give him "a few thumps as he passed, but not so hard as to break his bones," Dow applied his candle to the cotton bag.

"Come forth, old boy," he commanded.

Out from the bag, covered with flames, came the hidden visitor. He escaped, this story reported, with only one good rap of a cudgel. The woman's reputation was saved and Dow's reputation as a Yankee preacher of remarkable religious powers was enhanced.

More certainly realistic were Dow's reports of some of the religious activities he saw. Anxious as he always was to stir his listeners, he seemed still, as he wrote of them, a little appalled by the "jerks" which was to become a common phenomenon of the Great Revival in the West for which he was helping to pave the way. Passing by a meetinghouse he was amazed to see that the saplings about it had been left breast high "where the people had laid hold of them and jerked so powerfully, that they had kicked up the earth as a horse stomping flies." In the enthusiasm of a meeting near Natchez he observed at firsthand how "people are taken jerking irresistibly; and if they strive to resist it, it worries them much . . . but when they yield to it they feel happy, although it is a great cross. . . . Their eyes when dancing seem to be fixed upward, as if upon an invisible object, and they are lost to all below. . . ."

Some people came to such meetings to laugh and remained to jerk. Others found themselves dancing and shouting beyond self-control. Great crowds began to gather in Kentucky, Tennessee, and Mississippi to listen to relays of preachers warning of hell-fire and damnation, salvation and amazing grace. Not all the preachers whom he met regarded Dow with favor. Some questioned both his methods and his theology. He required favor from none. Still, on the Trace sometimes he needed the Lord's protection and used his own scraggly, matted head as well.

On that path he was frightened by panthers screaming at night like women crying in distress. He missed the trail in a great swamp. He was almost drowned in Pearl River—or "half-way river." And once he thought it "was a gone case" when Indians surrounded him. They had determined to take a life for a life, since a Kentuckian had recently killed an Indian.

"I felt the power of faith to put my confidence in God," Dow wrote; "at the same time I observed the Indians had ramrods in the muzzles of their guns . . . so it would take some time to pull out the ramrods . . . ready to shoot."

Then his horse shied, breaking the circle of Indians about him.

"I gave my horse the switch and leaned down in the saddle," he wrote, "so that if they shot I would give them as narrow a chance as I could to hit me as I supposed they would wish to spare and get the horse. I did not look behind me until I had got out of sight and hearing of the Indians. I was not long in going a dozen or fifteen miles."

Undoubtedly such circuit riders, as they were called when at last they had circuits and not merely a wilderness to ride, were often less dramatic men than Dow. Few of them were or looked so eccentric. Without them, both the consecrated and the fanatic, the taming of the West would have been a much slower process. Sometimes, however, they preached a grim gospel in the exuberant West. Often in their sternness harmless fun seemed almost transformed into deadly sin.

Before their preaching the fiddle music to which Rachel Jackson had danced fell into silence in the Cumberland and other settlements. The Great Revival, which swept with particular force across Tennessee and Kentucky, brought frowns on the fiddlers. Some dancing continued undoubtedly—and not only that kind of frenzied dancing which attended the jerks at the great camp meetings. "But,"

wrote Putnam, "instrumental music was condemned as
unsuitable." And many fiddlers of the old Mero District laid
their instruments "on the shelves or among old trumpery,
and a few broke them in pieces."

In Tennessee, God's angry men—preachers,
missionaries, evangelists—lifted their resounding voices
over vast congregations come from the whole surrounding
countryside in wagons, on horseback, afoot. Whole settlements came to campgrounds where bush arbors had been
built and straw pens prepared in advance for the groveling
of the repentant. The fiery sermons stirred even the gayest
boys and girls in the bushes. Lamentations and the cries of
exaltation by the saved made music with the soaring gospel
hymns.

Apparently the contagion, despite some testimony to the
contrary from Dow, seems to have been less violent down
the Trace in Mississippi. There "life though outwardly gay
and prosperous, was, in reality, cheap and easy to lose." So
despite the efforts of preachers, wrote Howard Mitcham,
some "believed in the virtues of whiskey as an immunizing
agent, that only the good die young, and since the dark
angel is an omnipresent brother, the best way to keep him at
a distance is to spit in his face."

And sometimes that was expressed by putting the boot to
the bottoms of the preachers' pants. Sometimes that was
justified in any case. There were fake evangelists who moved
with great unction in hope of profit from their eloquent
piety. Indeed, on some occasions the pretended character
of the missionary was worn as a mask by glib-tongued
marauders and other rogues.

Certainly, despite the best efforts of the best and bravest
preachers, Natchez-under-the-Hill remained loudly un-
repentant. There travelers were greeted not only by
brawny boatmen and gleaming black laborers, but by gangs
of idle and begging Indians as well. Thickening settlement
was often accompanied by degeneration as well as regenera-
tion. Certainly not all the Indians flourished under the ways

of the white men. Preacher Young told of those he saw when he, like Dow, moved over the Trace.

"They would run out partly naked," he said, "and hold up their little bowls, and cry out, 'bit.' "

Others whimpered: "We Chickasaw, we friend white men, give me two bits."

Old Colbert at the ferry was not without grounds for complaint about his people, even among those at the southern end of the Trace who were, he said, "great for preach." So at Natchez, even while religious fervor spread, travelers reported many Indians seeking a little money for a small portion of the cargoes of whiskey and provisions. Sometimes they offered in return screeching serenades played on a variety of instruments made from the joints of cane and of buckskin stretched over kettles. Men who had been warriors, squaws, girls, and children in tribal simplicity now danced to what one modern historian has described as an "Indian jazz band."

Such conditions obviously were not the fault of Crazy Dow or any of the other good preachers. Dow went on fighting the Devil. He gave some of his possessions to help build a church at Washington near Natchez. Sometimes he was accompanied by his wife Peggy, "as plain as a pipe stem" but a woman who found peace beside the Trace. A Massachusetts girl who long suffered from tuberculosis, she had married him upon his condition that she would never hinder him from his travels. Yet she wrote in her *The Journey of Life or Vicissitudes* of a period of brief happiness when they settled for a while near Port Gibson, founded by a relative of the Reverend Tobias Gibson.

Not all Heaven's blessings were vouchsafed them there. Lorenzo got into financial troubles over the operation of a mill and farm. He dreamed of a metropolis called "Loren, or the City of Peace." Also he planned a "Beulah Ethiopia," which was to be an asylum for "benighted Africans." All failed. Also, while living there, he was depressed by the disgraceful conduct of a sister-in-law. A backslider and worse, this lady left her husband and ran off with another, more lusty, man. Yet, perhaps strangely, it was in this period that poor Peggy found peace.

"There was a tract of land," she wrote, "lying in the midst of a thick cane break, on which was a beautiful spring of water, breaking out at the foot of a large hill . . . the cane was almost impenetrable . . . and likewise it was inhabited by wild beasts of prey, of various kinds, and serpents of the most poisonous nature. Notwithstanding these gloomy circumstances, Lorenzo got a man to go with him and look at it, to see if it would do for an asylum for us to fly to, provided we could get a little cabin erected near the spring."

The cabin was built. A way was cut through the cane to "the public road." They moved, Peggy said, "to our little place of residence, in the wilderness, or rather it appeared like the habitation of some exiles: but it was a sweet place to me, I felt at home, and many times the Lord was precious to my soul. . . ."

And she added: "The people were much surprised when they came to our little residence, how we came to fix on such a lonely place as this to retreat to. This is proof, that experience teaches more than otherwise we could learn; we had felt the want of a home in the time of trouble and sickness. This was a pleasant retreat to us: the wilderness appeared almost like a paradise to me."

While they were there Lorenzo was off preaching "as much as his strength would permit." After they left this spot, which was not far from the place where the young Jacksons had spent "agreeable hours," Peggy, who had briefly found paradise, died before him. Wandering, he became more cadaverous and unkempt than ever. He began to write more and preach less. More troubles plagued him. The Devil seemed raised, indeed, and in no mood to run away. Lorenzo traveled far and wide, in America and abroad. He grew ever more controversial. Other preachers shunned him. He quarreled and brought lawsuits. He damned

Whigs, anti-Masons, and Catholics. At the last he turned his fire even upon the Methodists, whom he claimed were becoming more and more tainted with popery.

Dow never doubted that he was a man headed for Heaven, even if unlike Peggy he never found the briefest paradise on earth. Still, by his lights, at the last he had reason to believe that on the Trace he had stopped short in their tracks some whom he was sure were making a beeline not only to eternity, but to a flame-billowing hell. There was always room on the Trace for men engaged in that enterprise.

XII: A MAN WITHOUT A COUNTRY

THE GREATEST preachers in the old west did not minimize
the great Dark Adversary in the gospel they preached. If on
occasion Dow did, few made a comic imp of him. They
wrestled with him respectfully in their struggle to save
sinners. In their long sermons they dressed the Devil, using
Biblical metaphors, in charming, persuasive, elegant,
dangerous fashion. The frenzy of their meetings sometimes
boiled over into other aspects of the people's lives. As the
preachers created the popular image of the Devil in
traumatic theology, so it was available in politics. And in
that process the diabolical picture of the most eminent
Trace traveler of the time stirred in some a frenzy almost
equal to the jerks. No one helped in that business more than
General Wilkinson.

This Devil, of course, was Wilkinson's old friend Aaron
Burr. Certainly Burr came West in much the guise of a fallen
angel. This often-damned gentleman, then recently retired
Vice-President of the United States, was sometimes called
by his enemies the "veneered profligate." There is much
evidence to support that epithet so far as ladies were
concerned. There is even more evidence to support the
melodramatic statement of Albert J. Beveridge in his
biography of Chief Justice Marshall, who tried Burr for
treason, that from the vice-presidency the debonair New
Yorker "marched steadily to his doom."

Certainly there seemed no sense of doom in Burr's
handsome head at the time. In the East he had the animosity

of Thomas Jefferson. He was under indictment in New York and New Jersey because, in their famous duel, correct in every particular of the code duello, he had killed Alexander Hamilton, saint of the Federalists, though, like Burr, he was sometimes a sinner with the ladies. Still, Burr looked by no means lost to fortune or fame. He did not mean to be.

If some seemed to have forgotten his military and civilian services, Burr had not. He came of the best American ancestry. His maternal grandfather was the great Puritan, Jonathan Edwards. His own father was president of Princeton. Burr as young patriot had been a hero at Quebec. He became an antagonist in politics worthy of Hamilton even before they met on the Jersey Palisades. His farewell speech as he departed from the vice-presidency had deeply moved even men ready to see him march to doom. Yet his first able biographer, James Parton (in a book published about the same time Edward Everett Hale used Philip Nolan's name for a figure in fiction), called Burr a man "without a country."

Many who knew him expected him to seek one. And in the West the handsome New Yorker was hailed as a brave and eminent man who in the past had been sympathetic with the problems of men beyond the mountains. Quick-tempered and pistol-ready men like Andrew Jackson were not appalled because he had killed an enemy in a fair fight. Jackson's hospitality to him in Nashville was marked by a "magnificent parade." Dark and sinewy at fifty, Aaron Burr looked, as he moved down the rivers on the journey from which he would return over the Trace, like a personage floating to a greater destiny. General Wilkinson had attended to that. Burr wrote about it to his brilliant and beloved daughter, Theodosia.

"The General and his officers," he told her, "fitted me out with an elegant barge—sails, colors, ten oars—with a sergeant and ten able hands."

The doors of great houses opened everywhere to him as he floated down the rivers. And no one of them could have better matched the romantic mood he created in those he visited than the island retreat of Harman Blennerhassett on the Ohio River near Parkersburg, then in Virginia. That expatriate Irishman, who was so nearsighted that he could hardly see across a room, had built a sort of private paradise for himself and his young wife there. The portrait of Margaret Blennerhassett which has been preserved is that of a beautiful young woman. Some, however, have questioned both the portrait's authenticity and the lady's looks. Apparently she was never listed among Burr's many loves.

Blennerhassett himself was a fumbling visionary. In the West he was an almost dainty idealist who longed for glory but whined of discomfort when he confronted it. However, he was an aristocratic, well-educated man with some fortune, more than was good for him perhaps. He had graduated from the University of Dublin with two degrees. In Paris after the French Revolution he became an ardent republican. Also he was much influenced by the writings of Rousseau. He had a talent for music. He brought a library and scientific instruments to his island, where he sank a good deal of his money in a house of "original ugliness." One who knew him said he had "all sorts of sense except commonsense." When Burr first met him, and afterwards, he must have seemed one of the best educated and most innocent of the pioneers.

Burr charmed other and all kinds of men and women as he moved southward. Even a judge, presumably of a judicial temperament, seemed almost ecstatic in describing him. The eminent visitor, he said, was "a man of erect and dignified deportment—his presence is commanding—his aspect mild, firm, luminous and impressive. . . . The eyebrows are thin, nearly horizontal, and too far from the eye; his nose is . . . rather inclined to the right side; gently elevated which betrays a degree of haughtiness. . . . His eyes are . . . of a dark hazel, and, from the shade of projecting eye bones and brows, appear black; they glow . . . and scintillate with the most tremulous and tearful sensibility—they roll with the celerity and phrensy of poetic fervour, and beam with the most vivid and piercing rays of genius. His mouth is large; his voice is clear, manly and melodious; his lips are thin, extremely flexible, and when silent, gently closed. . . . His chin is rather retreating and voluptuous."

As such a figure he came down the wide Mississippi to Natchez. The river no longer bounded the American West. From President Jefferson to the ordinary man, the imaginations of Americans had been fired by acquisition of the new, unmeasured, and unknown lands. Soon Jefferson would be sending his young secretary, Meriwether Lewis, along with William Clark to explore the vast area he had bought from France. Burr had known Lewis in Washington. Romanticists have long labored to create a love affair between Lewis and Theodosia Burr. Actually, Theodosia at seventeen had married a rich South Carolina planter, Joseph Alston, a month before Lewis came to Washington as Jefferson's secretary.

Of course, others besides politicians and explorers in Washington and the West were concerned with the Purchase. It not only brought much of the West to the United States. Also men saw beyond the western river shore, off where Texas would be, more open Spanish country. And some looked toward Mexico as to a land of legendary riches. Among those whose eyes turned westward were ordinary men—and Aaron Burr. In a war with Spain a man marching toward doom, or at least involved in great difficulties, might recapture glory. Some later spoke of dreams of an empire presided over by His Majesty Aaron I. There is no certain evidence that Burr moved in any such imperial plans.

Natchez pleased the former Vice-President very much. That neighborhood was to be a source of the first ugly rumors about his purposes. It was there, finally, that he began to be a fugitive and an exile. But first he enjoyed himself. He stopped on its clamorous shore on his way down the river to New Orleans. He came again when he headed homeward across the Trace. He found admiration, old friends, and perhaps one of the most charming women in a life filled with many lovely ones. Also there he met, unaware, the beginning of betrayal.

He wrote Theodosia how charmed he was with the place. Natchez was then, he said, "a town of three or four hundred houses; the inhabitants traders and mechanics, but surrounded by planters, among whom I have been entertained with great hospitality and taste. These planters are, many of them, men of education and refinement; live as well as yours, and have generally better houses."

Such a comparison with the rich South Carolina low country was a real compliment in 1805. The company of old friends on the plantations behind the Mississippi bluffs may have made the ebullient Burr expansive. Chief among them were Col. Benijah Osmun, a wealthy bachelor planter, and Maj. Isaac Guion, who had come to Natchez with the troops which took possession of it from Spain. Another friend was Lyman Harding, first district attorney of the territory under the administration of John Adams and his governor Winthrop Sargent. His first name suggests that he was kin to the Phineas Lyman of the early, troubled family in the Natchez country. Certainly, Harding later brought in the architect, Levi Weeks. Weeks claimed that the thick-columned, tall-porticoed Auburn he built for Harding was "the first house in the Mississippi Territory on which was ever attempted any of the orders of Architecture."

On at least one of his visits to Natchez Burr stayed with Colonel Osmun at his plantation on Half-Way Hill. Near the Osmun plantation, Windy Hill Manor, Burr, who may have been looking for an empire, found a lady. She was Madeline Price, scarcely twenty. She lived with her mother "in a little vine covered cottage" near Osmun's house. Her father had converted all his fortune into money with the intention of settling in Mississippi. Then the bandit Hare took his life and his money on the Trace. All that was left to

Madeline and her mother was a small farm and two or three slaves.

Historian Claiborne's prejudices in favor of this young lady are pleasant to read. As feminine facts they must have been appealing to Burr. Claiborne gave young Miss Price his favorite accolade of "a miracle of beauty." Indeed, he said, "In form and feature, in grace and modesty, she was all that the old masters have pictured the divine Madonna or that artist ever dreamed of maidenly loveliness." Burr, he said, had been introduced to her by Abbe Viel, a Jesuit priest who, some thought, Burr hoped would help him with religious orders "in his projected invasion of Mexico." Madeline and her mother were Catholics.

Burr did not tarry too long in Natchez on this trip south. He seemed a man in a hurry on his return journey. He moved swiftly in such July weather as slowed and plagued his poor friend Harman Blennerhassett when that whimpering visionary rode the pathway later. The New York adventurer crossed the rivers, undoubtedly paying Colbert in full and with a gesture (though on borrowed money). He reached Nashville on August 6. From there he reported to Theodosia from Jackson's hospitable house. It was still not the elegant Hermitage which Jackson did not have money enough to begin until a decade later. Burr did not compare it with mansions in the South Carolina low country. Still he was comfortable and gay in the log blockhouse quarters Jackson provided.

"You now see me safe through the wilderness, though I doubt (hussey)," he wrote his beloved daughter playfully, "whether you knew that I had a wilderness to pass in order to get here. Yes, about four hundred and fifty miles of wilderness. . . . The General has no children, but two lovely nieces made a visit of some days, contributed greatly to my amusement, and have cured me of all the evils of my wilderness jaunt."

Only Burr could speak of that journey, in 1805, as a

"jaunt." Hardly anything had been done to improve the path since the first military work upon it in 1802 and 1803. So it remained largely as it had been in the long past, except that the route constituted early cession of land rights in their nations by the Chickasaws and Choctaws. The description of the Trace Burr traveled depends upon the reports of other men, including those of the self-duped Blennerhassett, whose trip on the Trace resulted from his almost idiotic association with Burr.

Apparently no adventures attended Burr's "jaunt." Yet the wilderness was steaming and stinging with insects when he rode. Obviously at Jackson's he was in high spirits at the journey's end. He described himself as "lounging" at the general's house and clearly was still in the good graces of that gentleman, whom Burr regarded as "one of those prompt, frank, ardent souls whom I love to meet." On August 14, he was off through Kentucky toward St. Louis. He could not have been aware of a letter which moved northward after him, perhaps over the Trace, from Daniel Clark to General Wilkinson.

Clark, who had a finger in every financial and political pie in the southwest, had entertained Burr in New Orleans and provided him with horses and money for his journey northward. Now he wrote Wilkinson, who had introduced Burr to him, an ominous letter written in gay spirit. It was about "idle tales" and "absurd and wild reports" emanating from Natchez. They came from Wilkinson's old friend and associate in the sharing of Spanish bounty, Stephen Minor—no longer called Estevan in American Natchez.

Clark called Minor a "blockhead," an odd word for that man of successful passage from Spanish service to American wealth. The former Spanish official was, Clark thought, trying to make himself important. Still he was, as Wilkinson must have already known, "in the pay of Spain." Burr, in the things he was reported to have said, must, Clark believed, have been amusing himself at Minor's expense. Still the "blockhead" had "retailed the news to his employers."

"The tale is a horrid one, if well told," the letter to Wilkinson went on. "Kentucky, Tennessee, the State of Ohio, and part of Georgia and Carolina, are to be bribed with the plunder of the Spanish countries west of us, to separate from the Union."

It was all very funny as the New Orleans financier saw it in 1805: "Recollect that you, if you intend to become kings and emperors, must have a little more consideration for vassals. . . . Think of this and practice those formalities that are necessary, that I may have from my Illinois lands wherewith to buy a decent court-dress, when presented at your levee. I hope you will not have Kentucky men for your masters of ceremonies."

Wilkinson's reply showed no amusement. Almost curtly he called the rumors "the tale of a tub of Burr." Later, when he reported Burr's arrival in St. Louis, perhaps still ahead of the letter, the general said he made little of Burr's projects, "the nature of which he did not disclose." Burr, he declared, spoke of the imbecility of Jefferson's government: "It would moulder to pieces, die a natural death."

"No person was ever more mistaken!" Wilkinson quoted himself as saying. "The Western people . . . are bigoted to Jefferson and democracy."

If a Burr who would be king was a great knave, Wilkinson as a liar was an undisputed champion in our whole history. He was an energetic liar, however, and, until Spanish archives were opened long after his death, a successful one. Burr went East to engage in unquestionably devious dealings with both British and Spanish diplomats. He asked aid for strange projects. Also he needed money personally. If he had planned treason in the southwest, it was strange that he also asked Jefferson to give him a diplomatic job. Those hopes were dashed when Jefferson told him coldly that the country had lost confidence in him.

Burr started westward again just a year after he had come to Nashville over the Trace. Then a threat of war with Spain over the Louisiana-Texas border along the Sabine River seemed to stir the possibility of high adventuring for him. Actually, whatever his mysterious projects had been, they were disintegrating. On the surface at least his only enterprise seemed a land-settlement scheme in Louisiana, with the financial help of Harman Blennerhassett. That visionary with more enthusiasm than sense had helped increase the rumors that Burr was now fully embarked on a treasonable enterprise. The indiscreet or idiotic Irishman seemed responsible for articles in a local paper frankly discussing the possibility of a separation of the Western states from the Union.

Despite rejections and rumors, Burr was undaunted. When his little flotilla of settlers or "conspirators" reached the Natchez country on January 10, 1807, he had already been arrested twice on charges that he was seeking Western secession, and both times was triumphantly released. His popularity mounted with what seemed to be persecution of him. As frankly ready for glory in war as for prosaic settlement in peace, he was "sorry for it" when he learned that Wilkinson had patched up the quarrel with the Spaniards along the Sabine River.

He did not know, however, that the peace was only an item in Wilkinson's plans to save his own skin by saving the country from Burr. The former Vice-President became fully aware of the general's treachery only when he arrived at Bayou Pierre with a few boats and some young settlers. The general had not only arranged the boundary trouble with Spain; also, with his usual impartiality in such matters, he had sent messengers to both the American President and the Mexican viceroy. He warned Jefferson that a plot was on foot to disrupt the Union and invade Mexico. He dispatched a rider with a letter to the viceroy informing him of the danger to the Spanish dominions and, characteristically, asked for money to help in averting it.

This time the Spanish declined to pay. Jefferson, however, who had already sent an observer on Burr's trail, issued a proclamation. In it, without naming Burr, he called upon the country to beware of treason by a group illegally plotting an expedition against Spain. Its effect was electric. Suspicions soared. Virginian militiamen who did not like the strange Blennerhassett anyhow descended on his island retreat to damage and loot it. Even Andrew Jackson, who as businessman had undertaken to build and provision five river boats for Burr, momentarily roared his fears. And Wilkinson, whom Burr trusted and Jackson hated, moved his troops to New Orleans, spreading panic with the support of the President's proclamation. There the general cried that banks would be robbed and insurrection be rampant. Still, a good many people declined to be alarmed. Some were furious when Wilkinson went about saving the nation without regard for civil courts and civilian liberties At Natchez some patriots and politicians quickly arrested Burr again—and for good measure Blennerhassett and some others of his companions.

Burr was arraigned in the town of Washington on the Trace near Natchez. Its existence then as the territorial capital was due to the angry divisions of Jeffersonians and anti-Jeffersonians which attended so much of the story of the Burr conspiracy. Historian Claiborne described the town as a "gay and fashionable place" around which every hill was "occupied by some gentleman's chateau." A military cantonment nearby added much to the "punctillio and ceremony, parades and public entertainments" of the place.

"It was famous," he said, "for its wine parties and dinners, usually enlivened by one or more duels directly afterwards."

There is a legend, however, that it did not have a hall big enough to accommodate the crowd which gathered at the trial of Burr. So, it is said, the hearing was held under the "Burr Oaks" on the campus of the then recently established Jefferson College. If so, it must have been a shivering crowd, since Judge Thomas Rodney, who presided, recorded that the temperature was only ten degrees above zero. He was

approximately as cold to Burr. In the face of "the mighty
alarm" the approach of Burr's "armada" had aroused, the
evidence presented against him was almost ludicrous. No
case against him was found by the jury. Once again Burr's
popularity soared. A banquet and ball were given in his
honor.

Judge Rodney, appointed by President Jefferson,
refused, however, to release the supposed conspirator from
the $5,000 bond furnished by Colonel Osmun and by
Lyman Harding. Instead, Rodney required Burr to appear
daily in court. More "rumors" filled the district, these too
well authenticated to be dismissed. They were that
Wilkinson was sending soldiers "dressed in citizens
clothing" and "armed with dirks and pistols" to kidnap Burr
and carry him to New Orleans.

On advice of fearful friends, therefore, Burr did not
appear in court on February 5. On February 6, Governor
Robert Williams proclaimed him a fugitive from justice and
offered a $2,000 reward for his capture. Historian
Claiborne, who never let objectivity dull his pages, declared
that Williams, another Jefferson appointee, was too "repul-
sive and peremptory to please the country and refined
people among whom he resided." Certainly Burr's refined
friends did not trust the Jeffersonian governor. They urged
Burr's flight.

Perhaps he delayed too long. He visited his boats and
took leave of his men. He told them to go in the barges to the
Louisiana lands he and Blennerhassett had acquired and
settle there, or else sell the boats and divide the money. Back
at Windy Hill Manor, Colonel Osmun had one of his best
horses waiting. He also provided a guide who would lead
Burr, not northward over the Trace this time, but southward
toward the coast. Perhaps they might have made it if Burr
had not insisted upon stopping at the cottage of the lovely
Madeline Price.

"Those that saw her loved her," Claiborne wrote, "yet she was never conscious of the sentiments until she listened to Aaron Burr."

Perhaps it was not strange that Madeline had been stirred during the days when he daily met her on the "rural path . . . trellised with vines and shaded by evergreens" between Colonel Osmun's house and Madeline's mother's cottage. Burr was still the romantic Burr even though he was said to be disguised on the night of his flight "in a shabby suit of homespun with an old white hat slapped over his face."

Now, urgent as was his need of haste, Claiborne says that Burr halted till daylight at the cottage "imploring the beautiful Madeline to be the companion of his flight. He promised marriage, fortune, high position, and even hinted at imperial honors, not realizing, even then, a fugitive and branded traitor, the crushing downfall that impended over him."

So sings Claiborne. And in his song of Madeline he put Southern romance, too: "The maiden had given him her heart; she had listened to his witchery night after night, and loved him with all the fervor of a Southern nature. She would have followed him to the end of the earth, and to the scaffold, and her aged mother would freely have given her to this captivating man—for they looked on him as a demi-god—but as with most of our Southern women, the principles of religion, virtue and propriety were stronger than prepossession and passion, and the entreaties of the accomplished libertine were firmly rejected."

No one has seriously questioned Burr's gifts or guilts with the ladies. Yet this cherished tradition of his love for Madeline may deserve some such scrutiny as so many historians have given to the Burr conspiracy. In love, Burr was undoubtedly a fast worker. Certainly Madeline may have been as susceptible as she was young. Still, Burr had many problems besides love on his mind between January

10, when he landed in the Natchez District, and mid-February when, with the guide Osmun had provided, he rode away.

He never reached the coast. He had crossed what is now the Alabama line, however. Then his late riding on a moonlit night aroused the suspicions of a young lawyer, Nicholas Perkins, in the village of Wakefield, Washington County. Perhaps the hue and cry for Burr had preceded him. The story one of the two night riders told Perkins about coming down from the country of the Chickasaws seemed strange. It also seemed odd that they were unwilling to put up at the tavern. They preferred to seek the house of a Major Hinson, at night, "at a distance of 7 or 8 miles on a bad road, over broken and dangerous bridges."

Perkins took his suspicions to Capt. Edmund P. Gaines, who had helped survey the Natchez Trace. Gaines, then on duty at nearby Fort Stoddard, arrested the disguised Burr. The suspicious and zealous Perkins carried him under guard to Richmond. There the first thing Burr did was to get out of the shabby clothes he had worn when arrested. Perkins went on to Washington to receive the thanks of President Jefferson, and $3,331. He may have invested the money in the fine brick house he built later near the Trace in Tennessee.

Chief Justice John Marshall, the great judicial antagonist of Jefferson, presided over the trial in the Virginia capital in the summer of 1807. At first, after much discussion between court and counsel, Burr was held for a misdemeanor in organizing an expedition against Spanish territory. Then, when Wilkinson arrived late and gave his testimony, a charge of treason was brought against Burr. More than half a year after his arrest, the jury, basing its decision on the "evidence submitted," acquitted the former Vice-President and his associates of the charge.

The proceedings constituted a brilliant social as well as legal occasion. Of course, Burr's daughter, the beautiful Theodosia, was there. So was Meriwether Lewis, just returned from the great Lewis and Clark expedition. He was present as Jefferson's trusted and watchful friend. Romanticists have again put Meriwether and Theodosia together there in a farewell melancholy for Lewis. Perhaps the best picture of General Wilkinson, on the scene as the government's chief witness, was given in the words of Andrew Jackson, also in Richmond for the trial. That forthright Tennessean, certain now as to where the greatest villainy lay, called Wilkinson "a double traitor."

"Pity the sword that dangles from his felon's belt," the angry Jackson said, "for it is doubtless of honest steel."

Wilkinson barely escaped indictment himself. Indeed, as a result of his testimony that self-righteous general was forced to appear before a military court of inquiry. He outranked all the other members of this court. It acquitted him, but only after he had sought the aid and secured the deposition of Vizente Folch, Spanish commandant of Florida and nephew of old Governor Miró. That official vigorously lied that there was nothing in the archives of Louisiana, transferred to his keeping, which showed that Wilkinson had ever been a pensioner of Spain or received money corruptly from royal or provincial treasuries. Wilkinson he swore (in contradiction of facts the archives actually showed when opened long afterwards) was "an honest man," faithful to his country, and "entitled to the commission he holds."

Perhaps the most pathetic story connected with the trial was that of poor, nearsighted Harman Blennerhassett's journey to it over the Trace. He wrote to his wife from Port Gibson on Bayou Pierre.

"The road is pretty open, having been lately cut," he said of that first part of the trip.

Yet he was grateful for a cap and handkerchief which he could so adjust as "to parry the mosquitoes, or their more formidable companions the horseflies." By the time he reached Tockshish in the Chickasaw Nation, 310 miles from Natchez, he was writing of the "state of my tormented legs," of the "myriads of mosquitoes and horseflies," and of "almost incessant perspiration." He reassured himself that women and even children made the journey but declared that even the hardiest boatmen "swear that they will never again attempt it at this season of the year." He reached Nashville, which he said "appears very dull and ugly but tolerably cheap." The living at the inn was "rough and uncomfortable" except for the tea and coffee "which will redeem many sins of the table for me." What troubled him was that "the attendance is very bad everywhere and criminal, where I want it most, in the stables, at a time when I cannot walk. . . ."

After Burr was acquitted in Richmond of treason and of the misdemeanor charge which Jefferson insisted be pressed against him as well, similar charges against him were made in Ohio. The government did not press them. However, Burr, "free but no less a fugitive," sailed for Europe. In Britain and on the continent he spent three years as a penniless, hungry, often shivering exile, proposing fantastic adventures but unable to get a passport. He seems never to have been so poor, however, that he lacked for ladies. He wrote back to Madeline Price, Claiborne says, advising her to enter a convent. Instead, that young lady visited Havana. There her beauty was everywhere hailed. She was followed by cavaliers, and feted by the governor-general. When she returned to Half-Way Hill "she was followed there by Mr. K., an English gentleman, the head of the largest commercial house in Havana, and to him, on his second visit, she gave her hand."

Blennerhassett came back to the scene of his troubles in the Natchez area. He bought a plantation near Port Gibson which he called La Cache, the hideaway. Such wealth as he retained made Blennerhassett a man of affairs in Port Gibson but his continuing eccentricity prevented any congeniality with his new Mississippi neighbors. After eight years in the neighborhood, he sold his plantation and 18 slaves for $25,000 and moved to Canada. Restless there, he returned to Europe and died—as a man who loved the protection of water about him—on the island of Guernsey in 1831, a still confused gentleman in his sixties.

Port Gibson on the Trace seemed a strange retreat for such eccentrics as Blennerhassett and "Crazy Dow." Founded by Samuel Gibson, a cousin of the Reverend Tobias, it typified the plain strength of many who settled the area. There was little of the glitter of Natchez about it. It lacked the tough power of Nashville. Samuel Gibson never strutted in history. He is less remembered than the rogues who rode by his town. Yet from his coming from South Carolina in 1788, he was, as stockman, hunter, bee keeper, gardener, orchardist, and operator of a grist mill and cotton gin, the builder of an ordered and productive society. The inventory of his will showed 118 volumes of the kind which an inquisitive and cultivated gentleman might acquire.

History swept past his door. General Wilkinson came back to the southwest. Though so tarnished in reputation that Jefferson removed him as governor of the Northern Louisiana Territory, the President sent him back to command on the Southern frontier. Meriwether Lewis, perhaps already melancholy despite his fame, was made governor in St. Louis, where more troubles than those of an unknown Far West awaited him.

And Congress decided to spend some money on the Natchez Trace.

XIII: SO STRONG TO DIE

ONE FIGURE in the development of the west was at times more troublesome than the Indian or the outlaw—and occasionally more dangerous. He was the governmental clerk in Philadelphia, or in muddy Washington, who checked the accounts submitted by harassed officials from the outposts of American expansion. He even had his pompous and punctilious counterpart on the frontier itself. In 1802, Governor Claiborne wrote, with great patience by the still slow post from Natchez, about a voucher. It concerned his bill for stationery from S. Postlewaite & Co.

"If this bill should be passed by the accounting office," he wrote, "I will thank you to advise me."

The bill was for $37. Larger but similar difficulties troubled other eminent persons in the westward movement—notably gray Col. James Robertson and red-headed Meriwether Lewis. Robertson had, more than any other man, founded Tennessee, only to be brought to near bankruptcy by such pennysniffers. Lewis had shown the way to the Far West. In his case the bumbling or deliberate action of such men—or such a man—created the greatest mystery of the Natchez Trace.

Robertson's troubles were simpler than those of Lewis. Perhaps, as an older man, he was philosophically better able to bear them. In 1806, he had been so confident of getting the contract to improve the trail that he had leased his farm and bought supplies for those hands he meant to take from it for the work. He did not receive the contract, which was awarded to a Virginian by the politicians. Under sub-contract, however, he did the work of opening a twelve-foot road from the Indian boundary in Tennessee to the Chickasaw Agency in Mississippi.

He was to do the bridging at 66⅔ cents per foot and cause-waying at 76 cents per yard. Robertson knew the country as well as any man. He had the friendship of the Indians. Still it was quite an undertaking for a man of sixty-two suffering from neuralgia. He had more headaches coming. A draft in his favor for $1,175 was sharply scrutinized and its payment delayed. He received his money only after a late and thorough inspection in 1809, the year in which Meriwether Lewis, younger and angrier, came to the trail.

Lewis and his daring companion, William Clark, had come back in September, 1806, from their explorations up the Missouri River, across the Rockies and to the Columbia River which carried them to the Pacific. Their return from the crossing of the continent had been greeted with great rejoicing by the entire nation for it had been feared that they were lost in the unknown West. Their accomplishment also brought news of a great western promise to America. In the character of a national hero, Lewis had hurried to Washington. There, as one reward, Jefferson appointed him to succeed General Wilkinson, whose presence in St. Louis was no longer pleasing to many, as governor of upper Louisiana. It was no plum that the President gave Lewis.

In that autumn of 1806, Jefferson had accepted Wilkinson's warnings about the general's old friend Aaron Burr as a basis for his proclamation relating to treason. Yet earlier in that same year the President had finally been constrained to order Wilkinson to the southern frontier. The general's enemies had failed by a narrow margin in preventing his confirmation as governor. They made no secret of their suspicions that, as governor, Wilkinson had profiteered in a cantonment site at St. Louis and of their even stronger beliefs that he had decided tangled land titles in his own interest. Furthermore, the general had left behind him in office in St. Louis a relative of Aaron Burr whom Jefferson had named when Burr and Wilkinson were boon companions if not bound conspirators.

The President needed a man in St. Louis on whom he could depend. The measure of Jefferson's confidence in the 32-year-old Meriwether Lewis may be realized from the fact that he first offered the post to James Monroe, who had served with distinction as statesman, diplomat, and governor of Virginia. Showing his faith still further in a matter closer to his concern, Jefferson detained Lewis in the East for months after his appointment because he wanted his former secretary to attend the Burr trial as a private and personal observer.

At the trial Wilkinson seemed to many less than pure patriot in his testimony against his old friend Burr. Lewis apparently played no significant role in Jefferson's eagerness, with Wilkinson's aid, to prove his old Vice-President the enemy of the republic. The trial did not end until mid-September, 1807, and other matters continued to hold Lewis in the East. It was not until the winter of 1807–08 that he set out by way of Kentucky for St. Louis and he did not reach his destination until March 8, 1808. Much had happened in the year-long interim since his appointment as governor with the territory under the rule of its Secretary and Acting Governor, Frederick Bates—who, by his own account, had prospered in the post.

A younger man than Lewis, Bates had replaced Dr. Joseph Browne, Burr's brother-in-law, whom Jefferson had sent to the territory under Wilkinson's wing. At one time Bates had been close to Wilkinson. Indeed, as a new appointee, he seems to have been better known to Wilkinson than to Jefferson.

The President had known the Bates family in Virginia, including possibly Frederick who at twenty, in 1797, had moved west to Detroit where he served in the quarter-master's department of Wilkinson's Army of the Northwest. At one time he was "on very intimate terms with

Wilkinson," Bates himself wrote, though "misunder-standings" developed. An easy shift in relationships, real or apparent, marked the personality of young Bates. Though he had been, in his Virginia youth, "fired with the republicanism of Jefferson," in Detroit his friendships and his sympathies had been with the anti-Jefferson Federalists.

When Jefferson was elected, Bates, as a merchant who had time and desire for other employment, went after a succession of government offices in Michigan. He declared himself "staunch" in his Jeffersonian views. It was as a politician that he secured the post of secretary of Louisiana Territory (or second in command) at St. Louis. At that time Wilkinson was cutting all his ties with Burr and Burr's kin and Jefferson was depending upon Wilkinson's word in the Burr case. Wilkinson, too, needed a man in St. Louis on whom he could rely, even as did the President.

While Jefferson held Lewis in the East, Bates presided as acting governor. As a member of the board of land commissioners and recorder of land titles, he was close to the continuing suspicion that Wilkinson had handled land titles in his own interest. Before long the acting governor was quarreling with the other two members of the land board. By Bates's own report these differences had reached the point of feuding about the time Lewis arrived.

One of the members of the board was John B. C. Lucas, who had been a sworn enemy of Wilkinson. The other member, Clement Biddle Penrose, of a prominent Philadelphia family, was accused by Bates of being "nearly connected with 'the illustrious House of Wilkinson.' " Bates insisted that he himself was above all factionalism. This he emphasized by refusing to restore to office a man whom Wilkinson had discharged.

When Meriwether Lewis arrived in St. Louis the threats of Indian fighting were no more real than the rough conflicts of white men on that frontier. The late-coming governor may have been a political innocent. Indeed, every account describes him as a man who was woods simple and woods wise, honest, easy, courageous and kind. At first Bates was fulsome and obsequious to the governor whose arrival erased his acting status and power as top man in the territory. Within the week after Lewis's arrival, however, Bates began to show a personal resentment which seemed almost like fear. The situation, he said, was "squally."

Lewis, Bates soon wrote, had been spoiled by "elegant praises." Indeed, he declared that the young explorer had been overwhelmed "by so many flattering caresses of the high & mighty, that, like an overgrown baby, he began to think everybody about the House must regulate their conduct by his caprices." It was strange that the secretary should be confident of the incompetence of Lewis so quickly. There were reasons why they should have been friends. One of Meriwether Lewis's closest friends had been Frederick's brother, Tarleton Bates. Tarleton's influence had secured Frederick's advancement. There had never been any question about Tarleton's Jeffersonian loyalties. As a violent Democrat in the fiery politics of Pennsylvania he had horse-whipped one man and been killed in a duel by another.

Frederick Bates shared his brother's violence but not his loyalties and he began undercutting Lewis almost from the moment of his arrival in the tempestuous territory. Undoubtedly Lewis had faults. Also clearly he did not approve of everything Bates had done. Whatever the faults of the young explorer-executive, he had in Bates a pompous, pushing, unpleasant associate. It seems evident that some of the Washington red tape in which Lewis became entangled received extra twists in the hands of Bates in St. Louis. Almost from the beginning of their relationship it was clear that Bates wanted to get rid of Lewis.

Undoubtedly, Lewis was by temperament introverted and mercurial. Aspects of the administrative job may have galled the free explorer. Certainly he found feuds and factions. He confronted his complex and tainted inheritance from the Wilkinson regime with eyes that had pierced the distances of the West. Even as Jefferson's observer he may not have been impressed by General Wilkinson's patriotic candor in Richmond, as many others were not. Still as Jefferson's appointee Lewis served usefully as governor of St. Louis.

A man as clean as the West he had opened, he brought even-handed justice, humanity and honesty to the post Wilkinson had held. The militia was organized. He had the laws codified. With his old associate in exploration, Clark, who had been named superintendent of Indian affairs, he negotiated fairly with the tribes. And he tried to get along with Bates, though undoubtedly he gave that often raging bureaucrat some weapons with which to injure him.

Apparently the exasperated explorer drank more than was good for him. Records of drug purchases show that he worried much about his health. Other worries mounted as he became overextended in land speculations. He had to borrow small sums from Clark. Then, early in July, 1809, government clerks in Washington rejected a draft for $18 which he had drawn. As a poet wrote later, the explorer-turned-administrator was outraged at suggestions that he would "peck at dollars as a sparrow at dung."

Still the young governor rightfully feared that "the fate of other bills drawn for similar purposes to a considerable amount cannot be mistaken." He was right. Some special scrutiny for some special reason was apparently going on in the War Department which then had only eight clerks. On July 15, Secretary of War William Eustis, one of the most incompetent men ever to hold that position, refused to honor a draft for $500 which Lewis had submitted in connection with his dealings with the Indians.

Obviously Lewis was angry as the rising volume of protested drafts amounted to several thousand dollars. In debt and with a salary of only $2,000, he was naturally troubled and bitter when he wrote to Secretary of War Eustis that he was coming to Washington to defend his transactions.

"Be assured, Sir," wrote the young governor, "that my Country can never make 'A Burr' of me—She may reduce me to poverty; but she can never sever my Attachment from her."

That was a strange statement from such a man as Lewis. It suggests that the explorer-turned-executive felt that his country had made "A Burr" out of Burr, thus reflecting fears which had come into his mind when he watched General Wilkinson, his predecessor at St. Louis, arraying evidence in betrayal of Burr at the Richmond trial. Lewis had come upon Wilkinson's never pretty path in St. Louis.

However furious, Lewis was in "good health," according to the *Missouri Gazette,* when he left St. Louis in September, 1809. He traveled in no such style as that in which Wilkinson had sent Burr down stream on his first trip to Natchez and beyond. Riding a flatboat on which he drifted, he took with him but two servants. One was a John Pernia (spelled in a variety of ways), a man of unknown breed or origin. It was stated many years later by an historian of St. Louis that Pernia was "a Creole derelict" whom Lewis in kindness had picked up on the river front and made his body servant, "giving him clothes, whiskey, tobacco and an allowance." The other companion, called "Captain Tom," was a Negro slave who belonged to Lewis's brother.

Certainly the young governor set out to troublesome Washington with ill-will behind him. In advance of his departure Bates wrote a letter to his brother, Richard, who years later was to become a member of Abraham Lincoln's cabinet, in which he recounted the opposition he had had from the other two members of the land board. Then he tore into Governor Lewis:

"He has fallen from the public esteem & almost into the public contempt," he wrote. "He is well aware of my increasing popularity (for one scale sinks as the other rises . . .) and has for some time feared that I was at the head of a Party whose object it would be to denounce him to the President and procure his dismission."

Jefferson, who had been Lewis's close friend and patron, was no longer President. The Sage of Monticello had retired from Washington in March, 1809. He described himself as a wave-worn mariner approaching the shore. He was, he said, a prisoner emerging from the shackles and was eager for the tranquil pursuits which, he declared, Nature had intended him. Jefferson's departure undoubtedly weakened the position of his protégé in St. Louis, though it is possible that his stubborn opposition to Burr might not have made Jefferson sympathetic to any recital which added to the charges of corruption against Wilkinson. At this time it was Lewis, the child of Nature, who was shackled.

Bates evidently made it his business to receive news about Lewis as he drifted down the river. There are reports that the governor reached Fort Pickering, near Chickasaw Bluffs, in "a state of mental derangement." It seems possible that Lewis was drinking too much, yet his historians have noted that his notebook entries at the time were "eminently clear and sensible." Cap. Gilbert T. Russell, an old friend and then commander at Pickering, told Jefferson nearly four months later that Lewis's condition was such that "I tho't rendered it necessary that he should be stopped until he should recover which I done & in a short time by proper attention a change was perceptible and in about six days he was perfectly restored in every respect and ready for travel."

While Lewis was at Fort Pickering reports reached him that the United States and Britain were or might soon be at war. He feared that he might lose his disputed vouchers and the accounts of the Lewis and Clark expedition to British warships if he followed his original plan to go East by river and sea. He was also troubled by the heat, he wrote, and feared the greater heat further south. He turned eastward, therefore, through the Chickasaw country which he knew so well. As commander at Pickering a dozen years before, when Wilkinson had referred to his force as "rascals," he had made friends with the Indians and learned their language.

He was accompanied by his two servants and a Maj. James Neelly, then United States Agent to the Chickasaw Indians, who was traveling the same way. Dawson Phelps, official historian of the Natchez Trace Parkway, says of Neelly that "little is known of the man." One thing that is known about him is that a few years later the national government abruptly advised Neelly that he was dismissed as Indian agent and would be replaced by General Robertson. The reason given for his dismissal was the hostility of the Indians. They were often the best judges of the quality of the white men sent to them as agents.

On this journey, Neelly wrote Jefferson later, they rested two days because of Lewis's condition. They then crossed the Tennessee River on the 8th or 9th of October. They were now on the Natchez Trace. It was still no carriage road. The specifications under which Colonel Robertson had worked required only that no stumps were to be left on the trail which were more than 16-inches high, and to this rough way were always added the vicissitudes of weather which ran the gamut from blistering heat to blizzard.

On October 10, thunderstorms brought torrential rains on Lewis's little party. Two of their pack horses, loaded with Lewis's papers, broke and ran. Neelly said that he stayed behind to recapture them. Apparently the two servants lagged behind Lewis, too.

Meriwether Lewis was alone "dressed in a loose gown, white striped with blue," when he came to the first stand, or tavern, in Tennessee just inside United States territory beyond the Chickasaw lands. This stand had not long been opened. The wilderness came almost to its door. It was operated by a man named Robert E. Grinder (or Griner) who had settled in the area about 1807 on a farm on Swan Creek. The next year, still keeping the farm, he had opened the stand on the Trace. It was composed of at least two log houses, unplastered and unchinked, and a barn 100 yards away.

Grinder was not at home when Lewis arrived just before sunset. The stand keeper was said to be off on his farm, though his chief source of income was selling food, liquor and shelter to the increasing number of travelers who passed by. A legend grew later that Grinder, said to be part Indian, was not above looting his lodgers.

There were such inns on the frontier. Near Columbia, about 20 miles away, a woman called Mom Murrell kept a combination tavern, brothel and thieves market. One traveler said that the best way to pick—or not pick—a tavern was to note whether the landlord's ears had been cropped.

Folklore has multiplied tales of such hostels for murder. A favorite story concerns the son of parents who made a business of robbing and murdering their guests. After leaving home, the son came back older, bearded and a prosperous brigand in his own right. He planned a playful return. Not telling his ma and pa who he was, he talked of his riches and he got his skull cracked while he slept. Later a neighbor, whom the young man had let in on the joke, asked about the son. Sick and frightened, the old folks went secretly and dug up the body where they had buried it. On his breast they found the birthmark that their son had borne since the mother, who helped kill him, had suckled him long before.

There is no evidence that Grinder's was such a place. When Lewis arrived, Mrs. Grinder, who appears in all accounts as a remarkably timid woman for her place and station on the Trace, was present with her two children and two slave children. Lewis asked for accommodations for himself and his servants who would soon join him. She agreed to lodge him in the house and the servants in the barn.

Lewis drank a little. When his servants arrived he asked for his powder which he was sure he had in a canister. To this request, Mrs. Grinder said later, the servants made "no distinct reply." The governor seemed to her to behave strangely. He walked rapidly toward her, then wheeled and moved away. She fixed him supper from which he arose talking to himself "in a violent manner." Sudden flushes came to his face. Then quietly he sat down in a chair by the door and lit his pipe.

"Madam, this is a very pleasant evening," he said amiably.

He was by turn agitated and composed and again observed what a "sweet evening" it was. When she started to prepare a bed for him, he said he would sleep on the floor and sent his servants to bring his bearskin and buffalo robe. Pernia and Tom went off to the barn. In the kitchen, only a few yards from the room where Lewis was, Mrs. Grinder heard the young governor walking up and down and talking aloud, she said, "like a lawyer."

Then she heard the report of a pistol in Lewis's room and something fell heavily on the floor. A cry came, "O Lord!" Another pistol shot followed, and in a few minutes Lewis was at her door.

"O madam! give me some water and heal my wounds!" he cried.

Through the chinks in the cabin, she saw him in the yard. He staggered and fell against a stump. He managed to get back to his room, then to the kitchen door again. He did not speak but she heard him scraping the empty bucket with a gourd for water. Despite the evident distress of her lodger, the Grinder woman did not leave the kitchen until day broke, two hours later, when she sent two children to call the servants.

Her story, as she told it two years later to Alexander Wilson, who passed sadly by on a bird study tour of the Trace, was vivid and detailed.

"On going in," she said then in a story she had told many times, "they found him lying on the bed; he uncovered his side and showed them where the bullet had entered; a piece of the forehead was blown off, and had exposed the brains, without having bled much. He begged they would take his rifle and blow out his brains, and he would give them all the money he had in his trunk. He often said, 'I am no coward; but I am so strong, so hard to die.' He begg'd the servant not to be afraid of him, for that he would not hurt him. He expired in about two hours, or just as the sun rose above the trees."

That version was given convincingly to Wilson by Mrs. Grinder. An even more gruesome version was provided in the biography of Patrick Gass, the last survivor of the Lewis and Clark expedition, by John G. Jacob, which was published in 1859. Jacob said that Lewis was not only shot twice with a pistol but also that his throat was cut with a knife. The versions of the tragedy vary, even as to the spot where Lewis died.

John Bakeless, in his biography of Lewis, says that Robert O. Smith, one of the mail riders on the Trace, reached Grinder's stand during the morning of October 11 and found Lewis's body lying in the road, one hundred or one hundred and fifty yards from the Grinder cabins. Smith apparently observed no knife wounds. Examining the body, he thought a bullet had entered the back. Searching further he found a bit of wadding lying between Lewis's body and the stable, that looked as though it had come from a musket.

This account suggests the possibility of an assassin, standing near the stable, who fired at Lewis from behind — the theory being that the wadding would have dropped either somewhere between the muzzle and the target or would have been carried into the wound. It could not, according to this deduction, have carried clear through the body. Unfortunately, this post rider apparently made no written report for the Post Office Department records contain no reference to the affair. Phelps doubts that a Robert O. Smith ever carried the mail over the Natchez Trace.

Neelly, who is said to have come up after Lewis was hours dead, reported the tragedy to Jefferson. Other reports were made to the former President who rendered his verdict— the one generally accepted by history—from Monticello on August 18, 1813, nearly four years later. It has always been presumed that he had sought and received all available facts about the fate of his protégé. He pronounced it suicide based upon "hypochondriac affections."

"It was a constitutional disposition," the seventy-year-old Jefferson wrote, "in all the nearest branches of the family of his name, and was more immediately inherited from his father. They had not, however, been so strong as to give uneasiness to his family. While he lived with me in Washington I observed at times sensible depressions of mind; but, knowing their constitutional source, I estimated their course by what I had seen in the family. During his Western Expedition, the constant exertion which that required of all the faculties of body and mind suspended these distressing affections; but after his establishment at St. Louis in sedentary occupations, they returned to him with redoubled vigor and began seriously to alarm his friends."

It seems a little strange that Mr. Jefferson, knowing this hereditary taint, would have trusted Lewis in "sedentary occupation" as his secretary, sent him to Richmond as his trusted observer at the Burr trial and named him governor of Louisiana. It is possible that Mr. Jefferson was sensitive about "hypochondriac affections" when he wrote. He was closer to them than Meriwether Lewis. Just two years before he made his verdict and two years after Lewis's death, Jefferson's own nephews, Lilburn and Isham Lewis, had committed a crime which the founder of American democracy never mentioned. These young men were distant relatives of Meriwether. They were the sons of Jefferson's sister, Lucy, and of Dr. Charles Lewis, of Albemarle County, Virginia. The father, Dr. Lewis, was the son of Mary Randolph, sister of the President's mother.

On the night of December 11, 1811, in Kentucky at a

point not far from the conjunction of the Cumberland, Tennessee and Ohio rivers down which so many boatmen came to return by the Trace, the two young men committed a murder of classic horror. Because a slave had broken a pitcher which had belonged to their dead mother, Lucy Jefferson, they took him before their assembled slaves in the smokehouse and butchered him, hand after hand, foot after foot, then threw his carcass into the fire.

Not all violence had disappeared from the Trace or the West which it served when Meriwether Lewis died. Perhaps it was not in 1809, as Phelps avers, in minimizing the possibility that Lewis was murdered, "a dangerous road." Phelps may even be correct in his statement that "no robbery had been reported for years." Certainly for the moment the notorious outlaws were dead though others were to come again. That historian may have had all his facts in hand when he said of the place where Lewis died that "of those who passed the lonely grave not one reported rumors of murder or assassination."

Still dark legends grew. Lewis's own sister believed until she died that her brother had been murdered. There is even a tradition that Jefferson changed his mind about his verdict of suicide. So, apparently, did William Clark. Stories spread that Grinder had slipped back in the night and killed Lewis with the connivance of his wife who could talk so vividly afterwards about the suicide. The tavern keeper, it was rumored, went soon to the western part of Tennessee, from which Lewis had come to his door, and with money he had not had before Lewis came. There he was supposed to have bought a farm and a number of slaves. It was also reported that Grinder was hailed before a jury and released only because the jurors feared there might be bullets for them like Lewis got. The records are lost or confused.

As late as 1953, the *Dictionary of American Biography* stated that the "weight of evidence" was on the side of murder. That authority states that "no money was found on his body and his watch was later recovered in New Orleans." Such suggestions seem to point to the Creole Pernia. There was even a report that Lewis had found a fabulous gold mine while he and Clark explored the West and that men had followed him to steal the map showing the location. The certain things which followed Lewis to his death were the harassments and the venom of Frederick Bates.

Certainly no one was more excited about the matter. The acting governor was, of course, apparently safe from any blame in St. Louis when the death occurred. There he was receiving reports and writing letters about Lewis before and after his death. One letter to him, from one James Howe at Chickasaw Bluffs, stated that while at Fort Pickering Lewis "made several attempts to put an end to his own existence." Later Bates wrote flatly that "Gov. Lewis on his way to Washington became insane."

Except in conventionally pious phrases, Bates expressed no real regret for "the premature and tragical death of Gov. Lewis." He added in the same letter in which he used this phrase that he "had no personal regard for him and a great deal of political contempt." He had, he wrote, also borne "in silence the supercilious air of the governor for a long time."

It was in this same letter that he quoted in connection with Lewis's death, the Latin, "De mortuis nil nisi bonum" and a poetic passage apparently of his own making:

Oh Lewis, how from my love, I pity thee
"Those who stand high, have many winds to shake them
 And if they fall, they dash themselves to pieces."

Others, however, were apparently unwilling to leave the matter to such poetic piety. Indeed, as Bates himself reported on the arrival of news that Lewis was in a disturbed state at Fort Pickering and "before we heard of his death," he was being charged with responsibility for the condition of the governor. At that time, Bates said his steadily dissenting colleague on the land board, Clement Penrose, publicly "commenced a regular and systematic traduction of my Character." Bates gave a full report of this matter to his brother.

"He asserted in several respectable companies," Bates wrote of Penrose before Lewis had been dead a month, "that the mental derangement of the Governor ought not to be imputed to his political miscarriages; but rather to the barbarous conduct of the Secretary. That Mr. Bates determined to tear down Gov. Lewis, at all events, with the hope of supplanting him in the Executive Office with a great deal of scandal equally false and malicious."

Bates declared that he had forced Penrose to deny that he had made these statements and told him that "if you ever again bark at my heels, I will spurn you like a Puppy from my Path." Apparently, however, as Bates himself indicated, Penrose only told him that if the acting governor threatened him he would have him indicted for assault. Perhaps the oddest comment came from Bates's sister, Nancy, on December 6, two months after the event.

"I lament his death on your account," she wrote, "thinking it might involve you in difficulty."

It did not. Apparently no one except the angry Penrose has ever suggested Bates had any responsibility for the death of Lewis. Penrose only charged him with driving Lewis crazy with "barbarous conduct." None of those who have pursued the thesis that murder and not suicide took place on the Trace when Lewis died have undertaken to connect Bates with the supposed crime.

They have generally only examined such motives as theft by Grinder, Pernia, possibly even by the docile slave Captain Tom. They have looked sharply at the still mysterious Major Neelly. The theory of robbery by any of them is as transparently thin as must have been the purse of Lewis supposed to have disappeared at the time. Obviously Lewis's great trouble, as recounted by everybody, was that he was threatened with pennilessness, borrowing small sums, fearful of reduction to poverty. There was no secret gold mine and Lewis had less money than he needed to pay his bills. The only man known to have a credible motive for wishing Lewis out of the way was Frederick Bates.

Not even his motives are clear. His hatred of Lewis, as he expressed it himself, is certain. Yet ambition and jealousy do not quite account for the dimensions of his violent antipathy which seems almost to have approximated personal fear. His quarrels with his colleagues on the land board antedated his bitterness toward Lewis. From them and others Lewis might have learned things with which he confronted Bates. Certainly the fury of Bates seems something more than the contempt of a subordinate for a superior. He may have had something to hide about himself. Though he carefully dissociated himself in his letters from Wilkinson, so did many other men at the time. Bates may have been fearful of Wilkinson, with whom he had been once "on very intimate terms," about something that the general required him to keep hidden.

In 1809, as the already "tarnished warrior," Wilkinson was busily engaged in meeting a mounting mass of suspicions. It was in that year that the general's one-time friend, Daniel Clark, published his *Proofs of the Corruption of General Wilkinson.* John Randolph of Roanoke, aiming at both Wilkinson and Jefferson, was pressing for more and more investigations of the general's past conduct. It is, of course, not history but conjecture a century and a half after the event even to suggest that those who wonder about the manner in which Lewis came to his death need to look at a wider area than the clearing about Grinder's stand and at more people than were there on the night that Lewis died.

It could have been: At a time when Jefferson was listening to Wilkinson's lies, Wilkinson helped put the politically shifting Bates in office to cover up his corruption in St. Louis. Bates tried and failed due to the unco-operativeness of his colleagues on the land board. From them or other sources Lewis learned too much.

Wilkinson's slimy trail, of course, did not taint everyone he met along it. Bates may have been as righteous as he was

always self-righteous in Detroit and St. Louis about his relations with that general. Still Wilkinson was under wide
suspicion then from Detroit to New Orleans and in
Washington, too. The general was endeavoring to cover up
his crimes. He did not hesitate to use whatever men or
measures were required. If necessary, he regarded his
agents as expendable. He would not have hesitated to seek
the removal of anyone who knew much and might report
much to the authorities.

Philip Nolan's death, as the result of an order which came
originally from the general's friend Gayoso, is still a
mysterious affair. Wilkinson had not hesitated to try to hang
the noose of treason about the neck of his friend Aaron
Burr. Between the old governor of Upper Louisiana and the
new one, Bates's fury may have reflected his quaking in his
boots.

All sorts of theories have been advanced in this case.
Another one may be no sounder nor more strange:
Wilkinson could have convinced Bates, both now being
involved, that Lewis had to be put out of the way. As a
derelict off the St. Louis docks, Pernia might have been
available for that job; also, Neelly, lingering behind after the
horses when he let the man whom he thought needed care
go on, was a strange rider on the path to Grinder's stand.

No formal charge needs to be made. None now could be
made that would stand in a court of law or a court of history.
But, if Lewis was murdered, as good a guess as any is that
Wilkinson ordered it, Bates arranged it, Pernia did it.
Possibly, in his old age, Thomas Jefferson—sickened by the
horrid scandal in his sister's blood and bitter at anyone who
suggested that "A Burr" might have been made of Burr—
washed his hands.

Bates's subsequent story, of course, supports no such
possibility. He survived Lewis by sixteen years. He grew rich
and was respected in St. Louis. After serving as acting
governor three times, he became governor of Missouri in
1824, the year before he died. He lived on a 1,000-acre

estate and eulogists remembered that he had a wealth of curly hair, kind but brilliant eyes and "the countenance of a scholarly gentleman of the old school."

The documented certainty is that the tradition of murder goes back at least to the 1849–50 report of the Tennessee committee named to place a monument over the explorer's grave. It spoke of the impression of suicide which "has long prevailed." Then it added, "It seems to be more probable that he died at the hands of an assassin." To its statement of that probability it added the written suspicion of the son of William Clark who had explored with Lewis in more dangerous and more distant regions than the Trace and had been his friend still when the young governor left St. Louis on the journey which was to be his last.

Certainly, even before Jefferson rendered his verdict, the fate of Lewis seems to have been dismissed and the man's body almost forgotten. The former President, of course, made no personal investigation on the scene. Lewis was left where he fell like so many others who died on the Trace, and his grave was little more regarded. The certain witness of this is Wilson who, on one of his nature tours, made a special visit to the scene two years after the young governor died. He came down by old roads from Kentucky to Nashville which then, he said, "towers like a fortress above the river."

From that town he journeyed over the hills of Tennessee's Highland Rim and through the tall cane in the bottoms of Grinder's stand. This relatively short trip from the growing city took him, he said, through "the gloomiest and most desolate looking places imaginable." He heard and believed the Grinder woman's gruesome recital of her story of the death of Lewis. At the stand he felt more dismal than in the country through which he had come.

"He lies buried by the common path," Wilson wrote of the dead explorer whom as naturalist he greatly admired, "with a few loose rails thrown over his grave." It was a small resting place for a man who had encompassed the far, wide

West. The utter neglect in which the remains of Lewis were left depressed Wilson.

"I gave Grinder money," he said, "to put up a post fence around it, to shelter it from the hogs, and from the wolves; and he gave me his written promise to do it. I left this place in a very melancholy mood, which was not much allayed by the prospect of the gloomy and savage wilderness which I was just entering alone."

Perhaps in his melancholy he exaggerated the savagery and gloominess of the Trace. Phelps, who minimized the dangers of the Trace when Lewis came to it, noted that there were at least seven inns on the Natchez road in the year in which Lewis died. A man like Wilson could find accommodation as he studied birds. Eight miles south of the Tennessee River, which Lewis had crossed, was Buzzard Roost operated by Levi Colbert. There was a Pigeon Roost stand just beyond the Chickasaw line in the Choctaw Nation. This stand took its name from a wide area about it which was a favorite roosting place of passenger pigeons.

In Wilson's time these birds came in such numbers to the roosting area that their weight broke the limbs of the largest trees. In flight they darkened the sky. The expert on American birds calculated that a flock observed by him was some 240 miles long, and numbered two and a quarter billion pigeons. It would have been inconceivable to him that within a century the whole species would be extinct. Death and change were along his journey. He wrote in melancholy remembrance of death on the Trace when he reached Natchez in May, the brightest and sweetest of its seasons. Yet even in that town a greater ornithologist than Wilson, John James Audubon, noted not much later in the charming city above the river that "vultures unnumbered flew close along the ground on expanded pinions, searching for food."

XIV: ANNUS MIRABILIS

MANY things conspired to make the year 1811 the *annus mirabilis* of the West," wrote Charles J. Latrobe.

That Englishman, who became an Australian governor, wrote from reports he gathered later on a journey in the American West with Washington Irving. Irving was bringing his pen back to American subjects after a long sojourn abroad since, as a reporter, he attended the trial in Richmond of Aaron Burr. That occasion had made 1807 seem a year of calamity to the famous American writer. His heart had been with Burr when he paid him a melancholy farewell in a damp prison cell which had lately been whitewashed. He thought the prisoner then had been given "the cup of bitterness" and "with an unsparing hand." And General Wilkinson was on the scene, "swelling like a turkey cock." Latrobe wrote of the greater, less remembered events, of 1811.

"During the earlier months," he reported in *The Rambler in North America,* "the waters of many of the rivers overflowed their banks to a vast extent, and the whole country was in many parts covered from bluff to bluff. Unprecedented sickness followed. A spirit of change and recklessness seemed to pervade the very inhabitants of the forest."

Nature was Latrobe's field. Irving wrote of him as "a botanist, a geologist, a hunter of beetles and butterflies, a musical amateur, a sketcher of no mean proportions." Perhaps such a man "of a thousand occupations" was required to describe the events of 1811.

"A countless multitude of squirrels," this *Rambler* went on, "obeying some great and universal impulse . . . left their reckless and gamboling life and their ancient places of retreat in the North, and were seen pressing forward by tens of thousands in a deep and solid phalanx to the South. No obstacles seemed to check their extraordinary and concerted movement. . . . Multitudes perished in the broad Ohio, which lay in their path. The splendid comet of that year continued to shed its twilight over the forests, and as autumn drew to a close, the whole valley of the Mississippi, from the Missouri to the Gulf, was shaken to its centre by continued earthquakes."

Mr. Latrobe, as Thomas D. Clark has reported, "had little time for social and economic observation and comment." Squirrel, comet, and earthquake marked the marvels of the year for him. Yet even these phenomena seemed almost trivial compared to forces which moved from north to south that year. Men as well as Nature contributed to its wonders.

Change did not seem precipitate or explosive on the Trace. Stagnant pools stood around the cypress in the swamps. The drone of insects was soporific. Only bird cries broke the silences of the wilderness, except when gunshot suddenly punctuated it. And an increasing stream of flatboatmen and traders pushed northward and homeward across it. Longer coffles of slaves moved to supply the need for more hands in the cotton fields of Mississippi. It was still a road upon which wagons freighted with the wives and babies of missionaries sometimes got stuck in bogs. Yet ladies and gentlemen, well mounted and well attended, crossed the wilderness in relative safety and comfort. One lady left the record of her amusement that year when she met the wife of the Colbert who held the Tennessee River ferry.

This wife—or one of the wives—of the shrewd and active Colbert, wrote Mrs. Thomas Martin of the Nashville neighborhood, "was delighted with her trip to Washington;

said the President gave them a dinner, and had all the fashionable ladies and gentlemen there."

And Mrs. Martin added: "She was dressed in the latest Washington fashions, but was barefooted!"

Mrs. Martin's fastidious exclamation may have been justified. Yet, though seldom attired in Washington fashions, many white women, too, still went barefooted on this crowding frontier. And trips to seaboard states were not unique for Colberts. They had been received and courted in Washington. A few years after this meeting on the Trace of the Tennessee lady and the overdressed Chickasaw queen, another Colbert had his pocket picked of $1,089 in a Baltimore theater. He was reimbursed by the Federal government as a part of one of the treaties under which the whites were taking more and more Indian lands.

The tribal lands dwindled. On July 23, 1805, the Chickasaws ceded lands north of the "Big Bend" of the Tennessee River, which later became part of Alabama. Then a rush of white settlers pushed across Duck River at Gordon's Ferry, which was leased to Capt. John Gordon. Six years later, during the *annus mirabilis,* these lands which had been called a "howling wilderness" held about fifteen thousand Americans.

More were behind them, little squatters and big speculators. And long before the white men came to take land, they had left their blood in the tribes. Products of such blood blending were the Colberts. Others like them were bred among the Choctaws. Perhaps the great Choctaw, Pushmataha, spoke his origins to the confidence of his tribesmen.

"I had no father," he said. "I had no mother. The lightning rent the living oak, and Pushmataha sprang forth."

Oak and lightning may have been his parents, but he became the patriarch of a thriving family, not averse to the infusion of white man's blood—or white man's money, either. Pushmataha had won his title in 1805 by his exploits in tribal warfare on both sides of the Mississippi River. In that same year, tradition says he signed a treaty under a great oak with Lt. Edmund P. Gaines, who had helped survey the Natchez Trace. Pushmataha had then granted a cession of a large tract of Choctaw lands in Alabama and Mississippi which joined the Natchez settlements to those on the Tombigbee River. A part of the same treaty gave him a lump sum of $500 and an annuity of $150 as long as he was chief. He meant to stay chief.

Before Pushmataha attained that status, his sister had married a Frenchman. Their daughter, a "high-up lady" in Choctaw tradition, was the beautiful Rebecca Cravat. She had married Louis LeFleur, a handsome, dancing Canadian. LeFleur was supposed to have gotten his name because he was the "Flower of the Fete." He was not merely gay and handsome when he came to Mobile, in 1792. Shrewd and enterprising, he set up a trading post and stand at LeFleur's Bluff, the site of present Jackson. Later he operated a stand at French Camp, farther up the Trace. He was successful and Rebecca was fruitful. They had 11 children, one of whom, Greenwood LeFleur, was to become a chief as able as his uncle Pushmataha. He was only a boy of eleven when to the Southern country violent invitation came to the Chickasaws, the Chocktaws, and the Creeks to give true meaning to the old statement of Colbert at the ferry that the Indians were free, "and we intend to keep so."

Warning of this summons to the Southern Indians from Northern tribes whose lands were being taken came from Colonel Robertson. The Washington government which harassed him in road building still depended upon him for warning. Robertson was sixty-nine when he wrote President Madison on September 9, 1811. Younger men like Andrew Jackson were already more prominent. Robertson's neuralgia was growing worse, and he had only three more years to live. His friendship with many Indians and his vigilance among them had not abated.

He had learned from the son of Old John Brown, "a very

noted chief of the Chickasaws, a man of truth," that "there is a combination of the Northern tribes of Indians promoted by the English . . . to unite in falling on the frontier settlements and that they are about inviting the Southern tribes to join them. . . .

"That about the same time that Brown passed Colbert's ferry, there was passing south a deputation of the three nations one very far to the North; they would not name the tribes they were of, piloted by two Creeks to the Creek Nation."

Robertson had got his news promptly. The deputation to which he referred was that led by the great Tecumseh, who remains one of the greatest and most tragic American figures. In his time, says a modern biographer, his name was linked, by those who knew him, with those of Aaron Burr and the Comte d'Artois, later Charles X of France, as one of the three men possessing a courtliness above all others. The similarity ended there. No one even suggested that Tecumseh might betray his people. Gifted, studious, and abstemious, there was nothing in his character suggesting the young roué, stupid penitent, and blind Bourbon that Charles X was.

Tecumseh and his brother Tenskwatawa, a fanatic religious leader of his people called The Prophet, had combined their own Shawnees and other Northern tribes into a confederacy which hoped to stop the westward push of American settlement. Apparently a pure-blooded Indian, tall, erect and lean, the light copper-colored Tecumseh wished to avoid war with the United States "until he could effect a combination strong enough to resist them, or until the expected war with Great Britain should commence." He gave that counsel to his more mystic brother, The Prophet. Then, as Colonel Robertson had heard, the bold and dignified Tecumseh moved south to create the Indian unity he required. Apparently he had already been south on a preliminary errand the year before.

This time, with 24 magnificent young warriors in light canoes, he headed down the Wabash in August, and down the Ohio and the Mississippi. Autumn tinged the forests on the river shores. The pawpaws and chestnuts were ripening. The Indians moved southward along the ways the wild ducks flew in flocks to sun and feeding grounds. Near Chickasaw Bluffs they left the canoes and in single file struck overland toward the Trace, as Meriwether Lewis had done two years before. At the Tennessee River, however, old Colonel Robertson's work and years of friendship with the Indians were ahead of them.

Ferryman Colbert might talk of Indian freedom to a passing missionary. He was hospitable to the great Northern chieftain. He listened patiently. Undoubtedly he looked with admiration at the great Shawnee and at his warriors in buckskin hunting shirts and leggings, all wearing a profusion of silver ornaments. Their faces were painted red and black. Each warrior carried a rifle, tomahawk, war club, and scalping knife.

Colbert was impressed but, as rich realist, not moved to action. He told Tecumseh that the Chickasaws were at peace with their neighbors. They wished no part in any action which might lead to war. The Northern leader headed down the Trace toward the Choctaws. Somewhere beyond the point where De Soto had come west to the path, he turned eastward from the Trace. Then he moved southward among the Choctaw villages, close to the present Alabama line. Among the Choctaw chiefs, called mingoes, he found a sympathetic listener in one with the resounding name of Mashulatubbee. But he also found an implacable opponent in Pushmataha, the greatest of the Choctaw mingoes.

Their crucial debate took place in a glade at Mashulaville on Dancing Rabbit Creek, where two decades later the Choctaws sorrowfully ceded their Mississippi lands to the Americans. There and elsewhere on this journey Tecumseh made some of the greatest orations ever delivered in America. He had a voice which could be by turns whisper and thunder, blessing and curse, and the cry of fury and defiance. He had seen, he said, twice twenty and two springs come and go again, and during all that time the want of union among the tribes had brought disaster and ruin to them. The white people, he said, were like serpents: when chilled they are feeble and harmless, but invigorate them with warmth and they sting their benefactors to death.

He told the Southern Indians, you "were a mighty people. The pale faces trembled at your war whoop, and the maidens of my tribe, on the distant lakes, sung the prowess of your warriors, and sighed for their embraces."

He went on:

"But now your blood has become white; your tomahawks have no edge; your bows and arrows were buried with your fathers. You sleep while the pale face ploughs over their tombs, and fertilizes his fields with their sacred ashes. . . .

"The red men have fallen as the leaves now fall. I hear their voices in those aged pines. Their tears drop from the weeping skies. Their bones bleach on the hills. . . . Will no son of those brave men strike the pale face and quiet these complaining ghosts?. . . .

"Accursed be the race that has made women of our warriors, and harlots of our women.

"They have seized our country, and our fathers in their graves reproach us as slaves and cowards. Listen! Do you not hear their voices in the wailing winds?

"Kill the old chiefs, friends of peace. Kill the cattle, the hogs and fowls. Do not work—destroy the wheels and looms. Throw away the plows and everything used by the Americans. Sing the song of the Indians of the Northern lakes and dance their dance. . . ."

His voice rose in demand for the destruction of the Americans:

"Let the white race perish!

"Back whence they came, upon a trail of blood, they must be driven!

"Back—aye, back into the great water whose accursed

waves brought them to our shores!

"Burn their dwellings—destroy their stock—slay their wives and children, that the very breed may perish.

"War now! War always! War on the living! War on the dead! Dig their very corpses from their graves. The red man's land must give no shelter to a white man's bones!"

Persuasively he promised that in such a war on the Americans aid could be counted on from the British in the North and the Spanish in Florida. But he appealed also to the superstitions of his hearers. He had learned from British officers, it was said, that a comet would soon appear. Also, he repeated a still amazingly strange prophecy made by his brother, The Prophet, four years before in the summer and fall of 1807. At that time brother Tenskwatawa had said to the Chippewas:

"My children, listen to my voice, it is that of the Great Spirit! 'If you hearken to my counsel and follow my instructions for four years, then there will be two days of darkness, during which I shall tread unseen through the land and cause the animals, such as they were formerly, when I created them, to come forth out of the earth. . . .' "

The four years were nearly over when Tecumseh came to the Chickasaws, the Choctaws, and the Creeks. He repeated the prophecy.

"I will return to my country, to wash my hands in the blood of the pale face. My prophets shall tarry with you. They will stand by your side and catch the bullets of your enemies. When the white men approach your towns the earth shall open and swallow them up."

That prophecy, too, had been made by his brother, The Prophet. Indians in the North were to believe such magic to their doom. So were others in the South, particularly among the belligerent Creeks. But the greater prophecy seemed soon fulfilled:

"Soon shall you see my arm of fire stretched athwart the sky. You will know that I am on the war-path. I will stamp my foot and the very earth shall shake."

Young Choctaws in the glade stirred in restless eagerness to Tecumseh's speech. Some of them put their hands to their knives and tomahawks. But Pushmataha spoke the next day. Perhaps not the equal of Tecumseh, he still had great oratorical gifts. He spoke of the long and friendly relations between the Choctaws and the whites. No Choctaw, he said, had a drop of white man's blood on his hands. But, Tecumseh, he told the great Shawnee, you are on your way to visit the Choctaws' old enemies, the Creeks, whom he called the Muscogees: "You will enter their village and eat out of their bowls."

He predicted correctly that the Creeks would listen to Tecumseh's call. However, the Choctaws and the Creeks, he said, "will never travel on the war path together.

"Our old men, and our traditions forbid it. The ghosts of our fathers would meet us, and drive us back to our hunting grounds. The bones of our warriors, slain by Muscogees, are mouldering nearby, unavenged, and last night I heard their complaints around my camp. Even now I hear the voices of the dead in the passing breeze, and I see their spirits in yonder cloud. They hold the pipe of peace to the white man, and the Tomahawk to the Muscogee."

Then, turning to the other mingoes, he cried, "Return home with your warriors, and put to death any of them that join the Muscogees!"

Slowly, some reluctantly, the Choctaws accepted Pushmataha's counsel. And Tecumseh, rebuffed, departed abruptly, but uttering in his own tongue a bitter curse on the Choctaws. And even among the Choctaws memory remained, to be terrifyingly refreshed later, of the Shawnee's promise that he would stamp his foot and the earth would shake.

That same month in which Tecumseh moved among the Southern tribes, another man of less dramatic appearance and manner moved southward, too. No prancing warriors or confident prophecies accompanied Nicholas Roosevelt (of the same family which produced Theodore and

Franklin). Still, many were ready to believe that he was embarked on an adventure more improbable than Tecumseh's. As a partner of Robert Fulton, he had built a steamboat with which he calculated to overmatch the Mississippi's currents.

There were old reasons for skepticism. A man named John Fitch, who had preceded Fulton in the invention, had already tried it. And his life of hard luck and frustration ended when he saved up opium pills and killed himself in a garret in Bardstown, Kentucky, in 1798. That was four years before Fulton built his first American boat. And even in death Fitch had been denied his wish that he be buried "where the songs of the boatmen would enliven the stillness . . . and the music of the steam engine soothe his spirit." Perhaps his ghost in Bardstown alone was sure that a man would conquer the river with steam when Roosevelt set out.

Roosevelt built his boat in Pittsburgh. That frontier outpost then had already become a city such as that Wilson, the bird man, described when he set out south the year before Roosevelt sailed, "Bidding adieu to the smoky confines of Pitt." Smoke trailed behind Roosevelt when he sailed on his *New Orleans,* a vessel of 300 tons, in the fall of 1811. His wife of three years, who had been Lydia Latrobe, accompanied him. She was the daughter of a famous engineer and apparently not kin to the traveler who labeled the *annus mirabilis.* The boat also carried an engineer, a pilot, six hands, and a dog.

As they went down the river the explosive wonders of the year began to occur. Indeed, when the *New Orleans* arrived at Louisville in the midst of a moonlit night, on October 1, 1811, the "arm of fire" had been athwart the sky. The sound of the escape of the steam from Roosevelt's boat and the shower of its sparks caused many there to insist "that the comet of 1811 had fallen into the Ohio and produced the hub-bub."

That comet in the *annus mirabilis* was discovered first on

March 28, 1811, and was visible to the naked eye in April, but, according to Harvard astronomers, "only with difficulty." They added that "during the summer the comet was too nearly in the same direction with the sun to be seen at all, but [it] reappeared August 20th, and by August 26th was easily visible to the naked eye; it continued to increase in brightness during September, coming nearest to the earth on October 15."

That was two weeks after the *New Orleans* reached Louisville. It was only three weeks before the Battle of Tippecanoe. So, with its tail "132,000,000 miles long," it fell into darkness with the hopes of Tecumseh. Perhaps, as some historians have said, the comet was already too apparent for any purposes of pretended supernatural powers when Tecumseh pleaded with the Choctaws, the Chickasaws, and the Creeks. It may also be that he never made so ferocious a speech as that reported by Claiborne. If the speech, as some historians say, did not "breathe the well-established humane spirit of Tecumseh," then Claiborne or his informers made poetry which expressed the purposes of Indian resistance for which the great warrior came south.

Perhaps he did not stamp his foot. Still, on December 16, 1811, the first shocks came in the great Mississippi Valley earthquakes which continued until March 15, 1812. Of course, Tecumseh could not have foretold them. It seems unlikely that the "countless multitude of squirrels," which Latrobe reported as flying southward in the spring, could have been informed of the earth's convulsions in advance, by nature. Only a poet long afterwards, recalling sin, retribution, and a poisoned lineage, connected the event with the murder of their slave, committed by Thomas Jefferson's nephews on the night the earthquakes began. No historian can count any special significance in the fact that less than ten days after the quakes began, General Wilkinson was found "not guilty" by a court-martial verdict so worded that President Madison approved it "with regret." This was the trial prompted by the publication of Daniel Clark's *Proofs of the Corruption of Gen. James Wilkinson.* There was, indeed, much evidence of the general's treachery in the work, but Wilkinson once again appealed to Spanish officials for vindication. Later, this second coat of whitewash for the general seemed the product of a time when not only loftily lying Spaniards but the devil was really at work. Burr in England was examining models of steamboats and planning to sell his books for bread.

Tecumseh's stamped foot can be regarded in history only as a promise attended by remarkable coincidences. Still, white settlers feared Judgment Day had come when the skies darkened, the earth shook, and the red sun could be scarcely seen through clouds of dust. Indians, who had already crossed the Mississippi, hurried back, in panic penitence for having deserted their forefathers.

"The earth is ready to swallow us up," they cried; "it rumbles under our footsteps; it heaves and labors to vomit us forth. . . . We return to sit down, cover our heads, and weep by the graves of our ancestors."

It was a season of fear if not a signal for destruction. Villages were wiped out. New ravines were opened as far south as Natchez. In northwestern Tennessee, big Reelfoot Lake was formed when the ground sank and the Mississippi, reversing its current, poured in great waves to fill the hole. On the river the *New Orleans* seemed in special danger. Great hunks of bluffs fell into the stream. Smaller boats were flung up on the shore. However, steam dealt not only with ordinary currents, but also with catastrophe.

Fortunately, as the *New Orleans* descended the river it passed out of the regions in which the earthquakes centered. Still there was danger in the increasing volume of shoals, snags, and sawyers. Then Natchez was reached. Watching people crowded the shore under the hill and the bluffs above. The Roosevelts landed as calmly as if they had ended a pleasure journey. And to crown the journey, in Natchez the captain of the *New Orleans* married Mrs. Roosevelt's maid. Perhaps only tradition put the words of summation into the mouth of an old slave.

"By jolly, Mass Sam," he said to his owner, "old Mississippi got her massa dis time."

It would take more years for men to realize that the upstream push of steam would mean even more than that to the Natchez Trace. Not even the most enthusiastic then expected that in less than a decade and a half nearly 700 steamboats would be built for Western waters, thus making the overland trek homeward unnecessary.

The results of Tecumseh's journey were more quickly apparent. Soon after the earthquakes, messengers whipping foaming horses moved frantically over the old Trace. Some warriors from the Creek country moved over it, too. Tecumseh had stamped his foot, and the signal to join him, to rise, to burn, to pillage, and to kill had been given.

Yet not even the trembling earth served Tecumseh. He returned to the North to find disaster there. He had approved the encampment of his followers near the point where Tippecanoe Creek empties into the Wabash, despite the declaration of Gen. William Henry Harrison that, by treaty, the lands belonged to the whites. Tecumseh, however, had warned his brother, The Prophet, to wait and not fight. Yet when Harrison led his Indiana militiamen, Kentucky volunteers, and army regulars toward the Indian camp, The Prophet disregarded Tecumseh's advice. Promising that no bullet could wound them, Tenskwatawa sent his Indians in furious attack against the Americans. The magic did not work. Harrison flung the Indians back, though only with great loss among his own men.

More trouble and bitterness, too, awaited Tecumseh. As the War of 1812 began, the great chief found his British allies ready to retreat. In scorn he called Britain a "fat animal, that carries its tail upon its back, but when affrighted he drops it between his legs and runs off." Still, he helped cover their retreat and was killed at the Battle of the Thames River in Ontario.

"Brother warriors," Tecumseh had announced before the battle, "we are about to enter an engagement from which I shall not return. My body will remain on the field of battle."

He fell. Still, though many Indians who died there were mutilated and many of them were flayed to make razor strops of their skins, the body of Tecumseh was never found. The legend of his greatness grew. Harrison was elected President. Another man became a Vice-President on the basis of supporters' claims that it was he who killed the great chief. Even white men honored him. Seven years after his death it was suggested that the capital of Indiana be called Tecumseh. In that year, too, another fighting man, who would come south and fight in Tennessee and Mississippi, William Tecumseh Sherman, was christened with his name.

Tecumseh's plans had failed. But the anger he had stirred in the South among the Creeks had not subsided. He was not there to add humanity to fury when suddenly, on August 30, 1813, little more than a month before he died, the Creeks struck. They fell with unrestrained violence upon a stockade called Fort Mims, to the east and south of the Trace, at the meeting of the Alabama and Tombigbee rivers, in the present state of Alabama.

The attack became a massacre. Not only was the garrison wiped out, so were the settlers from the surrounding region who had come to the stockade for safety. Neither women nor children were spared. An accurate estimate of the victims was never made, for the Indians burned the fort over the bodies of the dead. When Americans bent upon retribution arrived they "found thousands of buzzards and hundreds of dogs, as wild and ferocious as wolves, devouring the rotting remains."

To the westward from Creek country the terror spread from Natchez to Nashville. Anger spread, too. The fury of the white men, from the Cumberland settlements down the road to Mississippi, was symbolized in Andrew Jackson. He had made money and lost it on the frontier. He had raced horses. He had by one vote been made chief of the Tennessee militia in 1802, though the last fighting he had seen was in the Revolution as a boy. Then, as the War of 1812 began, he was disregarded. Aaron Burr, who had landed in New York penniless after four years of exile in Europe, had explained this to Martin Van Buren, sometimes reputed to have been Burr's son.

"I'll tell you why they don't employ Jackson," the harassed old exile said. "It is because he is a friend of mine."

There were other reasons. General Wilkinson hated Jackson. Already the Tennessean had a bloody reputation, gained from his personal encounters, which was later to be documented in a "Coffin Hand Bill" circulated against him when he ran for President. Such personal violence did not seem shameful then at either end of the Trace.

It was in this year, 1811, that George Poindexter in Natchez challenged Abijah Hunt, who had established the first mail route on the Trace. Hunt had since grown richer and perhaps more arrogant in his conservatism. Poindexter was leader of rising Democrats who had learned to swagger as their power grew. He was a member of Congress and would be governor and senator. He met Hunt on the dueling ground on Stephen Minor's estate. Poindexter was damned—and damned long and loudly—only because it was charged that he put his fatal bullet into Hunt's abdomen before the signal to fire was given.

Just before the news of the Fort Mims massacre came, Jackson had been embroiled in a violent brawl in the Nashville Inn with his old friend, Thomas Hart Benton, and his brother Jesse. He had emerged from it soaking two mattresses with his blood. Jackson's left shoulder was shattered by a slug. A ball was embedded against the upper bone of that arm. Both had come from Jesse Benton's pistol. Doctors proposed the amputation of the arm.

"I'll keep my arm," Jackson said.

When the news came of the massacre at Fort Mims in Alabama, a committee hastened to his bedside at the Hermitage.

"By the eternal, these people must be saved," the lean, wounded Tennessean said.

He announced his command while propped up on his pillows. No lost blood or battered bone would stop Andrew Jackson.

XV: JACKSON'S ROAD

NOBODY knows how many times Andrew Jackson rode up and down the Natchez Trace before or after he and Rachel came home on the path on what they thought was their wedding journey. His journeyings back and forth upon it are so intertwined with the story of the road that they can only be described in the chronological record of the man upon it, and not compressed and compartmented into the calendar of other events. He moved on personal matters and national concerns, and he gave the color of his character to great and small incidents.

Indeed, where Jackson was concerned, it was always difficult to separate the tremendous from the trivial. He was the sort of man who put Colonel Butler's queue and the Louisiana Purchase in one bravo and blast to Thomas Jefferson. Certainly, he was known well on the Trace, and he knew it too well to let anyone trifle with him on it—and that included anybody from an Indian agent to a glittering general.

The years before the War of 1812 had not been a mellow time in Andrew Jackson's life. His public career seemed almost ended—and in honor. He had served as one of those chosen to draw the Constitution of Tennessee. Then he had served it in succession as congressman, United States Senator, and judge of its courts. By a close vote he had been chosen major general of the state's militia, a position regarded as next in importance to the governership.

Furthermore, his business affairs were apparently in better shape after a precarious period.

Yet, in 1810, he was ready to leave Nashville and settle on a plantation in Mississippi Territory. He even offered to sell the Hermitage to his rich, horse-trading acquaintance, Wade Hampton, of Charleston. Hampton was beginning to add to his South Carolina holdings the Western plantations which would make him the richest planter in America. Jackson was prepared to be content, he seemed to think then, with a $1,000 judgeship in Mississippi Territory.

In Nashville, talk that the lean border captain could not stifle persisted with regard to his belated marriage to Rachel. Some angry remembrance still remained from the duel in which he had killed Charles Dickinson in 1806. That encounter showed the character of Jackson. Skinny in his great cloak, he had let Dickinson, known as a sharpshooter, fire first. His bullet creased Jackson's side. Then, though Jackson's pistol missed fire once, he took steady-handed aim and put his lead in Dickinson's bowels. His nerve was as steady as his pride was implacable. Both were involved when he rode down the Trace on personal business before he first moved on it as a soldier.

In the process of dissolving the trading firm of Jackson, Coleman and Green, in which he was an inactive partner, Green had been sent to Natchez to sell some Negroes. This young man belonged to the family which had sheltered Rachel years before. Parton says he was a relative of Mrs. Jackson who had grown more portly and pious and also more precious to her husband with the years. Still, Jackson's scant patience snapped when he learned that Green had sold some of the slaves, from which Jackson was to get his investment back, at a poor bargain. Furthermore, the young man was squandering the proceeds in the gambling houses which flourished in Natchez-under-the-Hill and in the more sedate town on the bluffs as well. Trader Jackson rode off to get his Negroes. He got them and headed back up the Trace toward Nashville.

Jackson had no scruples about gambling. In one bout his fighting cocks had won 640 acres of land. The victories of his famous race horse Truxton, made Western turf history. Still he did not mean to let any whippersnapper, even a relative of Rachel's, gamble his money away. Neither, once he got his slaves, did he intend to let any government functionary, whose job was to protect the Indians and other men in the Indian country, too, keep him from taking his money in the form of black flesh home to Nashville. That brought him to his feud with Silas Dinsmore, United States Agent in the Choctaw Nation.

There was argument in Jackson's lifetime, as there has been since, as to whether he was a slave dealer. He did not build his career in that business as did Nathan Bedford Forrest or Isaac Franklin, both of whom got rich in the traffic. Forrest is remembered as the "fustest with the mostest" Civil War general. Franklin built a finer house in Tennessee than the Hermitage, and married the daughter of a highly respected Nashville preacher. He flourished. Long after his death, when his body was brought back from one of his Louisiana plantations preserved in three barrels of whiskey, his money made in slaves built an art gallery at the University of North Carolina.

Jackson's slave dealings were on no such scale. Still, the year in which he led his recouped colored folk up the Trace, the whole slave business had grown in terms of both profit and fear. His slaves were a trifling detachment in comparison with the march of black coffles down the wilderness path to the cotton fields. From 3,500 blacks in Mississippi in 1800, the number grew to 17,000 in 1810. And in the decade during which Jackson's collision with Dinsmore occurred, the number was doubling to 32,000 slaves, with only 42,000 whites beside them. The proportion of slaves was lower in Tennessee than in Mississippi. Still, by 1820, there were 80,000 slaves in a total population of 422,813.

Furthermore, the year before Jackson moved up the

Trace with his Negroes, terror came up the river to Mississippi and Tennessee with news of large-scale slave insurrections in St. Charles, St. James, and John the Baptist parishes near New Orleans. Five hundred organized slaves under grotesque flags had marched upon that city, setting fire to plantations as they passed. Their revolt was relentlessly suppressed. Many Negroes were killed. Sixteen black heads grinned in grisly warning from poles. This insurrection, like others before it, was traced in part to San Domingo slaves who had helped persuade Napoleon that he wanted no part of the Americas. Still, fear also attended some, like those Jackson had sent south by the undependable Green. In some cases, though not in Jackson's, there was fear that many "bad niggers" were "sold down the river."

Undoubtedly some such slaves were bought cheap to sell high. So were some sick ones shined up to look well. There were cases later in which slave drivers hid in swamps the corpses of blacks who had died of the cholera so they could sell as quickly as possible others who did not yet show signs of the disease. Sir Charles Lyell, commenting on the number and kind of slaves pouring into Mississippi, said that despite efforts of the newer South to bar slaves guilty of crimes in other states, "the negro-exporting portions of the Union will always make the newer states play in some degree the part of penal settlements." One commentator wrote that "for ingenious lying" all other rogues "should take lessons from the Southern Negro trader."

Lying was one fault seldom attributed to Jackson. His reputation as a slave owner was humane. Still Kenneth Stampp found that he "once offered $50 reward for the capture of a fugitive, and ten dollars extra for every hundred lashes any person will give him to the amount of three hundred." Once he was ready to have a soldier apply the whip to Mrs. Jackson's maid. These were rare cases. Certainly the Negroes he led up the Trace toward the Choctaw Agency seemed loyally ready to follow him. In a sense they were the first armed force he ever led.

So, before greater alarums, began his private war with Dinsmore. The evidence seems to be that, as United States Agent to the Choctaw Nation, Dinsmore was an official who tried to do his duty. Furthermore, his position, Parton thought, gave him "an almost regal influence" on the Choctaw portion of the Trace. Such agents were important men in the Nations, as was shown by the eagerness of a Colbert dowager to have her granddaughter, Peggy Allen, marry Samuel Mitchell, the Chickasaw agent, farther up the road.

Peggy was not intimidated. Neither now was Jackson. Still, Jackson's arrogance seems less admirable than Peggy's lack of ardor. Dinsmore had by law been given a job to do. It related to the apprehension of slaves who ran away for refuge to the Indian country. This function also involved watching white men who came with Negroes whom they only claimed to own. Some may have been early abolitionists. Some certainly were slave stealers.

Dinsmore's orders were to require passports of travelers through the Indian country, particularly those accompanied by slaves. He was never given any very definite instructions, however. And shortly before Jackson came he had been charged with leniency in this matter. So, in the month of April, 1811, he posted a sign beside his agency building. It pointed out that "complaints are made that runaway negroes effect their escape through the Indian countries, under the protection of pretended masters." Therefore masters would be required to show their papers. It seemed a reasonable procedure to most slave owners.

One such passport, preserved in the Library of Congress, is a document by which Governor Willie Blount of Tennessee attested to the character and property of Col. John Hamilton, "formerly of Pasquotanck County, North Carolina," who was on his way to Mississippi with his family and 56 black persons. This document was approved by Dinsmore. Some such westward-moving planters came not only with their families and slaves but with family physicians and private teachers for their children. No explanation has been made as to why Jackson felt this passport ruling was unreasonable when applied to him, except that Wilkinson's treaty of 1801 opened the road through the Indian nations to all white travelers, and presumably also to their slaves.

No exact description exists of the kind and number of slaves Jackson had entrusted to young Green or recovered from him. It is recorded only that when he got the Negroes, he marched them back toward Nashville. He was in no mood for bureaucratic details. So, aware of the vigilance to which the agent had been prodded by the United States government, he made preparations as he approached the agency where Dinsmore had put up his sign.

He armed "two of his most resolute negro men, and put them in front of his negroes." This statement, by one who reported that he heard the story from old Andy himself, suggests that there were quite a number of slaves in the company. Having armed his resolute slaves, he "gave them orders to FIGHT THEIR WAY, if necessary." The night before a friend had given Jackson himself "a good Rifle." Opposite the agency he directed the Negroes to go to a nearby stream and eat their breakfast. Then, alone, but apparently with his gun in his hands, Jackson went to the agency. Dinsmore was absent. So the angry Tennessee trader could only leave a message for him. It stated that he had been there. He would have been glad to see Mr. Dinsmore but could not wait. He was going on home with his Negroes—and nobody was going to stop him. Nobody tried.

"Jackson completed his journey," says Parton, "without molestation, and made no secret, on his arrival at Nashville, of the manner in which he had defied the power of the too zealous Dinsmore."

The zeal, if that be the word, was not limited to the agent. One item in Dinsmore's zeal, indeed, might have been expected to win his wrathful visitor's approval of the agent's activities. Considering Jackson's long memory of any mistreatment, he might have been pleased that one man caught in the passport net was Jessie McGarey. When Dinsmore stopped him, though he seemed a "young man of decent deportment," it was discovered that the Negro he had was actually the "property of Mr. Barnes, a planter of the Mississippi Territory." Young McGarey got away, but not before it was found out that he was the "son of Colonel Hugh McGarey, of Kentucky." Despite this normal frontier variance in spelling, this was clearly the Hugh McGary who had accompanied Andrew and Rachel on what they thought was their wedding journey in 1791 and who hurried afterwards to testify against them on the allegation of adultery.

If Jackson knew about this retribution on the Trace, he disregarded it. He was compiling complaints against Dinsmore, collecting affidavits and emphasizing such an impertinent action as the agent's stopping "a lady who was traveling through the Choctaw Country with a train of ten negroes, for none of whom she had passports or proof of ownership." The word "infernal" is not specifically recorded in the conversation of the quick-tempered Tennessean at the time. It was there. His pen swept across letters to Washington.

"The wrath and indignation of our citizens," he wrote, "will sweep from the earth the invader of our legal rights and involve Silas Dinsmore in the flames of his agency house."

Such wrath may have scorched the post rider's pouch. It still seemed a trivial matter in Nashville, as in Washington, when a galloping courier with "his horse's tail and his own long hair streaming in the wind" brought the news, welcome to the West, of the War of 1812. Though he had never fought a battle, Jackson as Major General of the Tennessee Militia proposed a rush of Tennessee men to Quebec.

Opinions of him then in Washington were still not high. As a political general his outspoken expressions about the "persecution" of Burr had not been forgotten. He had been for Monroe when Madison was elected. Therefore, when in October, 1812, the War Department asked for 1,500 Tennessee volunteers to reinforce Burr's "persecutor," General Wilkinson, in New Orleans, the request did not go to the Tennessee militia chief. Instead it was sent to Governor Willie Blount, Jackson's friend. Blount hesitated. He asked his tall fiery friend, who had already advanced money to buy rifles, if he could serve under Wilkinson. Jackson's reply was that "all I ask" is a chance to fight. Blount signed his commission as Major General of United States Volunteers.

Jackson set December 10, 1812, as the date for the rendezvous of volunteers. Fifteen hundred were called. Two thousand eager men arrived. They assembled at a time when, as happened two or three times in a century, the cold was such that the Cumberland had frozen from bank to bank. Deep snow lay on the ground. A thousand cords of wood had been gathered to last the encampment. It was burned the first night. From dark until nearly daylight Jackson moved through the camp looking out for the comfort of his men and, as Parton put it, "seeing that drunken men were brought within reach of a fire, and that no drowsy sentinel slept the sleep of death." At the night's end the weary commander finally reached his inn. There a comfortable Nashville man, who had slept warm in his bed, commented on the "shame" it was to have the men out on such a night. Andrew Jackson used his favorite oath or the one which has been steadily associated with him.

"You damned infernal scoundrel," he roared. "Let me hear no such talk, or I'm damned if I don't ram that hot andiron down your throat."

The volunteer commander's hard-fighting friend, Col. John Coffee, led the mounted men down the Natchez Trace. The general himself with two infantry regiments pushed down the rivers through crunching ice. He had a company of men as varied as the planters and settlers of

Tennessee. Also, he had at least one chaplain, the Reverend Learner Blackman, who had been a missionary in the West since 1802. In 1804, the Reverend Mr. Blackman had traveled down the Trace with Lorenzo Dow and nearly starved with that eccentric. Jackson's tough Tennesseans, the preacher feared now, were "very wicked," and it saddened him that "profane swearing prevales." Even Jackson troubled him. Apparently the tough commander did not care for his chaplain to tell a sick man he was going to die "if Simtoms were unfavorable."

"I find the Gen. cannot bare much opposition. He is a good General but a very incorrect divine."

Whatever may have been Jackson's theological views, he brought his army safely, with the loss of only one boat, to Natchez at dawn on February 15, 1813.

There the first disappointment awaited them. The Tennessee leader found Fort Dearborn, where they were to camp, "entirely out of repair, wood scarce, the old houses rotting down." Energetically he found a "handsome plain" one mile west of Washington and four miles from Natchez where he pitched his tents a week after he arrived. There, under orders from Wilkinson, they waited.

That "tarnished warrior" offered logical reasons for the delay. He mentioned difficulties of supply. Also he said he wanted the Tennessee volunteers where they could strike more swiftly if the British attacked at some point on the Gulf other than New Orleans. Clearly, however, Wilkinson's chief concern was keeping Jackson at a distance. The Tennessee commander's concern was fighting. He asked to go to the northern front. Instead, after three weeks, he received an astounding order on March 22. It came from the new Secretary of War, John Armstrong, old comrade of General Wilkinson's. One of Armstrong's first acts in office, after his appointment in January, had been to recommend his wily old associate for promotion to the grade of major general. Now he wrote Jackson:

"The causes for embodying and marching to New

Orleans the corps under your command," said the brief letter from the Secretary of War, "having ceased to exist, you will on receipt of this letter, consider it as dismissed from public service . . . deliver over to Major General Wilkinson all articles of public property. . . . Accept for yourself and the corps the thanks of the President of the United States."

One story is that Jackson received this order while attending a religious service. If so, he read it in no missionary mood. This was dismissal 500 miles from home. Some of his men were sick. No pay was provided for them. They lacked even wagons for a journey home. Their leader believed that he saw the slippery hand of Wilkinson in the order. Some grounds for his suspicions are to be found in General Wilkinson's friendship with the Secretary of War and his suggestion that Jackson's volunteers enlist in his regular army. The Tennessean ordered an army recruiting agent out of his camp and announced that any others found would be drummed out in the presence of his entire corps. He also dispatched letters to his superiors, couched in such indignation that an aide tried unsuccessfully to persuade him to make some "part softer."

As far as Andrew Jackson was concerned the United States government was just one big, bloated Silas Dinsmore. He told Wilkinson that if the Army contractors failed to supply provisions for his men or wagons for his sick, he would dismount his cavalry, carry the sick on them, and spend his own money for provisions. Once in Tennessee, he said, he knew he could count on supplies.

"These brave men, at the call of their country," he wrote, "voluntarily rallied round its insulted standard. They followed me to the field; I shall carefully march them back to their homes. It is for the agents of the government to account to the State of Tennessee and the whole world for their singular and unusual conduct to this detachment."

Certainly no such cavalcade had ever set out before over the ancient path. If his march constituted disobedience, it lifted the spirits of volunteers as impatient as he was. Still, it was a perilous passage. One hundred and fifty of his men were on the sick list. Fifty-six of them could not lift their heads from their pillows. Jackson pledged his own resources to hire 13 wagons and 26 packhorses. Those of the sick able to ride were put on the horses of officers, including three of Jackson's own horses. That rider and racer tramped on foot with his men.

The column of dismissed volunteers swung out of camp on the evening of March 25. By a steady and unbroken march of 20 miles along the high-banked route of the Trace, they reached the town of Greenville on the following day. This town, now extinct, was where the outlaws Mays and "Little Harpe" were hanged. When Jackson reached that place he found that he needed more horses for the sick and sent word ahead to his cavalry to send back to him 30 of their horses. He himself wrote from this journey, "I have not rode 20 miles, the field and staff are and have been on foot. . . ." Only the sick rode in wagons, which must have shaken their bones on the rutted road.

The march was rough. Still—and not worrying about Dinsmore—the corps arrived at the Choctaw Agency on March 30, where Jackson wrote the Secretary of War, "I have got on so far tolerably well. . . ." The corps reached the neighborhood of the Chickasaw Agency on April 8 or 9. In that vicinity Jackson learned that no conveyance from the Tennessee River to Nashville would be provided for his sick. Jackson wrote to the Army quartermaster:

" . . . is this the reward of a virtuous administration, to its patriotic sons, or is it done by a wicked monster, to satiate the vengeance, of a combination of hypocritical Political Villains, who would sacrifice the best blood of our Country, to satiate the spleen of a villian [sic] who their connections with in acts of wickedness they are afraid to offend . . .?"

Jackson made it clear that one of the villains to whom he referred was Wilkinson. However, on this march it was not the irascible toughness of the border fighter which marked

Jackson. Soldiers tramping beside him discovered that he was not the martinet many feared he would be. He shared their hardships and showed a gentleness few of them had expected. He shared his courage with them, too. One young soldier was lifted to his place in a wagon in an apparently dying condition.

"Where am I?" he whispered.

And General Jackson, standing beside him, heartily assured him, "On your way home!"

These men marching in the wilderness were not all gentle boys. They admired the tall, lean, tough officer marching beside them, sharing their hardships and fighting for their care. Such volunteers were a rough company, and the recollections of their passage are not all those of unhappiness and complaint. Indeed, at one of the many stands which had grown beside the Trace, one genteel traveler left a record of the rowdiness of some of the volunteers. Still, the roughest among them began to talk with admiration of how rugged the walking Jackson was. He was tough as hickory, some said. And Tennessee settlers knew which wood was toughest. Thereafter, his name in affection became then and forever, "Old Hickory."

By April 15, the corps arrived at Colbert's Ferry on the Tennessee River. Colbert was undoubtedly glad to see them. Never before in his monopoly had he had so much business. It is not clear exactly how much he charged this time. Popular report, however, is that when Jackson crossed with an army in a different state and mood two years later, the ferry keeper's bill against the government for provisons, horses, and ferriage amounted to $75,000. The certain fact is that when Jackson finally led his weary corps into Nashville on April 22, 1813, he had pledged his own credit to a ruinous extent unless the government reimbursed him.

In the public square, the governor's wife and other ladies presented the corps with silken flags of "the richest needle work." Politicians and newspapers praised them.

"Long will their General live," said the *Nashville Whig,* "in the memory of the volunteers of West Tennessee for his benevolent, humane and fatherly treatment to his soldiers; if gratitude and love can reward him, General Jackson has them. . . . We fondly hope his merited worth will not be overlooked by the government."

It was a fond hope. Washington protested his transportation drafts. Fortunately, however, a friend in Washington solved this problem. He pointed out that, if Jackson was left to suffer for his services "the state would be lost to the administration." Then he suggested that the Secretary of War issue an order to General Wilkinson to pay for so much transportation as General Jackson's command would have been entitled to if it had returned under regular orders. The Secretary of War, who understood his politics if not the logistics of war, considered it an admirable idea.

There is no record of exactly what Wilkinson thought. He vas on his way to Canada, incompetence, and another ourt-martial, in which, of course, he was again found not uilty. This time, however, he was not tried for corrupt ealings with Spain. After an ineffectual campaign in the War of 1812 in which he had quarreled with American associates and superiors more violently than he fought the British, he faced a long list of allegations. He was charged with disobedience, failure to make the best of his opportunities, conduct unbecoming an officer and a gentleman, and of being drunk "on divers occasions, on wine or spirituous liquors or both." Also it was said he had let loose with profanity at the whole Army, the expedition, and himself. However, the president of the court was an old friend. Sober and shining, Wilkinson conducted his own defense well. After the trial he was dropped from the Army only because Congress reduced the number of its officers and nobody seemed anxious to retain Wilkinson. He was given neither retired pay nor pension.

So "the most finished scoundrel that ever lived," as the sharp-tongued John Randolph of Roanoke called him, fell out of the story of America and of the Natchez Trace. He passed that way again, however. Possibly he visited his friend Stephen Minor on the Natchez estate where the first Mrs. Wilkinson was buried. With a new wife, he settled on a plantation he had managed to save below New Orleans. There he began writing the arrogant apologia for his life in his *Memoirs of My Own Times*. In his sixties he moved on to Mexico, where he undertook to advise the briefly reigning Emperor Iturbide. In some fashion he represented the American Bible Society there. He died, in 1825, of chronic diarrhea aggravated, according to tradition, by overindulgence in opium.

Jackson's first real fighting was when, after the brawl with the Bentons, he went to meet the Creeks. This campaign, too, was hindered by inefficiency in transport and provisions. It was free, however, of the finagling and interference of Wilkinson. In his first fighting campaign as a soldier, Jackson defeated the Creeks at Horseshoe Bend on the Tallapoosa River in Alabama, on March 27, 1814. During that fighting he had the militant aid of old Pushmataha and General Colbert, both of whom had repulsed the overtures of Tecumseh.

George Colbert led 200 mounted Chickasaws, noted for their horsemanship, into that fighting. Nearly 600 Choctaws attacked the Creek settlements. Meanwhile, Creek marauders hit Colbert's Ferry and threatened the safety of travelers on the Trace. All along this path Indians drew their families back from the Creek threat. Fear spread, too, among white settlers from Tennessee to Natchez. With the Tennessee volunteers in the fighting were Gen. Ferdinand Leigh Claiborne and Mississippi militiamen.

No one now wished to dismiss Jackson from the fighting scene. His victory at Horseshoe Bend established his military reputation, lifting him above the level of militia leadership. It brought him a commission of Major General in the United States Army. It was as such a soldier that he was called from his battles with the Indians to defend New

Orleans against the veterans of the armies which had defeated Napoleon. Despite his enhanced reputation, however, he did not look like an adequate hero when he arrived in the metropolis at the Mississippi's mouth to command American defenses in the Battle of New Orleans, in the first days of January, 1815. To a Creole lady who prepared breakfast for him as he arrived to meet the threat of the veteran British army, he looked like no *grand général* but "an ugly old Kaintuck flat-boatman."

The defending army he led seemed less than prepossessing. There were handsomely uniformed companies in it such as the New Orleans militia, composed of the elite of the city, and some soldiers of fortune who had fled from Haiti. There was also a battalion of free Haitian Negroes who had stood with the whites against the slave insurrectionists there. Some of the city's defenders were fearful about arming and using them. There was also reluctance about enlisting the aid of the famous Baratarian pirates under Jean Laffite. All were arrayed. Still, the force of Jackson counted for its strength on the tough boys who came pouring down the river and road from Mississippi, Tennessee, and Kentucky. The immaculate British soldiers called them, perhaps with some justice, the Dirty Shirts.

Undoubtedly the differences in the appearance of the two armies were striking. The British fleet brought tried and disciplined troops. Four regiments had been among those which not long before had burned Washington and sent President Madison scurrying to safety. There was a brigade of Wellington's veterans who had made the victories over Napoleon in Spain. Color and strength was added by a "praying regiment" of Scottish Highlanders and two West Indian regiments composed mostly of Negroes. All were magnificently equipped. Moving on already romantic New Orleans, their battle cry was "Beauty and Booty." And the beautiful and the rich trembled in that elegant city.

There is neither place nor reason in a story of the Natchez Trace to tell the details of that battle. No complex military problem was involved. The brave, red-coated British had to move toward the city over a narrow strip of land between the river and the marshes. Jackson chose as his main line of defense an old canal across this strip. Behind a palisade there Old Hickory arrayed his Creoles, his Negroes, his pirates, and, probably with most faith in them, his sharpshooting militiamen from the states served by the Natchez Trace. Three times, with ordered movement and desperate bravery, the British attacked. Three of their generals were killed. Then the thinned red line fell back, and New Orleans was saved.

Old Hickory was then not only the *grand général* in Louisiana, he was also symbol of the American strength which had risen in the West. He was, of course, feted in New Orleans, where Rachel had come to join him in a well-refurbished Cumberland keelboat. It was her first visit to a city larger than Nashville. Her clothes seemed quaint to the elegant ladies of the Creole city. Also, though her hair was still dark, she had plumpened to a point where those who honored her husband recalled a French proverb: "She shows how far skin can be stretched." And when she and the general, at a Washington's Birthday dinner and ball in their honor, agreed to show their hosts how the young had danced in a Tennessee blockhouse in the old days, a member of the committee on arrangements made a wry note about it:

"To see these two figures," he wrote, "the general a long, haggard man, with limbs like a skeleton, and Madame la Générale, a short, fat dumpling, bobbing opposite each other . . . to the wild melody of *Possum up de Gum Tree* . . . was very remarkable."

It does seem remarkable in more ways than one. Not only did Rachel still seem a backwoods woman to those who honored her and the victorious general in New Orleans and Natchez. She was not merely a dumpling. She had lost her looks and kept her bitter memories. She had become more and more religious, and far more interested in Jackson's

spiritual salvation than his political success. She had turned
to a "spiritual father," the Reverend Gideon Blackburn. He
may have been kin of that Reverend Learner Blackburn who
had traveled over the Trace with Jackson's angry army on its
way back to Nashville in 1813. At the end of that journey
Learner Blackburn had written that he went "to General
Jackson's dwelling to see his family according to his
request."

This chaplain Blackburn concluded his journal of the trip
that produced Old Hickory: "Prayed with them at night—
They seemed solome."

Near that dwelling Jackson built a little brick church.
Though Parton thought it "the smallest church in the
United States, and one of the simplest construction," it was
"incorporated into the presbytery and supplied by it with a
minister." To Mrs. Jackson, he said, it was all "that a
cathedral of sublimest proportions could have been."
When away from Tennessee with her hard-driving husband
"it was for this little house of brick and unpainted wood that
she longed."

Still the bands had played as the triumphant Jackson had
marched home. Balls were held. The music was as gay as
that which Gamble had made on his fiddle long before.
Natchez was enthusiastic in its welcome as the Jacksons
came northward—and, so far as the record goes, less caustic
in its comments about "the dumpling" who had been so
lovely a girl when she first rode up the Trace, sure she was
young Jackson's bride.

They arrived in Natchez on April 20, at the season when
the old town begins each year to be its most beautiful. Not
only was there a ball. Also, the whole town was illuminated
in the victor's honor. Natchez was both crowning its hero
and hoping for better times. The war with Britain had
brought down the price of cotton. Furthermore, for three
years in succession the river had overflowed. Crops were reduced by rot. In these hard times, historian Claiborne wrote
of the sharp feeling about tax collectors as "official

vermin . . . that swarm at all periods of distress, in arrogance and pride of place . . . like vultures scenting their prey afar off."

Yet the oldest and most conservative families joined in the jubilation for the Tennessee General who was soon to be the great American Democrat. Claiborne wrote that his father, who had fought with Jackson, returned to his family near Natchez with his constitution broken by exposure and his fortune totally wrecked in the public service. Soon to die, "the last act of his life, and the last dollar of his fortune, were expended in illuminating his house and grounds" for the victorious Jackson. This was the gesture of the gentility. General Claiborne, who honored the conqueror of the British, had married a daughter of that famous old Tory and loyal subject of the British King, Col. Anthony Hutchins.

The ovations continued up the Trace—at Washington, Selsertown, and Greenville. The Jacksons passed within a few miles of the mouth of Bayou Pierre, where they had lived for a brief, happy time, years before. Then after reaching Port Gibson on April 24, 1815, the Jacksons and their party moved on rapidly toward Nashville. Apparently this time the Trace was in such condition that the haggard commander and his plump wife could ride in a carriage. At least Jackson's great lieutenant, Colonel Coffee, who rode ahead, sent word back that "I have left the road in bad condition for your carriage. . . ." It was still a bumpy way.

The path was certainly cleared by the tramp of many feet, however. The Reverend John G. Jones wrote later of having seen Jackson and his army moving up the Trace after the battle. Speaking of himself in the third person, he recalled:

"For many months he had often seen soldiers marching southward; but now they were seen marching, with light step and merry heart, in the opposite direction. First came a heavy brigade of Tennessee infantry; then came regiments of mounted riflemen, and squadrons of light dragoons of various sizes. These were fellowed [sic] by smaller detachments of both infantry and cavalry, and last came the sick and their attendants; and for months we seldom looked up or down the Natchez Trace without seeing passing soldiers."

Following the troops, the Jacksons found much improved accommodations or stands along the road—though none so fancy or comfortable as the many inns in Nashville and Natchez. Indeed, for this year *The Louisiana and Mississippi Almanac* listed nearly 40 such stands. Their names, often variously spelled, were well known to boatmen and planters: Trimble's, Woolridge's, McCraven's, Brashier's, Carney's, Norton's, M. LeFlo's (obviously the Le Fleur which became LeFlore), Widow Watson's, D. Folsom's, Big Town, Indian Factor, Good Spring, and many others. There were several Colbert stands. And there was one listed named Dinsmore.

It is unlikely that it belonged to Silas Dinsmore. He was no longer agent at the Choctaw Agency house at which the Jacksons arrived on April 27. He was not actually dismissed because he tried to enforce the law about Negroes and passports. Evidently, however, that factor entered into what Parton called the "quieter, politer and meaner way" of getting rid of him. He was called to Washington to explain some expenditures which the Secretary of War held were too large. The Secretary was not in Washington when Dinsmore got there. Trying to find him and explain, the Choctaw agent following the Secretary found himself at Lake Erie on the eve of Commodore Perry's famous battle. He volunteered and fought on one of the victorious American ships.

It was while he was in the northern Lake Country that the Creeks went on the warpath. An agent with the Choctaws seemed essential then, so a substitute was named who did his job well. When peace was restored, the power of Jackson's fame was sufficient to keep Dinsmore from getting his job back. Benjamin L. C. Wailes, who served as a clerk in the agency under Dinsmore's successor and was later to become famous as Mississippi naturalist and historian, knew Dinsmore's story well. He wrote that as a result of pressures in which hard Old Hickory had a part, the former agent was "reduced to poverty and made a wanderer in the regions where he had formerly borne sway." By then, as Wailes saw with a young man's eyes, Andrew Jackson had climbed up as far as he had pushed Silas Dinsmore down.

Triumph was not all-embracing. Colonel Robertson had died on September 1, 1814. He had been succeeded as agent to the Chickasaws by William Cocke, a pioneer who had followed Daniel Boone into Kentucky in 1775. At the end of a tumultuous career in politics, Cocke had at the age of sixty-five enlisted as a private in the Creek War. He fought with such bravery as to win the praise of General Jackson— also probably as to win the agent's post. He convened the Chickasaws at their council house on the Natchez Trace on March 2, 1815. He explained that the war had ended. He expressed the appreciation of the United States government for their fighting loyalty. Then he advised them to lay aside the tomahawk and turn to agriculture and industry.

Maj. Levi Colbert, who had led mounted Chickasaw warriors against the Creeks, spoke for his people.

"Yesterday," he said, "we expected to march under your Orders, against our enemy, today you tell us it is peace . . . my family have been very sick, & some of us was obliged to stay at home to take care of the nation but when you let us know that you wanted us, you see we are doing the best we can, & that we are willing to venture our lives with our friends."

The test of friendship was not far ahead. Uneasy Indians realized it. "Thousands of adventurers" were waiting, looking toward the Indian lands. Levi Colbert, who answered Cocke, knew that many of these white men had their eyes on the lands of his Nation as the "favorite tract." More white men were coming hell-bent down the Natchez Trace, determined to possess it and other areas. They were eager for the country from which the buffalo had disappeared and where the Indians would have to bargain for the best they could get. Friendly red men faced white pressure and white impatience, of which the great hero, Andrew Jackson, was only the sternest and most irascible symbol. Silas Dinsmore was only one man who could be swept aside.

XVI: THE TRAIL TO TEARS

CHANGE was as perceptible as the cloud of dust which had risen above Jackson's victorious army as it moved up the drier stretches of the Natchez Trace. The end of the War of 1812 not only re-established the market for cotton in the British Isles. It also pushed more Americans, many with slaves and some only with slatterns and brats, toward the Mississippi cotton country. They stood waiting for a greater and greater share of Indian lands.

Old men and young men watched the change. No white man was more articulate or better placed to see the change than young Benjamin Wailes, in his job as assistant at the Choctaw Agency on the Trace, seven miles northwest of the present Jackson. As a boy of ten, Wailes had come with his family to Mississippi Territory in 1807. Educated at Jefferson College in the little town of Washington, he had also learned surveying in the field with his father. He began to acquire his great knowledge of Mississippi geography, flora and fauna, and men, too, at various land offices in the territory before he got his job at the agency.

That agency was no such rude stand as many of those travelers had described along the path. Indeed, some ascribed the dismissal (or departure) of Dinsmore to the extravagance with which he built the $10,000 house. Mail riders and travelers kept it from ever being lonely. Kentucky boatmen who went up the Trace were already talking more about Henry Clay, who had gone to the United States Senate, than about Daniel Boone, who had left the more and more crowded "dark and bloody ground" to die in Missouri in 1820.

Travelers talked, too, of George Poindexter, the rough Virginia Democrat, who was governor of Mississippi, which had been set up as a state in 1817. Some already gossiped about the possibility that, though Tennessee was the sixteenth state to be admitted to the Union, it might be the third state to provide a President in Andrew Jackson.

At the agency house there were slaves to handle the chores and the housekeeping. Wailes was comfortably established there. He worked at his job of helping reward Chocktaw Indians who had fought for the United States in the war. Also, he had "a pretty good collection of books" to read. Perhaps more important in his education there, he watched Andrew Jackson. There he met also, not for the first time, the famous Choctaw chief, Pushmataha.

This mingo of the Choctaws was only fifty when he came home from the Creek War. He had been vigorous enough to lead 500 warriors to Jackson's aid in that fighting. Already, however, Wailes was referring to him as "the old chief." Also, Wailes described him as a man who, even at a critical treaty negotiation, could talk in a "spirit of pleasantry and bandinage."

Perhaps, as Pushmataha proclaimed, he had sprung fully armed from the oak. He could also be as pliant as the willow. He had seen what had happened to the Muscogees and had helped to bring it about. He had held back the Choctaw hotheads from Tecumseh, who now was dead somewhere by the Thames River in Ontario. In negotiation he showed more shrewdness than anger. Pushmataha understood hickory. And he understood, too, the American pressure represented by the nationally acclaimed Tennessean, a little younger than himself, with the long, narrow face, the hair which stood stiffly erect on his high forehead, the long teeth, and the heavy upper lip.

Pushmataha and Jackson faced each other in the autumn of 1820 at Doak's Stand, on the Trace, in present Madison

County, Mississippi, between LeFleur's Bluff and French Camp. This stand was established in 1810 by William Doak. Pushmataha came with other mingoes. Also by his side was his nephew, Greenwood LeFlore, who was only twenty then.

That young man, born June 3, 1800, had apparently shown great promise since childhood. His charm and intelligence had attracted the attention of one of the post riders on the Trace—Maj. James Donly, of the Nashville neighborhood. The major also owned a sort of stage route on the rough road. He asked to take Greenwood to Nashville for a proper education. Greenwood got more than that. In Tennessee dialect his name was corrupted from LeFleur to Leflore. Also, he fell in love with the major's daughter, Rosa. He was only seventeen then. Rosa was fifteen. Such youthful marriages were not unusual in Tennessee. Major Donly vetoed the match. Greenwood waited. Then, weeks later, young Greenwood spoke casually to his mentor and patron.

"Major, if you were in love with a girl and her parents objected to your marrying her, what would you do?"

For once the major's guard was down. "Why, I should marry her first, and then tell her parents."

Greenwood did just that. This elopement took place shortly before young Greenwood came with his uncle to the treaty grounds. There Greenwood's action, following the major's counsel, seemed to be a course also followed by white men who longed for the Indian lands at least as much as young Leflore had wanted the Donly girl. Andrew Jackson, who came as white leader to Doak's Stand, had, in his drumhead peacemaking after the Creek War, run off with more lands than the Indians were willing to give. He had taken more lands than just those belonging to the defeated Creeks. Some were those of his Chickasaw and Choctaw allies. Other thousands of acres were the property of friendly rather than hostile Creeks and Cherokees.

Afterwards the Federal government, in its efforts to

secure an enduring peace, sent Jackson, who had grabbed too much, to the task of dealing with "the restless and sorrowful Indians in the Southwest." So, in 1816, after a grand review of troops in New Orleans, where he had won the battle the year before, he moved up the Trace again, through the lands of the Indians. With each tribe he held ceremonial talks. At the Chickasaw Council House he had met Chinnubby, called the King, and Tishomingo, known as the orator. Also, equally important there were William, George, and Levi Colbert.

As a result of the meeting the Chickasaws ceded to the United States all rights to the lands north of the Tennessee River and relinquished claims to certain lands south of it— 13,000 square miles of land on both banks of the Tennessee, above and below Muscle Shoals on Duck and Elk rivers and on Buffalo, Beech, Caney, and Bear creeks. In return, Jackson agreed to pay the Chickasaws $10,000 a year for ten years. To the Cherokees, for lands which they claimed belonged to them and not the Creeks, he gave the same sum annually for eight years.

In the course of such settlements, Jackson came to Doak's Stand. Old Hickory had there as his chief associate in the negotiations Gen. Thomas Hinds, who had led his dragoons at New Orleans. Other Americans came as aides and spectators. Young Wailes, as a well-placed witness, wrote that among them was "a plain-looking old gentleman" in "straightened and embarrassed circumstances." He wore "the homely garb of the backwoods traveler." He was Silas Dinsmore, Jackson's old, unequal, and almost irritably chosen enemy.

Wailes saw more than treaty making. A perceptive observer, he was soon to become the friend of John James Audubon, who aroused his interest in the nature of the land about him, and in human nature as well. Audubon was to help him to see everything more clearly, including even the familiar town of Natchez. It had grown to the point where the young ornithologist hoped to make a living painting portraits, and teaching French, drawing, and dancing to an aristocracy tracing its gentility to cotton dollars. Audubon reported that a part of the bluffs above the river had fallen to make a basin or bowl, which was used as a "depot for the refuse of the town." Wailes's friend Audubon was describing nature, not making a parable of the struggle in the region, when he told how he saw there a white-headed eagle chase a vulture, "knock it down, and feast on the entrails of a horse, which the Carrion Crow had partly swallowed."

Human nature as displayed at Doak's Stand was not exactly similar. Still, the struggle for possession of ancient Indian lands was not always pretty. Jackson was certainly the eagle on the treaty grounds. And, though Wailes was in the American service there, he was not a partisan of Old Hickory's in history. That may have been because Wailes became a Whig in the struggles with Jacksonian Democracy. He was delighted, however, when he could help James Parton write in such a way as to lay "all Old Hickory's sins & imperfections bare."

For Pushmataha the young agency clerk had affection. He gave Dinsmore a far more attractive personality than was reflected in the overzealous stubbornness for which Jackson gave him credit in 1812. Though Wailes was only 23 years old then, he referred to Dinsmore as "my old acquaintance." He said that Dinsmore, then living at St. Stephens, Alabama, near the Tombigbee River, "was a gentleman of highly cultivated mind, of much experience and knowledge of the world, a man of unbounded wit, and possessing extraordinary conversational powers, which rendered him the life of every convivial party."

Perhaps Dinsmore was sometimes too witty. Some thought he had lost the collectorship of customs at Mobile by joking with a high Washington official who asked "how far the Bigbee river ran up?" with the reply "that the Bigbee river did not run *up* at all." Impertinent in his humor or not, Wailes admitted that Dinsmore had a "passion for disputation and argument."

At the Doak's Treaty negotiations, Dinsmore apparently did talk too much. To a young lawyer from New Jersey who had come "to witness the novel spectacle of Indian life and manners," he spoke of American Indian policy as too harsh. Perhaps the old man was merely garrulous then. However, when this young lawyer learned that Dinsmore, as former agent to the Choctaws, was "a great favorite, and of unbounded influence with them," he was disturbed. Swiftly he sent the news of Dinsmore's talk to General Jackson, giving the impression that the old agent was present to use his influence against the treaty.

"What brings him here?" demanded Jackson's chief associate, Gen. Thomas Hinds.

Wailes, who had heard this conversation, gave it as his understanding that Dinsmore was there for no such purpose as Hinds and Jackson feared. The old man only hoped that in any land cession a little area could be set aside for him "to indemnify him for the destruction of some of his stock and other property, many years before . . . by some turbulent young Choctaws, during his absence from the agency." This explanation, Wailes said, served to prevent General Jackson from placing Dinsmore "under personal restraint, of which, although he may never have known it, he stood in great peril." Jackson's ready wrath was apparently reduced by this explanation about Dinsmore.

The treaty making went forward. The negotiations were not easy. A mingo named Puckshenubee spoke with such vigor against any cession of more Choctaw lands that those who favored it threatened to remove him as one of the tribe's three chiefs. Pushmataha traded. He brought his eloquence, which earlier had rejected Tecumseh's pleas, into full play. It was met by Jackson's determined forcefulness.

At the end of one of the days of negotiations, Pushmataha

seemed content, as the parties turned to light, free conversation at a bench before Jackson's tent. Wailes began the conversation with inquiries about some old friends with whom a few years before he and Pushmataha "had spent some months in the woods." The old chief told some ludicrous incidents of the time. All tension was broken. And Dinsmore entered the talk perhaps in the character which Wailes said made him "on all occasions of social intercourse the center and attraction." Conversation turned to the next session of Congress. Dinsmore asked Jackson if he planned to attend and hear the debates. It was, Wailes thought, a "friendly overture and adroitly made—but it failed." Jackson paused with a long coldness, which could be felt in the twilight.

"No, sir," he said, "I never go where I have no business."

Finally, a treaty was shaped. Pushmataha gave more than his people wished to relinquish. But Jackson did not get all he sought. He had wanted virtually all of the Choctaw territory, but dealing with Pushmataha, hickory against oak and willow, he settled for less than half. The Chocktaws ceded about six million acres of land in exchange for a tract beyond the Mississippi between the Arkansas and Red rivers. The treaty extended the American area which had once been only the old Natchez District as far north as Doak's Stand, where the treaty was made. So swift was the insweep of settlers that within a few years it was divided into nine counties. Still, in the treaty which conveyed the great cession "there was no clause reserving land for Silas Dinsmore."

The Americans, of course, were not content with what they got. More and more land-hungry men pressed against the Indian boundaries and moved with envious eyes down the Trace, which now ran for less of its length through Indian country. Pushmataha, probably using the old path, visited the city of Washington. There he and his party of warriors met Lafayette, then revisiting the country whose freedom he had helped assure. They enjoyed the hospitalities of the Federal city. Then, in the cold Washington winter, the old chief was taken with diphtheria and died on Christmas Eve, 1824. A sandstone shaft was erected over his grave in the Congressional Cemetery on which his words are engraved: "When I am dead, let the big guns be fired over me." A grateful government complied.

So Greenwood Leflore, who had won election as chief of the tribe at the age of twenty-two, succeeded to the old chief's position. He was persuasive to a great degree in pressing his ideas about adjusting the Choctaws to the civilization of the advancing whites. He divided the Nation for law enforcement purposes, provided for trial by jury, and tried to prevent the bringing of liquor into the Choctaw Nation. The tribal council, which had seen the destructive effects of the white man's liquor on the red man's character, decreed flogging as the punishment for smuggling liquor. And when the first man found guilty turned out to be the husband of one of Greenwood's sisters, he personally applied the lash.

Educated among white men himself, he recognized the need for the education of Choctaws in a land in which old tribal ways were no longer possible. Before he became chief, other Choctaw mingoes—Puckshenubee, who had opposed the cession at Doak's Stand, and Mashulatubbee— had endorsed the mission school set up among the Choctaws with the Reverend Cyrus Kingsbury in charge. The views of these chiefs were not shared by all the Indians.

White ways were associated with the white pressure ever pushing the Indians westward. In 1826, General Hinds and Colonel Coffee tried and failed to get either the Chickasaws or the Choctaws to agree to their removal to Oklahoma. And four years later, in September, 1830, blood bitterness among Choctaws attended the negotiation of the Treaty of Dancing Rabbit beside Dancing Rabbit Creek, where Mashulatubbee had wished to yield to Tecumseh's oratory.

When a young half-breed named Killahota spoke in favor of new American demands, an old squaw rushed upon him and tried to stab him to death.

The situation was tense. Six thousand of the 20,000 citizens of the Choctaw Nation gathered at the treaty ground. Despite Leflore's efforts, liquor peddlers moved among them. Andrew Jackson was in the White House at this time, but he had sent his old comrades in arms, General Hinds and Colonel Coffee, to speak his determinations. Fortunately for peace, Leflore spoke for his people. They knew that this Greenwood was not intimidated even by Old Hickory.

The story is told that before this treaty time he had gone to Washington to complain about one John Smith, who had come to the Choctaws as a Congregational missionary but remained as a crooked Indian agent. After futile protests, Leflore went to Washington to see Jackson about this man who had strong political backing. He poured out his protests in a tirade. Jackson met them coldly.

"I, Andrew Jackson, President of the United States, know this man to be an honest gentleman."

Leflore stood as straight as Jackson.

"I, Greenwood Leflore, Chief of the Choctaw Nation," he said, "know him to be a damned rascal."

Smith was fired. Still, beside Dancing Rabbit Creek, Leflore spoke against the folly of Choctaw resistance to the Great White Father. He proposed a compromise. The Nation would cede its lands for others in the Indian Territory across the great river. However, any Choctaw who wanted to remain would be given a section of land in Mississippi, plus more for each of his children. The die-hards hated him and his plan. Still angry and with much grumbling, the Choctaws agreed. Many prepared for the exodus to the West. Leflore preferred to stay. He received a plantation site among the rich bottom lands, where the Tallahatchie and Yalobusha joined to make the Yazoo.

The Chickasaws held out a little longer. Then, in 1832, at

the Treaty of Pontotoc, they came to a similar agreement. Ironically, Pontotoc was close to the field of the battle where the Chickasaws had held their lands against the early thrust of the French nearly a century before, in the defeat of D'Artaguiette in 1736. Perhaps symbolically, the place took its name from the Indian words, *ponti* and *tokali,* "battle where the cattails stood." Now a land office was set up here to sell the Chickasaws' lands to new settlers. It was a crowded, busy place while the Americans who had poured down the old Trace waited for the Chickasaws to vacate their ancient lands.

The migration of the Indians themselves away from their homeland was a last, sad march on the declining road. Some of the Indians set out for their westward trek from the Choctaw Agency over which Silas Dinsmore had presided. Some crossed the Mississippi at Walnut Hills, which was to become Vicksburg. For many of them it was a journey in stoic acceptance of a fact they had faced with increasing bitterness but with diminishing confidence.

If Greenwood stayed behind, there were Leflores among those who departed. Indeed, the county in eastern Oklahoma to which most of them moved is called Le Flore. Their chief village there was called Scullyville, deriving its name from the Choctaw word *iskuli,* meaning "money." Appropriately, Choctaws called the Agency Building where they got their government aid the pay house. There lived Mashulatubbee, who had approved the mission schools in Mississippi. Basil Leflore, as Choctaw chief, fittingly lived in an area where the counties were named Choctaw and Pushmataha.

The Chickasaws came to join them in the Indian Territory. Perhaps their journey was a "Trail of Tears," like that along which Gen. Winfield Scott led the Cherokees a few years later, in 1838. It was also an escape. In May, 1835, the register and receiver at the land office at Pontotoc wrote a letter about the situation of the Indians there. White settlers and speculators waited impatiently. Immediately over the line, among these waiting whites, he said, "a number of shops have been established whither the Indians resort, and drink spirits to an intoxication of almost unparalleled extent. . . ." Many were outrageously cheated in the process.

The situation had a sobering effect, even among the Colberts. Most of them moved with the tribe. And despite the waste and corruption of money-mad contractors who profited from their journey the Chickasaws went West with a dignity which impressed even the whites they passed on the way. They were observed as presenting "a handsome appearance being nearly all mounted, and, with few exceptions well dressed in their national costumes. It has been remarked by many of our citizens, who have witnessed the passage of emigrating Indians that on no previous occasion was there as good order or more dispatch. Not a drunken Indian we believe was seen in the company. . . ."

Colberts, Leflores, and Indians whose names were never recorded moved in the company. One of those who went West with her people was a daughter of the Colberts by James Allen, whose sister Peggy had declined to marry the Indian agent despite her grandmother's delight at such a match. She had in her veins the blood of the Chickasaws, the Choctaws, the whites. Historian Claiborne, who regarded himself as somehow the spokesman of Southern womanhood, wrote in his history that at the time she was "the most beautiful woman in Mississippi."

Greenwood Leflore, who stayed behind, was condemned as a traitor by his tribe. But among white men his prestige grew with his wealth. In the increasing torrid politics of Mississippi, he was elected to both the House and the Senate of the state. It was a time when oratory was in its flower. Not all speakers had the eloquence of the sonorous Seargent S. Prentiss, nor the ability of the violent George Poindexter.

Some, indeed, were perhaps as illiterate and ignorant as the one who wished to amend a proposed law dealing with the premise that "if enny man by making false promises,

shall seduce eny chasd female Etc." He wanted to insert the
words "an cotchd" after the word "chasd." There were also
some dandies at politics and law who heavily decorated
their orations with Latin quotations. Leflore put an end to
that by making an hour-long speech in Choctaw.

He flourished in business. On his place, well west of the
Old Trace, he imitated the mansion builders around
Natchez by erecting a palatial house called Malmaison,
naming it for the home in which the Empress Josephine
found refuge after her divorce from Napoleon. He had the
furniture for the rambling white two-story structure
designed in Paris. He built it for his third wife, Priscilla, the
sister of Rosa Donly, with whom he had eloped in his
youth.

For a while he filled it with hospitality. Yet at last
hostilities grew around him. Having preferred to stay as an
American in Mississippi rather than go with his people, he
refused to give up his American citizenship and support the
Confederacy when war came. Once, militant Confederates
threatened his life. An incendiary fire broke out in
Malmaison. When he died in 1865, however, he was
wrapped for burial in the American flag he loved.

In a strange way his life paralleled that of Benjamin
Wailes, to a sad end in a lovely land. Wailes was not a man
for gestures, at his death or before. Increasingly, though he
managed at least two plantations and 150 slaves, he became
more interested in science. The clerk who watched the treaty
making at Doak's Stand searched the earth about him. He
collected the shells and fossils, rocks, and plant life of the
old Natchez region in a private museum. He dug into the
great, mysterious mounds which the earliest Indians had
left behind them centuries before. He wrote valuable early
works on geology. Yet as a scientist and a gentleman, he still
did not escape the violence which persisted among
gentlemen in Natchez as on the flats below it.

William Johnson, the free Negro barber, who left a diary
much more objective if less literate than Claiborne's history,

conveyed an idea of this violence in almost stenographic fashion. Wailes's daughter, he wrote, "ran away to night with young Jo. Winston and gets married to him on the other side of the river. Mr. Seth. Cox assisted him in the Snap."

And next day Johnson made the entry: "Col. B. C. Wailes and Mr. Seth. Cox has a fight. They were sepperated amediately. Mr. Cox was about Choaking him, had the Col. against the Banisters of the Court House yard."

No reason for the elopement or the fight appears. Joseph Winston was a member of a wealthy planter family. Generally Wailes's life was studious and placid. As a Whig, he did, however, hate the Democrats, and watched with apprehension their angry movement toward disunion. Fortunately perhaps, morphine, required by fatal illness, dulled his last hours, when war later came to the old city at the foot of the ancient road. Wailes did not stand against the South whose secession he had opposed. He was put quietly into the earth he loved in the family graveyard in the decaying little town of Washington, where in unhurried years before he had planted live oaks, Napoleon willows, and magnolias.

All this runs far ahead of the story of the Natchez Trace, but it marks the end of many journeys made upon it. Perhaps, indeed, the years after Jackson left to be President stressed the inevitable ends of the many difficult passages across the old road—to unexpected gentleness and to violence and frustration, too.

As much as any other event, Rachel's death may mark the time of the death of the Trace. Rachel had died as Andrew prepared to be President in 1828. She never lived to see in its final finished form the beautiful Hermitage, which emphasized the elegance of Nashville. Diagnosis and historical post mortem may set the cause of her death down as heart disease in a lady who carried too much weight. She was no longer young. The Nashville to which she had come as a girl was now a city. Yet she carried a weight greater than her flesh. There were those who felt that the slander of politicians was a burden a woman could not carry who had danced in danger on a flatboat half a century before.

Jackson himself carried that burden to Washington. At the beginning of his administration, so soon after Rachel's death, he looked old and wrinkled. His eyes were sad and his heart empty. Yet he seemed less sad than sinister to the Eastern conservatives whom he supplanted. "King Mob" seemed triumphant, thought a chagrined member of the old order. Perhaps some of Jackson's friends did seem rowdy. But actually, it was the free, strong West, which had come back over the roads, the trails, and the traces by which it had accomplished a continent and reshaped a nation's character. Jackson's arrival was a revolution and a returning.

That was seen less readily than was a smaller tumult. In unfamiliar fighting, Old Hickory confronted the superior, stiff-necked wives of members of his own Cabinet. They refused to accept socially Peggy O'Neill, pretty Washington tavernkeeper's daughter, after she married Secretary of War John Henry Eaton of Tennessee. Old Hickory, who remembered the political sneers at Rachel, was ready to break up his Cabinet to take her side. History has given Peggy an attention society denied her. Yet another woman more clearly and more gently symbolized the wound which Jackson carried to Washington.

The youngest daughter of Abner Green, of the old Natchez District, came to call at the White House. She was welcomed as the child of the mansion close to Bayou Pierre where Rachel had found refuge so long before. Also, she was the granddaughter of old Col. Anthony Hutchins, who had roared and prospered near the Natchez Trace. Her husband, W. H. Sparks, in his *Memories of Fifty Years,* recalled the time when aging Jackson met his bride.

"He did not speak, but held her hand . . . gazing intently into her face," he wrote. "His feelings overcame him and clasping her to his bosom he said, 'I must kiss you my child for your sainted mother's sake'; then holding her from him . . . 'Oh! how like your mother you are—She was the friend of my poor Rachel when she so needed a friend.' "

Not many such happy encounters are reported in the Trace's final story. Other details in history were more important. There were many of them. Back in the old West, the Indians continued their full-scale departure. Yet Mississippi had brought in more black men than all the red ones pushed to the West. Their labor built the fortunes of those to be called the Cotton Snobs. The legends of faithful slaves had affectionately grown, but the folklore of black violence had flourished as well. As early as 1823, Governor Gerard C. Brandon had proposed the prohibition of the importation of any more slaves into the state. However, the coffles still trudged down the Trace. Other men were concerned with this black tide. United States Senator George Poindexter wanted, it was rumored, laws preventing the congregation of slaves even for religious worship. Devout whites not only rejected the proposal but politically punished Poindexter for it.

Poindexter was no fair symbol figure of the period. In both strengths and weaknesses, he represented extremes such as have often been romanticized in the differences in sin and gentility between the hovels of Natchez-under-the-Hill and the mansions upon the bluffs. Though an intense Democrat, as a young man he had been put out of the Baptist Church in Virginia because he wore a queue, "then the custom in fashionable circles." The church acted not because the queue was an aristocratic and Federalist symbol, as in Colonel Butler's case, but because of a pronunciamento by St. Paul against long hair.

As an ardent Democrat in Natchez, Poindexter had been a great supporter of General Jackson, at the other end of the Trace. Then he became his bitter enemy. Coarse and boisterous, as Claiborne thought Poindexter, he had married Lydia Carter, the daughter of a wealthy planter. Afterwards Poindexter accused her unjustly, according to

Claiborne again, of adultery with the elegant Col. Thomas G. Percy. He divorced her and abandoned their not very bright boy, who died "a pauper, vagabond and criminal."

Poindexter collected enemies by the score. They continued to charge him with shooting Abijah Hunt before the signal to fire in their duel. Also, they said he was guilty of cowardice in the Battle of New Orleans. Claiborne was charitable enough to acquit him of these charges. But the historian pictured Poindexter in the years of Natchez' greatest glory as a man spending the last years of his life chiefly at the gambling table, and "with bar-room companions, sneering at his former friends, and inciting the sectional hatreds which, in a few years, produced such bitter fruits."

"Neither the rattle of dice, the lucky run of cards, nor the jests and jibes of low associates," said Claiborne, "brought a smile to his lips. . . . He had contracted a habit of looking frequently over his left shoulder, as though he heard unexpected and unwelcome footsteps."

That last was not symbolic of him alone. Anger and fear grew together where the red men had departed and black men teemed in the white cotton fields. Good men in graceful houses shared both the fury and the terror. The sense of the wilderness and its dangers did not disappear as more and more fields pressed back the forests from which the game and the Indians were gone. The oldest road led to folly and the feeling of danger at the door.

XVII: THE ENDLESS ROAD

AMONG his shells and fossils, Colonel Wailes kept specimens of reptiles, too. He stuffed and mounted "Two Diamond Rattle Snakes. Two Harlequin or Bead Snakes." By various methods he tried to keep the colors of some such specimens from fading. Once he put "a beautiful *bright green* grass snake alive in White or Spanish Brandy & wraped the Jar in paper to exclude the light and prevent it from fading if possible to retain the original colour."

On larger specimens he omitted the alcohol bath. When a slave boy brought him a large, live rattlesnake with seven rattles, he used chloroform, then "had him skinned and prepared for stuffing." With chloroform, he noted, a rattlesnake "was rendered insensible and quite rigid in about ten minutes."

No such anesthetic methods attended the death of the serpentine Natchez Trace. The demise of that road, which had run north from Natchez from before the days of the Great Sun's relative, Tattooed Serpent, was more like the death of the glass snake, or joint snake. That creature of the region is really an elongated, legless lizard. It takes its name from the brittleness of its tail, which is more than twice the length of its body. Its vertebrae are so slightly connected that a part or all of the tail will easily break off, or may be cast off, without resulting death.

The Natchez Trace fell apart in that way, but it remained in some respects reptilian to the last. It never was much of a road, as highways are counted now. Except apparently for the pay of military surveyors and laborers, little more than $20,000 was ever spent by the Federal government specifically for the road. During the same period the government spent $1,875,659.54 on the "Old National," or Cumberland Road, which was surveyed to run from Cumberland, Maryland, to St. Louis, but was never completed.

The Cumberland Road served greater population areas. No rivers served as alternates to travel upon it. Money from the public lands was available for the Cumberland Road. The United States never owned the public lands of Tennessee through which approximately 100 miles of the Trace ran. Since the Trace went only 40 miles and touched only two counties in Alabama, that state was not much interested. Mississippi, in which 300 miles of the old path lay, never received any money for public lands sold within its borders.

Furthermore, the jurisdiction of the Federal government diminished as Indian lands were ceded. After the Louisiana Purchase, postal officials figured they could cut a third of the distance from Washington to New Orleans by using a road through the South Atlantic states rather than the roundabout way by Knoxville, Nashville, the wilderness, and Natchez. Still, as late as 1823, the Trace, though "circuitous," was regarded as the "safest and best" by Post Office authorities.

Despite much discussion of the "true route" of the Natchez Trace, the probability is that alterations were constantly being made in its course. Indians, and afterwards boatmen, made slight deviations in terms of water and weather. Promoters like Andrew Jackson sought shorter trips from Nashville southward. Settlements grew with Indian cessions, and new links ran between them. Some parts of the old path were abandoned. Negroes and mules moved through cotton fields where mounted gentlemen, highwaymen, and boatmen with Opelousas packhorses had passed. The Trace fell into parts like the long spine of the glass snake.

Yet the Natchez Trace, in terms of its tough and romantic meaning in the American past, died of one fatal cause: the great, white-plumed, spark-showering steamboats. On them even such a long-legged flatboatman as Abraham Lincoln could ride upstream cheap. Such tramping boatmen as "Walking Johnson," who could outpace the post riders, became legends. Indeed, as the old road declined, the legends of the Trace grew greater in the memories of old men—of gaffers who had been lusty boys in Natchez-under-the-Hill, of old veterans who had given Jackson his name of Old Hickory when they were that tough, too.

The steamboats did not mean safe travel, however comfortable and elegant they were. Murders on the Trace never compared in quantity with deaths on the river. In the forty years after Nicholas Roosevelt steamed down between the river's astonished shores, more than 4,000 people were killed or maimed in steamboat accidents or explosions on the Mississippi. Nor had all hardships of Northern travel disappeared. A man who took the kind of deck passage Abraham Lincoln got when he came up the river reported that such passengers were treated "like dogs, and had nothing but a plank to sleep on." Still, in the palatial cabins among the high-piled cotton bales, passengers moved to danger in decorum—or drinking, dancing, gambling, making love in the moonlight on the waters. The boats were beautiful. A little Natchez poem described the riverside feeling about the handsome, speeding boats:

> Aladdin built a palace,
> He built it in a night,
> And Captain Tobin bought it,
> And named it "J. M. White."

Handsome John W. Tobin, in the steamboat's greatest days, was one of the boldest racers on the river. He named his boat after J. M. White, one of the captains involved in the famous race between the *Natchez* and the *Robert E. Lee.* Another Captain White appeared in the first days of floating palaces. He was Capt. James Hampton White. He had married Jane Surget, of a rich and aristocratic Natchez family founded by a French sea captain (some said pirate) who had settled in the district around 1785. Soon left a widow, Jane White decided, around 1819, that she wanted a palace on the shore. So in building Arlington, with the aid of an architect from Philadelphia, she was one of the founders of the mansion-building period for which Natchez became renowned.

Her red-hued house with its high white Doric columns was furnished with materials from New York, France, England, and Holland. She opened it with an elaborate ball. Then, when the last strains of music had died away and the last guest had gone, she went up to her huge four-poster mahogany bed, carved in acanthus design. It was so high that a matching mahogany stair stood beside it. Next morning they found her there dead in the great bed. It was generally believed that she died of an attack brought on by the excitement of the gala night before. Still Harnett Kane in his *Natchez on the Mississippi* reported the persisting tradition that "Jane's slim throat bore finger marks, that a slave had strangled her."

Violence had not disappeared. And uneasiness about slaves and slavery had already begun to grow from Nashville to Natchez and in other parts of the South as well. In May, 1822, Colonel Coffee advertised in the *Nashville Whig* for a slave who had run away from General Jackson's plantation near the Trace in Alabama. There were many other such advertisements. In August of that year, in the same paper, such a notice of special interest appeared:

250 REWARD

A man by the name of George W. Harvy, after loitering in few days about the plantation of Maj. Thos. B. Scott . . . did on Friday last steal a remarkable likely bright mullato woman, named POLLY, about twenty years old, light hair, inclined to curl a little . . . They will no doubt travel as man and wife as she . . . would . . . pass as a white woman. . . . They will undoubtedly try to reach the free states . . . or some Spanish Territories. . . .

John Scott

The Natchez Trace was still then a path of slave stealers, as it had been in the time Jackson began his feud with Dinsmore. The traffic was reputedly built into big business by John A. Murrell, whose activities extended beyond the great days of the Trace but are associated with travel along that disintegrating road. Indeed, born around 1804, he could have been already active in 1820. Virgil A. Stewart, who later claimed to have uncovered a great slave insurrection plot planned by Murrell, quoted that great rogue as saying that "my mother learned me and all her children to steal as soon as we could walk, and would hide us whenever she could."

Tradition, or fiction built high above tradition, presents the Murrell mother as a woman married to an itinerant preacher who only waited for his absence to make money as eager whore and avaricious thief. Preacher Murrell, it was said, left her to preach the gospel, fearful that otherwise he "would be after her all the time like a boar during the rutting season." When he was at home he tried to break her of "walking as she did, hips swinging and breasts undulating, and long thighs molding themselves against her skirt with each step." When her husband was away she made theft for her son easier because the traveler he robbed was "so weary from the sport she had given him on his bed . . . that he probably would have slept through an earthquake."

John Murrell was an apt pupil of his mother. Stewart's story of his criminal career has a dime-novel quality which does not build confidence in its accuracy. Other writers since have elaborated sensation. Nevertheless, court records show that Murrell was fined for "riot" near Nashville in 1823. In 1825, he was arrested for gambling.

Twice, in 1826, he was tried for horse stealing, being sentenced the second time to a year in prison. Later he had the letters "H.T." for horse thief branded on his thumbs.

By his own admissions, as Stewart recorded them, he was a ready killer and robber, using the old Harpe and Mason method of disposing of bodies by filling their abdominal cavities with stones and sinking them in streams. He enjoyed his loot. Like Hare, he loved fine clothes. And his recollections of high times in whorehouses from Nashville by Natchez to New Orleans capture forever the picture of those pleasure places. He had no poetic concern with "still unravished brides of quietness." Still, his statement of frolic and "high fun with old Mother Surgick's girls" almost creates an eternal frieze of wanton middle-American girls in the gay and obscene positions of harlotry.

Apparently, however, he had organizing ability as well as a ready pistol. The *Police Gazette,* founded as a rowdy scandal sheet in 1845, rewrote Stewart's narrative and called Murrell the Great Western Land Pirate. All tales about him agree that his slave stealing began in a small way. He would promise a slave to lead him to freedom if the Negro would let him sell him once or twice on the way. Then, when the Negro had been sold and stolen again so often that he might be recognizable as what we now call hot goods, he would kill him and dispose of his body. Once he dealt with a whole Negro family that way—father, mother and children all.

He was moving ahead, organizing other rogues—including some who put up a respectable front—into a clan which he called the Mystic Confederacy. He worked out channels and found "fences" by which loot, horses, or Negroes were traded and disposed of. But his master plan, as Stewart reported it in a book he published in 1835 and made more lurid in subsequent revisions, was a great Negro rebellion in the southwest. During the panic it created, he calculated that he and his associates could loot plantations and whole towns. How much of this conspiracy was real and how much conjured up by abolitionist activity and

Southern fears can only be conjectured. The Nat Turner insurrection in Virginia, in August, 1831, had put whites on edge throughout the South. The certainty is that reports of such a planned insurrection circulated in the South in July, 1835.

Apparently they rose first in Madison County, between the Big Black and the Pearl rivers. The old Trace ran through it. There, scorning old Silas Dinsmore, Jackson had made the Treaty of Doak's Stand. Now it was a changing land. A newspaper in the newly established state capital, where Louis LeFleur had built his first stand, reported on the change early in 1824. There then, it said, "immense bodies of rich land are all being converted into cotton fields, and negro quarters—leaving so sparce a white population, as to preclude the possibility of building up anything like an interesting state of society. Many of the owners of those large plantations reside in other settled parts of the state, and not a few of them in other states—leaving on a plantation containing perhaps, several sections of land, no white person except the overseer. . . ."

If Murrell planned an uprising there on Christmas Day, 1835, as Stewart said he did, he was not there. Stewart already had him under arrest on a relatively petty Negro-stealing charge, on which he was sentenced to ten years in the Tennessee penitentiary. Stewart, as the story goes, also informed authorities of the planned revolt. Rumor and fear were, however, all too present. Toward the end of June, the wife of a planter named Latham stepped out on the north gallery of her house near Beattie's Bluff on the Big Black River. She was startled by what she overheard the nurse of her baby saying to a huge, glossy black field hand.

"But this here is such a pretty little baby!" the girl was saying. "You-all ought to know I never could kill that child!"

The man answered coldly. "When that day comes you-all got to, gal. Won't be no never-could about it. Us got to kill them all."

"Go on kill all you-all wants," the nurse whimpered. "Won't nobody touch this lamb here. I won't let them touch him."

An hour later planter Latham was riding from plantation to plantation. On June 30, quickly armed and assembled white men seized several suspected Negroes. Under the lash, a black boy named Joe broke down. Others admitted that they had planned a revolt on July 4, because on the holiday slaves could assemble without being suspected. On July 2, the suspected slaves were hung. Then two white men were seized. They were Joshua Cotton and William Saunders, both "steam doctors" in a therapy then in vogue.

Under Mississippi law, however, no testimony by Negroes against a white man was admissible. This undoubtedly seemed at the time and place and under the circumstances adequate excuse for setting up an extralegal court of planters and slaveowners, which confronted the white men with the slave confessions.

The newspapers which had grown at Nashville and Natchez and sprung up in smaller towns along the old Trace told a sensational and frightening story. The *Gazette* in Clinton, once known as Mount Salus, which earlier had been one of the Choctaw Six Towns called Mount Dexter, told a story which was widely reprinted. Cotton, a New Englander and newcomer, under steady questioning admitted that he was a member of Murrell's gang. The date of the planned revolt had been advanced from Christmas to the Fourth of July because of Stewart's revelations. He implicated some other white men from Hinds County, just below Clinton on the Trace, and from its neighbor, Warren County, which contained Vicksburg, on the Mississippi River. Also, Cotton said that the project "embraced the whole slave region from Maryland to Louisiana, and contemplated the total destruction of the white population of all the slave states."

The Nashville Banner reported that the conspirators planned, after first striking in Madison County, "to proceed thence, through the principal towns to Natchez, and then on to New Orleans—murdering all the white men and ugly women—sparing the handsome ones and making wives of them—and plundering and burning as they went." Thus, killing, and recruiting a black army, the entire South would fall under their control. In such a dark dream the Southern states would be turned into a blazing, bleeding replica of the conditions which drove even Napoleon from San Domingo.

On the Fourth, when the revolt was supposed to have begun, according to this fantastic story, the unofficial jury sentenced Cotton and Saunders to be hanged. Saunders maintained his innocence until the rope on a makeshift gallows silenced him forever. But Cotton publicly confirmed his guilt and warned the gathered populace, according to the *United States Telegraph,* of Washington, D.C., to "beware to-night, to-morrow, and the next night."

No such warning was needed in the frightened plantation country. Armed posses spread. Bloodhounds sought out the suspected. More white men whom Cotton had named were arrested and questioned. A better gallows was built for them. More men were hanged. One, who had been tortured by his questioners, committed suicide. Some, held to be less guilty, were "slicked." This punishment, according to the *Telegraph,* was one in which "the prisoner is stripped naked, laid on his belly, his hands and feet fastened o four pegs; when with a coleman, he receives the stripes from different hands."

Still the panic persisted. The *National Intelligencer* in the Federal capital quoted one planter as saying, "I have not slept two hours in the twenty-four for six days and nights and have been on horseback more than four-fifths of the time." *The Nashville Banner* said that "a dreadful alarm exists, particularly among the females." Anger grew until fury turned even on two wealthy planters, who as unofficial judges freed two accused men for lack of evidence. The house of one of these planters was attacked by a mob. He had to flee the county.

"It is no longer the negroes, but white men against white men," the *United States Telegraph* quoted the Lexington, Kentucky, *Intelligencer* as saying. "The Mississippians are ruining their own State. By their own high-handed and violent measures, they are giving a magnitude and terror to the contemplated insurrection which it otherwise never could have attained."

And George Wyche, a Madison planter who seems to have kept his head, wrote Governor Hiram G. Runnels, a land speculator and political gamecock who this year was engaged in a political campaign in which bloodshed was narrowly averted. He urged the governor to issue a proclamation "exhorting to peace and moderation, & submission to the Civil Powers. The danger from the slaves vanished at the detection of the conspiracy & another danger has taken place far more formidable than that." Runnels refused to take promptly his advice. His kin and friends were in the ranging mobs. He waited until the violence had worn itself out before he urged that suspected persons be turned over to proper authorities.

Some have doubted that there ever was any such conspiracy as triggered this violence. Murrell, who may have been an imaginative braggart, died, ten years after the supposed revolt, of tuberculosis he had contracted in prison. Stewart, the informer, was a hero in Mississippi, but Claiborne wrote later that Stewart was "a notorious scamp."

"The whole story was a fabrication," he wrote, in 1860, when a greater and sadder revolt was about to begin; "Murrell was simply a thief and counterfeiter, and Stewart was his subordinate, who, having quarreled with him, devised this plan to avenge and enrich himself. The whole 'plot' and its tragical consequences, may now be regarded as one of the most extraordinary and lamentable hallucinations of our times."

Whether the plot was fact or fabrication, it was a part of the reality of violence at the time. Terror and indignation at abolitionists rode the roads between Natchez and Nashville. It was lynch law's great day. In Vicksburg, in the July of the slave terror, "respectable citizens" turned their indignation against the professional gamblers who rode between the river towns gaudily clad on the beautiful boats. In a pitched battle there, one citizen was killed and five gamblers were captured and promptly hanged.

Three months later in Natchez, when William Johnson, the free Negro barber, began to keep his diary, he noted on October 25 that "Bills came Out in the morning Ordering the Gamblers to Leave the City in 24 Hours." Nice distinctions were made about gambling. On Christmas Day, the day Stewart said the revolt was originally planned to take place, Johnson's notation was not of terror but of sport: "A Race between Mr Rushlows Arabb horse and Mr Claibournes Sorrel mare Antelope Twas won by Antelope by about a quarter of a mile Col B. won about $1600 from 2 men, 15.00 from Mr Beasly & one hundred from Elias Burns. . . ."

The "Col B," of course, was Adam L. Bingaman, who with William J. Minor, son of the early Don Estevan, became the most prominent turfmen in Natchez. They were men of the generation which grew up as the Trace flourished and died, and as increasing estates and multiplying slaves served as the basis for flowering elegance and architecture. While some raced imported horses, others moved in truly gentle quietness through "unhurried years." Benjamin Wailes collected his specimens and wrote his books.

The famous Irish actor, Tyrone Power, came to play at the Natchez theater, located in a graveyard, and to see all these gentlemen at about the time of the reported Murrell slave insurrection. The weather was cold when he came, "below zero," he said, but the atmosphere quickly became serene and warm. He admired the company which came in carriages, on fine mounts, and on foot to see him play.

"A finer set of men I have rarely looked upon," he wrote: "the general effect of their costume, too, was picturesque and border-like: they were mostly clad in a sort of tunic or frock, made of white or of grass-green blanketing . . . broadleafed white Spanish hats of beaver were evidently the *mode,* together with high leather leggings, or cavalry boots and heavy spurs."

He dined in the country at "the very beau ideal of a Southern dwelling." It was the house of "Mr. M——r," who had been "an officer in the Spanish service," and was evidently Stephen (or Estevan) Minor. Behind the deep porticoes of the house were all the evidences of wealth and grace. Duelists had often fought in its grounds. The Philadelphia Biddle girl who had been the wife of slippery General Wilkinson was buried there. And Minor's Yellow Duchess, whose sister had married Philip Nolan, still presided over the wide plantation.

The observant actor also went to look at the race horses of "Colonel B——n," or Colonel Bingaman. He had a long conversation with "Colonel W——s," clearly Wailes, "on the former and present condition of these frontier states." He "derived much in the way of both information and amusement from this intelligent and well-informed gentleman." Also in the West, which was turning into the South, he met another stranger who was an old friend. This was John Howard Payne, who a decade before, writing abroad of a changing America, had composed "Home, Sweet Home." He was trying to get subscribers for a magazine, and though Payne did not know it at the time, he was also on his way to arrest on suspicion that he was an abolitionist.

The weather warmed quickly. The gardens bloomed

around the mansions. Already, as an observant British traveler said later, not only were the country houses elegant with "some of the gardens belonging to them laid out in the English, others in the French style." There were also terraces with statues and cut evergreens, "walks through borders of flowers, terminated by views into the wild forest, the charms of both being heightened by the contrast." Some of the hedges were of "Gardenia, miscalled in England the Cape jessamine, others of the Cherokee rose, with its bright and shining leaves."

Contrasts were sharp in foliage and society. Natchez-under-the-Hill had begun to wane. Yet the day of the gamblers and hell-raising flatboatmen had not completely passed, despite the handbills ordering the gamblers out of town. Short generations of amiable girls had become grumbling crones. Still, there were more and younger smiles for sale.

There were also belles on the bluffs whose behavior became the prototype the future looked back to for daintiness, dancing, and decorum, yet who had strength under their silks. There were gentle songs, anger, and mellifluent speech like that of Seargent Prentiss, the Maine-born master of Southern oratory. His voice seemed as sweet to the South as that of Jenny Lind, who came later to sing for the planter aristocrats. Gentlemen still crossed the river to the Vidalia dueling ground where Poindexter had killed Abijah Hunt, who got the first mails going over the Trace. In 1836, Poindexter nearly killed himself when he went drunk from the gambling table at the Mansion House and fell 20 feet to the brick paving below. Perhaps he uttered a parable as well as a snarl when a preacher inquired what he fell against:

"By God, sir, I fell against my will."

The hard-riding Cotton Snobs felt that way about the increasingly querulous inquiries from the North about their slavery. More and more men were crossing the river now. They went the ways Philip Nolan had gone long before to catch his wild horses—and many to the same fate. Hardship trails led to a new, deep, and farther West. Men like the pioneers were uncomfortable in the Old Southwest, which had become the epitome of the South itself—the South of the slave (fawning or furtive), of the mansion, the silks, the spur, and the magnolia. The spirit of the Trace itself moved westward, where the buffalo and the Indians had already gone.

With its spirit moved such men as good, brave James Bowie, who may or may not have invented the knife. He certainly fought a knife duel with a crooked gambler who had fleeced a young planter in a Natchez-under-the-Hill gambling den. They fought, close-slashing, with their left wrists tied together with a sash. Bowie and his friends and enemies fought a mass duel called the battle of the sandbar at Vidalia, in 1827.

Gentlemen still fought, sometimes brawling, under the chinaberry trees on the streets of Natchez. Now, however, Tennessee and Mississippi were black-and-white crowded. They were no longer places for men like Bowie and David Crockett, who would joke even in the face of death. The cotton seemed to them to grow too placidly under the sun where the wilderness had stood. And perhaps the story of the Trace ends when, beyond it, in the 1830s, they and men like them moved to Texas.

Westward and southward they pressed as De Soto had moved, and Jackson. Theirs was the continuing stream of hunters and traders before the planters; of soldiers, both sick and triumphant; of towheads and slaves; of patricians and piney-woods people. Over still-perilous trails, the journey of Bowie and Crockett and young, gallant, doomed Col. William Travis took them only to the Alamo.

The golden vision of Mexico, which may have dazzled Burr into betrayal, was still before their eyes. There was once again a West which the American hand could take. Its grasp was still strong and perhaps, as men may have hoped, better protected by the parrying guard of Bowie's knife.

Some hands fell open as they relaxed in death. Their blades fell. Other men with knives and guns, too, followed them. And all knew always that the Natchez Trace did not merely run from the old Cumberland settlements to the rich and rowdy city by the greatest river. It ran—and runs still—from the vision of bounty to the farthermost stretch of the grasping hand.

EPILOGUE: THE OTHER HAND

THERE was—and is—another hand beside the old Natchez Trace. This one is not grasping, but golden. High on the spire of the Presbyterian Church in Port Gibson on Bayou Pierre, the conventional cross is replaced by a great gleaming hand, with thumb and three fingers closed, its index finger pointing imperatively to heaven.

Tired travelers long ago saw it. Tourists stop now as they follow the Natchez Trace Parkway. Ulysses S. Grant's great blue army, which had crossed the Mississippi from Louisiana in April, 1863, on its way to the capture of Vicksburg, looked up at it. It may have been part of the reason for the statement of General Grant, which Port Gibson still proudly repeats, that that little town was too beautiful to burn. The story of this hand is an inescapable part of the tale of the trail, from the wilderness years to the landscaped times.

Not all hands were raised to heaven. A little way off the Trace between Port Gibson and Natchez, in Rodney, once a great cotton shipping center, now a ghost town, fortune-seeking cavaliers opposed any church. These gentlemen, each "spry as a gamecock, proud as a peacock," wanted no preaching to interfere with their gaming and racing. Evidently Port Gibson, where Dow and Blennerhassett found refuge, was different. Beyond it, on the trail north, was where the wilderness began even when Jackson marched back over the Trace in triumph from New Orleans in 1815. Yet in 1807, the year in which Burr landed a few miles westward near old Bruinsburg on his way to arrest and trial in Richmond, a little Presbyterian Church was established at Port Gibson.

It must have been little more than a mission among the plantations and by the bayou. Its first regular pastor, Reverend Zebulon Butler, as a young man of twenty-five, came south to it from Pennsylvania in 1828, the year in which Jackson was elected to the Presidency. Evidently Butler was a power in the pulpit and in the surrounding countryside as well. Shortly after his arrival the little wooden church was replaced by a brick one. The church grew, and its increasing congregation noted and honored one pulpit mannerism of their pastor: "the upraised and clenched hand, with the index finger pointing heavenward."

This gesture became so much a part of his powerful preaching that members of his church took it as the symbol of his work and their worship. A young local woodcarver, Daniel Foley, later fashioned its replica in a great wooden hand for the steeple. Covered with gold leaf, it glistened in the Southern sun. As time passed and the church grew, the gleaming hand became the area's highest visible sign of the best in its spirit.

Like the Trace, and the cotton fields and woodlands through which it ran, Foley's carving was not immune to time and change. As the years passed, the wooden hand was riddled with the holes of woodpeckers, which Audubon found as common in the South as mockingbirds. The gold leaf peeled and cracked. And around the church in Zebulon Butler's lifetime, not all things pointed to goodness. Courage as well as aspiration was required in a region where faith and fanaticism flourished side by side.

Today, those who stare at the high hand and those who are inspired by it forget much of the story of the man whose gesture it perpetuates. Not even the present keepers of the church recall all that story when they write about it. Important things in Butler's life are less remembered than the acquisition by the church after his death, of its chandeliers which gleam within. They came from the great steamboat *Robert E. Lee,* which beat the *Natchez* in the most famous race on the Mississippi which was also a famous gambling event.

Despite the respect of his congregation in the pews before his gesticulatory preaching, Butler also gambled in a land where stakes were high and tempers sometimes trigger-quick. He put himself at hazard as the furious slavery argument, and some men's consciences about that "peculiar institution" were stirred. He was no fanatic. Neither was he frightened. He stood for what he believed, together with some of the richest and most eminent men along the lower end of the old Trace. One was Dr. Stephen Duncan, who, Benjamin Wailes said, was "a 4000 bale planter and the owner of 500 negroes." Another was David Ker, equally prominent if less rich. Both were active leaders in the American Colonization Society, which proposed the return of Negroes in emancipation to Africa.

This humanitarian concern about slavery drew the scorn of ardent abolitionists, who wanted men free where they were. Its efforts also aroused the fury of Southerners who opposed any emancipation at all. With such conservatives as Duncan and Ker, who distrusted the growing power of angry Democrats, Butler was involved in a case which created great excitement in the cotton country. It grew from efforts to nullify the will of a planter, Capt. Isaac Ross, of Jefferson County, which lies between Port Gibson and Natchez. Ross, who died in 1836, made the astounding provision that most of his slaves be transported to Liberia under the auspices of the American Colonization Society.

Anger, cold and hot, spread at the news of this plan to free so many Negroes. Some men whom Captain Ross had named as his executors refused to serve. In determination to see her father's will carried out, his daughter, after conferring with Dr. Duncan, left the slaves involved to Ker and Preacher Butler. Efforts to prevent the emancipation were made in the courts. In angry sessions legislators undertook to pass laws nullifying the will. Angers were thick around the church which bears the golden hand. They were even more intense northward in the country through which the old Trace ran. After the greatest legal and financial difficulties, between 235 and 300 Ross slaves were transported to Africa by 1849. Ker as politician waged an open, dramatic fight against hysterical opposition. But Zebulon Butler never lowered his hand.

Tempers everywhere were stiffening. Yet, in his church in the plantation country, Butler still punctuated the preaching of his faith with his clenched hand and stiffened forefinger. His pews continued to be filled. In 1859, a larger church was clearly needed. As the new church was completed, Butler, after thirty-three years as its pastor, died on December 23, 1860. Only two weeks later, on January 9, 1861, Mississippi seceded as the second state of the Confederacy. The secession convention was held in Alabama less than a month later. Farther up the way the old Trace had run, Tennessee resisted secession until late in the spring.

The older and wealthier families in the region around Butler's church were reluctant to leave the Union. So were many of the poorer people along the way where the Trace had run. The great bulk of the middle class, particularly in Mississippi, were rampant for rebellion. Pride rose high, but the golden days were done. The first ceremony to take place in the new edifice of the church of which Butler had been minister so long was his funeral. Yet about it already the young were dancing to war. And in a land of great expectations as the war began, Windsor, regarded as the finest house in Mississippi, was built near Bruinsburg. There Rachel and Andrew Jackson had been lovers. There, after landing, Burr found friends. And there Grant would land, too.

Windsor's observatory was as high as Butler's hand. It rose in magnificence within 22 gigantic stone Corinthian columns, joined by Italian wrought-iron railings.

Confederates used it as an observation tower. After the Battle of Port Gibson, Union forces used it as a hospital. After the war's end it continued to stand, frayed within but monumental still, as a symbol and a landmark. Mark Twain, as a young river pilot, sometimes charted his course by its towering majesty. Its destruction came late. Fire in 1890 left its columns standing in magnificent ruins. And around ruin poverty spread where people had poured to promise.

General Grant found no Natchez Trace to follow in his movements in Mississippi, though pieces of the roads, which Yanks and Rebs took in their fighting, had once been parts of the old trail. Even when Grant came to Bruinsburg and Port Gibson, led by a Negro who knew the ways, the roads were rutted and difficult through a country of ridges and ravines filled with timber, cane, vines, and thorn. Long lasting postwar economic collapse caused more destruction than Grant or his great lieutenant, William Tecumseh Sherman. In the early twentieth century, men like Thomas D. Clark, who gathered the history of the old frontier, traveled roads on which "every mudhole, rutted hillside, and rickety bridge had to be negotiated according to its own peculiar bit of treachery." Wasteful methods of cultivation, he said, had gutted the hills. Cotton poverty was at the throats of all the people.

Only pride remained. As poverty seemed increasingly permanent, memories were enriched and often revised. In the first decade of the twentieth century, the Daughters of the American Revolution and the Daughters of the War of 1812 began to mark with boulders the Natchez Trace, along which not only revolutionists, but rogues and gentlemen, too, had moved long ago. There were arguments about exactly where the old Trace had run. Traditions went to battle with documents. Then, as the argument lengthened, a new, more intensified poverty descended on the land, not only between Nashville and Natchez but also upon the whole nation which men on the old trail had helped develop. At last, as one Roosevelt with his steamboat had doomed the Trace, another, Franklin D. Roosevelt, agreed to make the lost path a national parkway.

Many deserve credit for that development. Certainly patriotic ladies and energetic historians built interest in the story of the Trace. There was a Mississippi character named James Walton, who almost made a livelihood of organizing interest in the old road. His success would have been doubtful if there had not come with the depression of the 1930s an interest in public works which would provide jobs for people. Certainly the Old Southwest (now the Deep South) needed them. The poverty of people and not mere historical interest stirred Congressman Thomas Jefferson Busby, of Mississippi. He was born in Tishomingo County, a few miles from the ferry General Colbert had operated across the Tennessee River, and had been a lawyer in the town of Houston, below Tupelo, near which the Trace once passed.

Busby introduced a modest resolution in 1934 asking the Department of the Interior to make "a survey of the old Indian trail, known as the Natchez Trace . . . with a view to constructing a national road on this route to be known as the Natchez Trace Parkway." Though many Mississippians had appeared to approve it, the National Park Service was not enthusiastic. Apparently the Department of Interior was about to urge a Presidential veto, though only $50,000 was involved in the proposed survey.

Then, as luck together with hazard has always attended the story of the Trace, Roosevelt needed some help in Congress from the then Senator Pat Harrison, of Mississippi. Some resistance was growing against Roosevelt's spending, which seemed big then. Pat Harrison was chairman of the powerful Senate Finance Committee. Bitterly he let it be known that he did not feel he was getting his due in Presidential favor and patronage. Harold Ickes, who described himself as an old curmudgeon, was then Secretary of the Interior and as such was in charge of the National Park Service. In February, 1935, he went to see

Harrison and came away liking him less than when he went.

"He was," said Ickes, who seldom failed to be uncharitable where his prejudices were involved, "like an old complaining woman and, also like a woman, he keeps running around in circles and coming back to the point of departure . . . he kept whining about his grievances."

If Harrison whined, he whined effectually. The survey was approved. Also, late in 1935, funds totaling $1,286,686 for the construction of the Trace in Mississippi were allotted from the President's "emergency funds." Then, a year later, Ickes conferred with the President on public works projects.

"He is approving very few," Ickes noted in his diary, "although necessarily we have to take care of some rescissions and amendments. He told me that it would be necessary to give Pat Harrison $5 million more for Mississippi roads, making a total of $15 million in all."

Harrison, born in Copiah County, Mississippi, not far from the route of the Trace, knew the old, almost forgotten path was still a way upon which a man could go to get what he wanted. The first contracts on the parkway were awarded by June 30, 1937.

As happened in the days when Colonel Butler would not give up his queue and General Wilkinson waited for mule loads of Spanish gold, war and other troubles slowed the completion of the project. Now, however, cars will move along landscaped ways where boatmen trudged long ago. And beside the parkway there are not only restored cabins, parking lots, campsites, lunch tables, displays of flora and fauna, and museums, but also "stands" equipped with the most modern plumbing.

From the Hermitage beyond Nashville to the old mansions in Natchez, the ancient path is monumented. Decorous roadside signs along the way tell the old Trace's story. Tourists move by the busloads to pageants, on pilgrimages, to eager hostesses of the Old Southwest now a new South, too. Certainly the belles of the past were no lovelier than those who point out the antiques in refurbished mansions. And along the Trace the golden hand of Zebulon Butler never gleamed more brightly than now.

It is an erect symbol still. Many travelers stop and write their thoughts about it in a book kept in the old Presbyterian Church for that purpose. Today as in the past, some feel as did a successor of Butler in the church's pulpit who wrote about The Hand. He said it was "a reverent sign from a people who knew and loved their God—and it speaks today, also, as a reverent sign from a people who know and love their God."

It may be that the earth and the people from which the great finger points upward have not greatly changed. America under heaven is America still, good and bad, tough and beautiful, and still not always safe, comfortable, or satisfied in the directions to its destiny.